THE NEWBORN AND THE NURSE

MARY LOU MOORE, R.N., M.A.

COORDINATOR, MATERNAL AND CHILD HEALTH,
NORTH CAROLINA BAPTIST HOSPITAL SCHOOL
OF NURSING, WINSTON-SALEM

Saunders Monographs in Clinical Nursing — 3

W. B. SAUNDERS COMPANY
Philadelphia, London, Toronto

W. B. Saunders Company: West Washington Square
Philadelphia, PA 19105

12 Dyott Street
London, WC1A 1DB

833 Oxford Street
Toronto 18, Ontario

The Newborn and the Nurse ISBN 0-7216-6490-3

Print No: 9 8 7 6 5 4 3

To Richard Dudley Moore,
my husband

"La puericulture est une science précise; elle est aussi une oeuvre d'amour." Childcare is a precise science; it is also a work of love.

L'Attente de Bébé
Brusells: Oeuvre Nationale de l'Enfance

Preface

Caring for a newly born infant constitutes a very special kind of nursing. Those of us who care for him directly, in newborn, premature and intensive care nurseries, in clinics, and in his own home, have to recognize and appreciate his special characteristics and needs and help his parents to understand them too. When he has extraordinary problems — prematurity, malformation or illness — he needs very specialized attention from nurses who not only understand what kind of care is needed but why such care is important.

Many nurses are never directly concerned with the care of newborns, yet they contribute a great deal to their well-being by guiding mothers through a safe pregnancy, by teaching family planning so that pregnancies will not come so frequently as to risk abnormality or at a time when the mother's own health is poor, by teaching basic nutrition to girls who are still in school and by working personally and professionally to improve living conditions and the quality of health care.

Even those nurses whose career interests are in no way related to infants find that friends and relatives are likely to seek advice from them about their own new babies.

It is for all those nurses whose lives — professional and personal — touch the life of an infant that this book is written, in the belief that with an increased awareness of physiological, psychological, and sociocultural factors we will offer to every baby the very best of nursing care.

MARY LOU MOORE

Acknowledgments

Few books are written without the help of many people; this one is no exception. I am particularly grateful to Dr. Harold O. Goodman, Professor of Medical Genetics, Bowman Gray School of Medicine, Wake Forest University, for his suggestions concerning the genetic material in the first chapter; to Miss Camilla Hanes, R.N. and Mrs. Marley Willard, R.N., who read and commented on various sections; to Mrs. Thelma Belton, R.N., head nurse in the premature and intensive care nursery and Mrs. Florence Hampton, R.N., head nurse in the newborn nursery, North Carolina Baptist Hospital, who shared their knowledge and experience with me; to the embassies of Belgium, Denmark, the Federal Republic of Germany, Finland, Great Britain, Norway, Sweden, and Switzerland who helped me gather literature from their countries; and to those companies and agencies which contributed many of the illustrations used throughout the book.

M.L.M.

Contents

CHAPTER 1

The Unseen Infant

For 9 months the infant to be grows unseen. The chromosomes, with their genes, which are inherited from the parents, interact constantly with the environment surrounding the fetus and determine what he will be at birth and to a certain extent what he will be in the months and years that follow. By understanding what happens to the fetus during the first 9 months, we are better able to understand why a newly born infant behaves as he does and we are in a better position to answer the many questions posed by his parents. This knowledge also helps to reduce the number of ill and malformed newborns, and enables us to plan for the improved health of all infants.

Gestation

THE FIRST MONTH

As yet it has not been determined exactly when fertilization occurs in humans, but it is within 24 hours after ovulation and coitus. Between 24 and 60 hours the fertilized egg begins to divide; at the same time it passes from the fallopian tube to the uterus. The *morula*, a solid ball of cells, has been found in the uterus approximately three days after ovulation (Fig. 1–1).

Fig. 1–1

Figure 1-1. The morula, a solid ball of cells, about 3 days after ovulation. (Courtesy of the Carnegie Institution of Washington.)

Figure 1-2. A 58-cell blastocyst, 4 days after ovulation. (Courtesy of the Carnegie Institution of Washington.)

Figure 1-3. A 107-cell blastocyst, 4.5 days after ovulation. (Courtesy of the Carnegie Institution of Washington.)

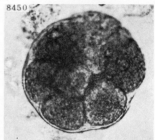

inner cell mass ——

trophoblast ——

blastocyst cavity ——

zona pellucida ——

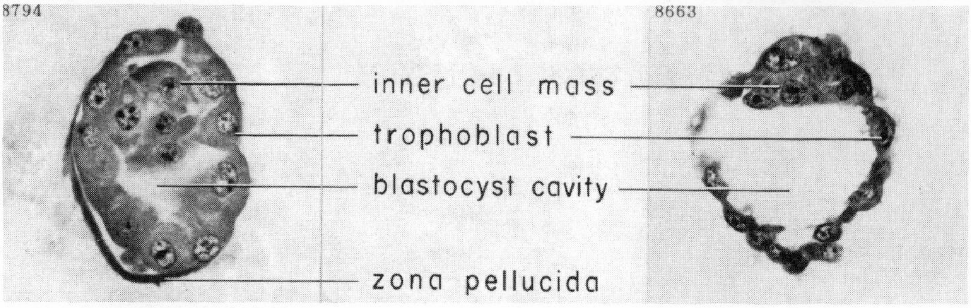

Fig. 1–2   Fig. 1–3

Toward the end of the third day or early in the fourth day the morula begins to change from a solid mass of cells into a ball with a central cavity called the blastocyst. The cells from which the embryo will develop (embryoblast or inner cell mass) remain at one end of the blastocyst, while those cells, which, along with uterine tissue, will form the placenta (trophoblast) gather around the periphery (Figs. 1–2, 1–3).

During the time in which the blastocyst has been dividing and traveling to the uterus (Fig. 1–4) the secretory phase of the menstrual cycle has been preparing the uterine endometrium for the ovum, just as it does during every menstrual cycle. By the beginning of the second week after fertilization the trophoblast has begun to attach itself to the endometrium; by the end of that week it will be completely implanted and will then have access to the food materials available in the maternal blood supply. Until that time the embryo is dependent upon its own rather meager store of nutrients and any food and oxygen it can derive from the fluids of the uterine tube and uterus.

While the blastocyst is becoming implanted in the uterine wall, changes are also taking place in the inner cell mass. The amniotic cavity forms, splitting the inner cell mass into an outer layer of cells, which will become the amniotic sac, and an inner layer, the embryonic disc. The amniotic sac forms above the embryonic disc; the yolk sac forms below it (Fig. 1–5). The human yolk sac does not contain

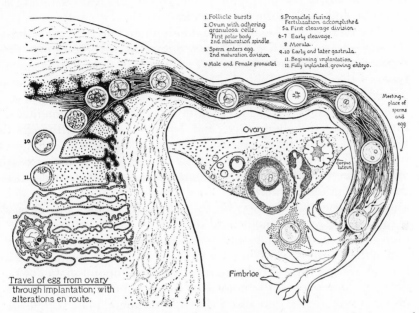

1. Follicle bursts
2. Ovum with adhering granulosa cells. First polar body 2nd. maturation spindle
3. Sperm enters egg. 2nd maturation division
4. Male and Female pronuclei
5. Pronuclei fusing Fertilization accomplished
5a. First cleavage division.
6-7. Early cleavage.
8. Morula.
9-10. Early and later gastrula.
11. Beginning implantation.
12. Fully implanted, growing embryo.

Ovary

Corpus luteum

Meeting-place of sperms and egg

Fimbriae

Travel of egg from ovary through implantation; with alterations en route.

Figure 1–4. As the fertilized ovum divides to form the morula, the blastocyst, and finally the trophoblast, it travels through the fallopian tube to the uterus. (From Dickinson *In* Arey: *Developmental Anatomy.* 7th Edition. W. B. Saunders, 1965.)

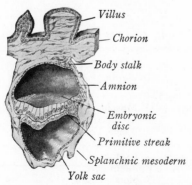

Villus

Chorion

Body stalk

Amnion

Embryonic disc

Primitive streak

Splanchnic mesoderm

Yolk sac

Figure 1–5. Right half of the human embryo (Brewer) of 14 days (× 85). The chorionic villi have partially penetrated the mucosa of the uterus. (From Arey: *Developmental Anatomy.* 7th Edition. W. B. Saunders, 1965.)

yolk; it is so named only because it resembles the yolk sac in birds and reptiles. Thus of all the cells which have resulted from the cleavage of the original egg, only those which form the embryonic disc will be a part of the developing embryo. All the rest—amniotic sac, placenta, and cord—form his environment.

The embryonic disc begins to differentiate into two layers during the second week. By the third week there will be three layers—ectoderm, mesoderm, and entoderm. From each of these layers specific types of tissue arise (Table 1–1). These germ layers are, in a sense, assembly grounds. During the early stages of development each germ layer has had the potential for a variety of types of development. Cells first differentiate chemically, and later physically. Although the master controller of this process is the genetic code, cell differentiation is more immediately influenced by *induction*, the process by which one tissue transmits a chemical stimulus that leads to the development of another tissue. For example, the nervous system begins with a median cord of cells, the notochord, which forms from the embryonic plate. The notochord then induces the cells above it to form first the neural plate and subsequently the neural tube by the end of the fourth week. When contact between the notochord and the cells above it is prevented experimentally, the neural plate does not develop. Moreover, if the notochord tissue is implanted under ectodermal tissue somewhere else in the body, a neural plate will develop there.

Should induction fail either because of inadequate inductive stimulus or because the tissue does not react, an organ may fail to

TABLE 1–1. *The Germ-Layer Origin of Human Tissues**

ECTODERM	MESODERM *(including mesenchyme)*	ENTODERM

1. Epidermis, including:
    Cutaneous glands.
    Hair; nails; lens.
2. Epithelium of:
    Sense organs.
    Nasal cavity; sinuses.
    Mouth, including:
      Oral glands; enamel.
    Anal canal.
3. Nervous tissue, including:
    Hypophysis.
    Chromaffin tissue.
	1. Muscle (all types).
	2. Connective tissue; cartilage; bone; notochord.
	3. Blood; bone marrow.
	4. Lymphoid tissue.
	Epithelium of:
	5. blood vessels;
	    lymphatics.
	6. Body cavities.
	7. Kidney; ureter.
	8. Gonads; genital ducts.
	9. Suprarenal cortex.
	10. Joint cavities, etc.
		Epithelium of:
		1. Pharynx, including:
		    Root of tongue.
		    Auditory tube, etc.
		    Tonsils; thyroid.
		    Parathyroids; thymus.
		2. Larynx; trachea; lungs.
		3. Digestive tube, including:
		    Associated glands.
		4. Bladder.
		5. Vagina (all?); vestibule.
		6. Urethra, including:
		    Associated glands.

*From Arey: *Developmental Anatomy.* 7th Edition, W. B. Saunders, 1965, p. 83.

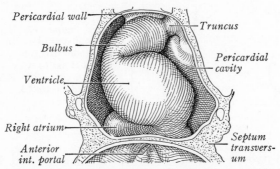

Pericardial wall — Truncus

Bulbus

Pericardial cavity

Ventricle

Right atrium

Anterior int. portal

Septum transvers- um

Figure 1-6. The heart at approximately 3 weeks. Even before the anatomical structure of the heart reaches its final form, the heart has started to beat in order to maintain circulation within the embryo and to provide a placental circuit. (After Davis *In* Arey: *Developmental Anatomy.* 7th Edition. W. B. Saunders, 1965.)

appear (agenesis) or may be smaller than normal (hypoplasia), or may be incompletely differentiated. Irregularities in induction can also lead to organ duplication, such as a double kidney and ureter, or to abnormal positioning of an organ.

During the third and fourth weeks of embryonic life, a time when the mother is scarcely aware that she is pregnant, several major systems undergo remarkable development. The rudimentary nervous system has already been mentioned. The neural tube, at first, is open, but by the end of the fourth week the anterior end has closed to form brain tissue, while the posterior portion has closed to form the spinal cord. If for some reason the neural tube fails to close, anencephalus will occur at the anterior end; if the posterior neural tube fails to close, myelomeningocele results. For whatever reasons these defects occur, they occur very early in pregnancy.

Heart formation also begins early, at about the sixteenth day. In just eight days the circulatory system progresses from young blood cells clustered in the walls of the yolk sac, to a fine network of blood vessels, to two symmetrical tubes, to a single heart tube which is present on the twenty-second day and which begins to beat about the twenty-fourth day (Fig. 1-6). Further heart and circulatory development will take place over the next several weeks so that by the end of six weeks the exterior heart form is essentially what it will be at birth. By the seventh week the heart valves are present.

In the third week the rudimentary respiratory and digestive tracts exist as a single tube (Fig. 1-7); the potential for tracheo-esophageal fistula is not difficult to imagine. By the end of the fourth week the esophagotracheal septum has begun the initial division of the two systems and lung buds have appeared on the trachea.

Embryonic skin, a bud which will become the liver, arm and leg buds, and rudimentary kidneys are also present by the end of four

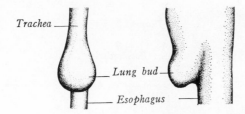

Trachea

Lung bud

Esophagus

Figure 1-7. Both trachea and esophagus develop from a single entodermal tube. (After Grosser and Heiss *In* Arey: *Developmental Anatomy.* 7th Edition. W. B. Saunders, 1965.)

weeks, only two weeks after the mother has missed a menstrual period (Fig. 1–8). Yet the embryo is no larger than a fingernail (Fig. 1–9).

THE SECOND MONTH

Equally crucial to the embryo is the second four-week period. At the start of this period, the embryo looks something less than human; before the four weeks are completed he is not recognizable, but he has begun to develop every one of his systems, several of them to a very high level. It is hardly surprising that disturbances in normal development during this period can lead to serious malformations.

Nervous system and muscle tissue. During the second month, the brain becomes the largest and also the most complex of the embryo's developing organs. Both motor nerves, which innervate muscle tissue, and sensory nerves, which carry messages from receptors to the central nervous system, have begun to form and, in some instances, to

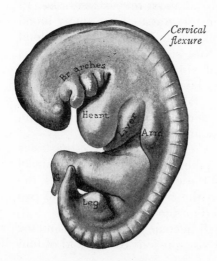

Cervical flexure

Br. arches

Heart

Liver

Arm

Leg

Figure 1-8. A human embryo at 4 weeks. (From Arey: *Developmental Anatomy.* 7th Edition. W. B. Saunders, 1965.)

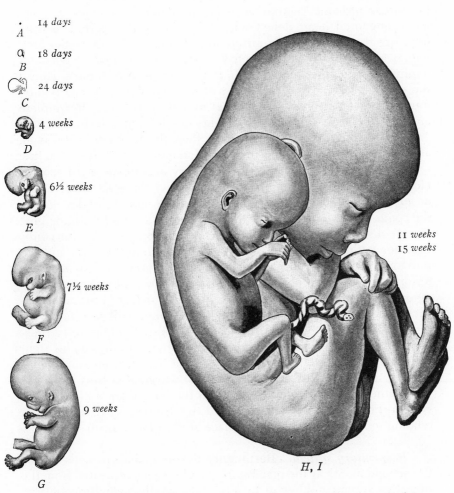

A   14 *days*

B   18 *days*

C   24 *days*

D   4 *weeks*

E   6½ *weeks*

F   7½ *weeks*

G   9 *weeks*

11 *weeks*
15 *weeks*

H, I

Figure 1–9. Human embryos at natural size. (From Arey: *Developmental Anatomy.* 7th Edition. W. B. Saunders, 1965.)

function. Meanwhile the muscle tissue is also developing; if for some reason innervation fails to occur, the muscle will subsequently atrophy.

Heart and circulatory system. The septa which divide the heart into chambers develop during the sixth to seventh week. Failure of the interventricular septum to close completely is a relatively common congenital heart defect which dates from this period. During fetal life there is normally an opening between the atria—the foramen ovale—which is important to fetal circulation but which becomes nonfunctional at the time of birth. It may not close anatomically until the end of the first year and never closes completely in nearly one-fourth of all adults with otherwise normal hearts. This incomplete anatomical closure apparently presents no problem in heart function. A defect in the atrial septum, other than the foramen ovale, is an anomaly, as is premature closure of the foramen ovale during fetal life.

In looking at one phase of circulatory development it becomes clear why the combination of defects known as tetralogy of Fallot occurs simultaneously. At 28 days, before the septa have developed, the *conus cordis* forms outflow tracts from both ventricles. In the next few weeks the *aorticopulmonary septum* develops to divide the conus together with the adjacent truncus arteriosus into the aorta and the pulmonary artery. If the aorticopulmonary septum is displaced anteriorly, the opening of the pulmonary artery will be narrowed (pulmonary stenosis), there will be a consequent defect in the interventricular septum, and the enlarged aortic opening will rise from both the right and left ventricles. Because of the position of the aorta, pressure increases in the right ventricle and hypertrophy of the right ventricular wall results. A different type of defect in the aorticopulmonary septum results in transposition of the great vessels.

As the heart is developing, so too is the remainder of the vascular system. Fetal circulation is described in Chapter 2 (pages 82–83) in relation to the changes that take place at the time of birth.

Respiratory system. Respiratory development proceeds during the second month as the respiratory tract becomes separated from the digestive system and begins to subdivide into the main bronchi (Fig. 1–10). Unlike some systems, respiratory development is not completed until after birth, with significant changes occurring at virtually the moment of delivery, one reason, perhaps, that the respiratory system is so highly vulnerable in the newborn.

Until the seventh week, the diaphragm does not completely separate the thoracic cavity from the abdomen. Large openings on either side of the septum transversum, the major component of the diaphragm, are known as the pleural canals. During the sixth week, fast growing lung buds extend down into these canals, but further

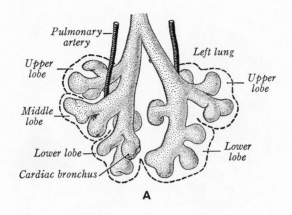

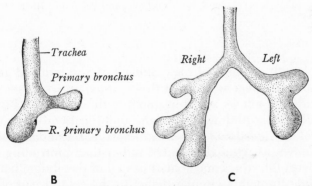

Figure 1-10. Anatomical development of the respiratory tract. *A*, At 4 weeks; *B*, at 5 weeks. (After Heiss and Merkel.) *C*, At 6½ weeks. (After Ask.) (From Arey: *Developmental Anatomy.* 7th Edition. W. B. Saunders, 1965.)

longitudinal growth of the chest enables the lungs to re-enter the thorax and the diaphragm to be completed in the seventh week. Failure of the canals to close results in a diaphragmatic hernia which in the majority of instances is on the left side. The stomach, spleen, liver or intestines may then enter the thoracic cavity, compressing the lungs and displacing the heart (Fig. 1-11). Babies with diaphragmatic hernia have severe respiratory difficulty at birth and require immediate surgical treatment.

Digestive system. The intestinal tract grows so rapidly during the second month that the abdominal cavity temporarily becomes too small to contain it. During the sixth week a portion of the intestinal loop enters the coelom (i.e., cavity) in the umbilical cord, where it will remain until the ten-week gestation period by which time the

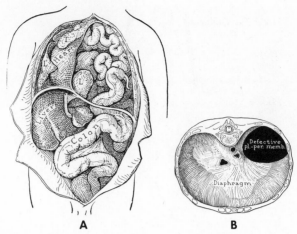

Figure 1–11. A, Herniation of intestines into the left pleural cavity. B, The actual defect in the diaphragm. (From Arey: *Developmental Anatomy.* 7th Edition. W. B. Saunders, 1965.)

expanded length of the fetal torso along with the reduced growth of the liver and the degeneration of the *mesonephroi,* one set of rudimentary kidneys, allows sufficient room in the abdomen (Fig. 1–12). Occasionally this withdrawal from the umbilical cord fails to occur and some of the intestinal loops remain outside the abdominal wall in a defect known as *omphalocele.* Or, rather than protruding through the umbilicus, intestines and sometimes all of the abdominal viscera may protrude through a circular defect in the central part of the abdominal wall. Viscera are covered by peritoneum and amnion but not by skin. The thin covering sac often ruptures at the time of birth or very shortly afterward.

Between the fourth and sixth weeks the *cloaca,* a common tube at the caudal end of the digestive tract, is divided laterally by the urorectal septum into the anorectal canal and the beginnings of the urogenital sinus. Urorectal and rectovaginal fistulas are anomalies related to this part of development.

Virtually faceless at four weeks, the embryo at eight weeks is recognizably human (Fig. 1–13). During this period of preliminary facial development a cleft lip and palate may develop. A cleft lip results when the lateral and medial nasal process fails to fuse; a cleft palate is due to a failure of the maxillary palatal shelves to fuse at a slightly later time (Fig. 1–14). More than 40 per cent of the time these two defects occur in conjunction with one another.

Skeletal system. While there is no bony skeleton in the second month, cartilage prototypes in the shape and position of future bone

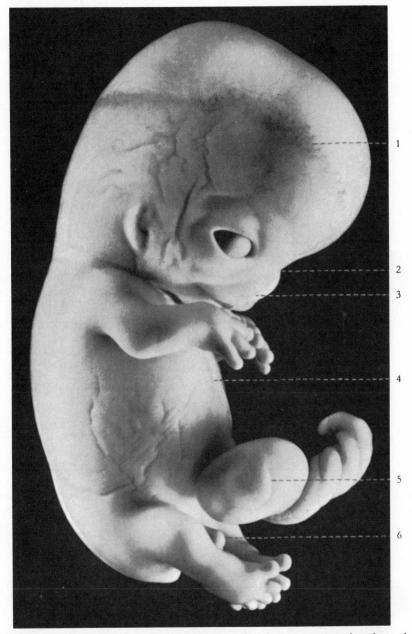

Figure 1–12. Fetus at approximately 8 weeks, showing intestinal coils in the umbilical coelom (5). Note the genital tubercule (6); males and females do not differ anatomically during the first 8 weeks. Other numbered items: (1) vascularization border; (2) sulcus interorbitis; (3) external naris; (4) sulcus medianus alongside the ventromedial ligament. (From Blechschmidt: *The Stages of Human Development Before Birth.* W. B. Saunders, 1961.)

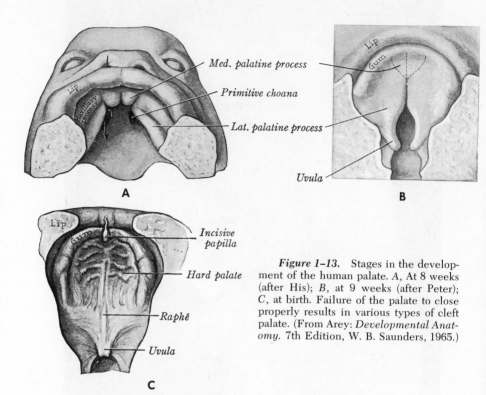

Med. palatine process

Primitive choana

Lat. palatine process

Uvula

A

B

Incisive
papilla

Hard palate

Raphê

Uvula

C

Figure 1-13. Stages in the development of the human palate. *A*, At 8 weeks (after His); *B*, at 9 weeks (after Peter); *C*, at birth. Failure of the palate to close properly results in various types of cleft palate. (From Arey: *Developmental Anatomy.* 7th Edition, W. B. Saunders, 1965.)

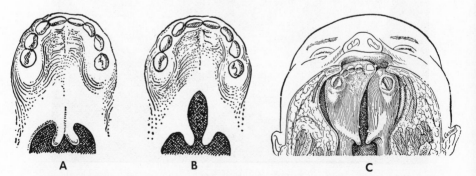

A   B   C

Figure 1-14. Three varieties of cleft palate. *A*, Cleft uvula; *B*, cleft of the total soft palate; *C*, cleft of the soft and hard palates combined with severe cleft lip. (From Arey: *Developmental Anatomy.* 7th Edition. W. B. Saunders, 1965.)

already support the embryo to some extent. Ossification, the replacing of this cartilage with bone tissue, begins in the second month and continues not only throughout fetal life but until adulthood, some 18 to 20 years later. Once the cartilaginous vertebral column has formed, the embryo begins to straighten. A distinct difference in curvature can be seen in comparing the embryo at 6½ and at 7½ weeks (Fig. 1–9).

And so the embryo reaches two months, still only an inch long, with his head accounting for approximately half of that length. Yet many of his organ systems now function in a rudimentary way. A great many of the most common congenital defects present at birth will already have occurred during the eight-week gestation period. The mother has missed her second menstrual period by now; if she is a middle- or upper-class patient she has probably been seen by a physician. But if she is poor, though she may be quite sure of her pregnancy, it may be weeks or even months before she will visit a clinic or doctor.

THE THIRD MONTH

The third month brings continued growth and differentiation. The embryo triples in length, from 1 inch to 3 inches. At the same time his proportions change. At the end of the third month his head accounts for only one-third of his total length rather than one-half as in the second month. His arms and legs also increase in length.

Genital systems. Sexual differentiation is one of the major changes in this period. Although sex is determined at conception by chromosomal inheritance (see page 19), there is no way of dis-

TABLE 1–2. *Homologues in the Male and Female Genital Systems**

Male	Indifferent Stage	Female
Testis	Gonad	Ovary
Seminiferous tubules	Germinal cords	Pflüger's tubules
Bladder; prostatic urethra	Primitive urogenital sinus	Bladder; greater part of urethra
Appendix testis	Paramesonephric duct (Mullerian duct)	Uterine tubes Uterus Vagina
Glans penis	Glans of phallus	Glans clitoris
Floor of penile urethra	Urethral folds	Labia minora
Scrotum	Genital swelling	Labia majora

*Adapted from Hamilton:

TABLE 1-3. *Menstrual and Embryonic Timetable*

Last Normal Menstrual Period ———→						
Fertilization	2	3	4	Blastocyst	Implantation begins	7
8	9	10	11	Implantation Completed		14
First Missed Menstrual Period				19	20	21
22	23	Heart beat	25	26	27	28
29	Lateral Separation: trachea & foregut					
Fusion: lat & medial nasal processes						
Second Missed Menstrual Period						

tinguishing males from females during the first eight weeks of development. Both gonads, which form in the sixth week, and genital ducts are initially identical for both sexes during the "indifferent stage." Table 1-2 documents the development of some major portions of the genital systems.

Red blood cells. It is during the third month that the liver takes over the major part of the production of red blood cells, with some blood formation also beginning in the bone marrow. Prior to this, red blood cells were produced in the yolk sac in the third and fourth weeks and by numerous blood islands scattered throughout the embryo in the ensuing four weeks.

Table 1-3 depicts the events of the first trimester in calendar form.

THE SECOND TRIMESTER

After the first trimester the infant-to-be is considered a fetus rather than an embryo; some embryologists would make the differentiation at the end of the second month.

While development in the second trimester is less obvious than it was in the first, it is only at the very end of the sixth month that the

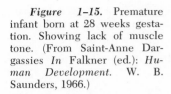 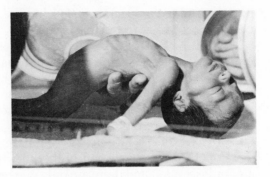

Figure 1-15. Premature infant born at 28 weeks gestation. Showing lack of muscle tone. (From Saint-Anne Dargassies *In* Falkner (ed.): *Human Development.* W. B. Saunders, 1966.)

fetus has any real likelihood of survival, and even then the mortality risk is high. Much of the change during this second trimester involves the continuation and occasionally the completion of earlier development.

Ossification and Hair.   Ossification, for example, which began in the eighth week, is widespread by the end of the fourth month, although the carpal, tarsal and sternal bones do not ossify until near the time of birth. Hair begins to appear on the head in the fourth month. The vernix caseosa, that thick, white material which covers newborn skin, begins to form in the fifth month. From the fifth month until birth, bone marrow begins to play an increasingly important role in blood formation.

Size.   A major change of the second trimester is in size and proportion. Body growth continues to be more rapid than head growth. At the end of the second trimester the fetus weighs roughly 2 pounds, more than ten times what he weighed at the end of the first three months, yet this is less than half of his full-term weight. His length is approximately 14 to 15 inches.

THE THIRD TRIMESTER

With some exceptions development in the third trimester parallels rather closely the extrauterine development of the prematurely born infant. Since weight alone is not always a good indication of the baby's gestational age, developmental indices are very helpful in knowing what can be expected of an individual baby and the kind of care that will serve him best.

At 28 weeks the premature baby has a general lack of muscle tone (Figure 1-15) and very little subcutaneous fat, so that his skin has a wrinkled appearance. He sleeps almost continually. Pupils do not react to light before 29 weeks.

By 32 weeks he will wake more easily and stay awake for brief periods. He has a sense of taste and may "fight" a gavage feeding which seems unpleasant to him; he also begins to suck on the gavage tube. The Moro reflex (page 97), incomplete at 28 weeks, is now complete with all three movements. Before 33 weeks there is no raised area where the nipple will be.

Muscle tone continues to improve and by 35 weeks is well developed in the lower half of the body. Before 36 weeks the testes are undescended and there are only one or two transverse skin creases on the sole of the foot, in contrast to the complex of criss-cross creases at term.

Two major changes which occur in the respiratory tract and eye during the third trimester have a direct bearing on the pathology that may develop in prematurely born infants.

Respiratory tract.   In the respiratory tract alveoli begin to appear in the lung between the 26th and 28th weeks. At the same time capillaries proliferate around these terminal air spaces. Until both alveoli and capillaries are developed there can be no exchange of gases; babies born before this period of development will die.

In addition, beginning at about the sixth month, certain cells (called Type II cells) within the alveoli begin to secrete a lipoprotein, surfactant, which keeps the lungs expanded when the baby exhales. It is now believed that the absence of surfactant is a major factor in respiratory distress syndrome. This would account for the observation that respiratory distress syndrome rarely occurs in term infants who have had sufficient time to develop and store adequate surfactant.

Eye.   Until the fourth month of gestation the retina of the eye has no blood vessels. During the fourth to eighth month, vessels grow anteriorly toward the retina. In a baby born at seven months much of the anterior retina still lacks these vessels and is consequently highly susceptible to damage by oxygen. Once vascularization is complete, the retinal vessels are no longer in danger. Unfortunately it is the young premature baby who is most susceptible and most likely to be in need of oxygen because of other problems (see page 150).

Kidneys.   The structure of the kidney continues to change as glomeruli form throughout the third trimester. In spite of this there is not much difference in kidney function in surviving premature infants and in term infants. However, the kidneys of both early and term infants do not tolerate stress well, and the smaller premature infant is more likely to encounter the stress of illness, unstable temperature, and the like.

Size. The most striking difference between the infant born at term and the one who is in an incubator during the last weeks of what ideally should have been gestation is size. The term infant weighs about 3000 to 3400 gm. (6½ to 7½ pounds), is approximately 50 to 53 cm. in length (20 to 21 inches), and has a head circumference of 34 to 36 cm. (13½ to 14½ inches). In contrast, the prematurely born infant reaches 41 weeks weighing about 2500 gm. (5½ pounds), measures 45 cm. in length (roughly 18 inches), and has a head circumference of 32 cm. (approximately 12½ inches). He continues to have less subcutaneous fat than a term baby. His skin is fine and his muscles are thin. He tires easily; muscle contractions are briefer than those of a term infant. In spite of our ever-improving technology, we do not seem to have developed an environment which can compete with the maternal womb under normal circumstances.

The Genetic Basis of Development

The development of a single fertilized egg into a marvelously complex human infant is governed continually by hereditary factors, by the infant's own internal environment, by the environment of his mother's body, and by the environment surrounding his mother. After several decades of debate it now seems evident that both the genetic potential of the *gametes* (the single sperm cell and the single ovum which it penetrates) and the environment interact continually from the time of conception until death.

How does a gene determine development? Deoxyribonucleic acid (DNA) is the substance in which the structural and functional potential of each individual is encoded. The theory, hypothesized by Watson and Crick and subsequently supported by other researchers, describes the nucleic acid molecule as consisting of two sugar-phosphate strands arranged in helical fashion around a hypothetical central axis, together with purines and pyrimidines which are attached to this sugar-phosphate backbone and which stretch inward from it. As the two strands of the molecule unwind, the halves separate to form new, identical molecules (Fig. 1–16).

The sugar in some nucleic acid is ribose, hence ribonucleic acid (RNA). A similar sugar, lacking one of the oxygen atoms of ribose, is called deoxyribose and is found in DNA.

Two purines, adenine and guanine, and one pyrimidine, cystosine, are found in both DNA and RNA. The pyrimidine thymine,

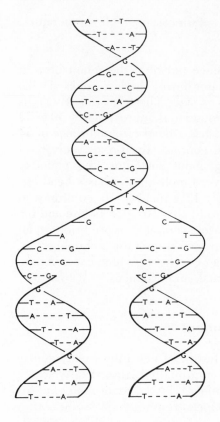

Figure 1–16. Diagram of DNA structure according to the Watson-Crick hypothesis, showing how strands identical to the parent strand are formed at replication. (From *Genes, Enzymes, and Inherited Diseases* by H. Eldon Sutton. Copyright © 1961 by Holt, Rinehart and Winston, Inc.)

found only in DNA, is equivalent in terms of the genetic code to the pyrimidine uracil, found only in RNA.

A single segment of the helical strand, involving one sugar portion to which one phosphate group and one purine or pyrimidine is attached, is termed a nucleotide. Each individual gene is estimated to be made up of a chain of from 200 to 2000 nucleotides. As many as 3000 genes, in turn, make up a single chromosome.

Unlike genes, whose numbers can only be approximated, the number of chromosomes for a given species is known and is specific to the species. For example, there are 20 chromosomes in corn, 48 in the chimpanzee, and 46 in man. Since chromosomes exist in pairs, except in the gametes, man has 23 pairs of chromosomes.

The genes associated with each chromosome are transmitted as a group, called a linkage group. They are inherited as a group, rather than independently. If chromosomes (or linkage groups) always remained intact, and man always inherited 23 groups of genes, possible combinations of traits would be somewhat more limited than they are. However, because of a process termed *crossing-over*, in which two

chromosomes of a pair may interchange sections and thus genes, linkage groups do not remain constant (Fig. 1–17).

The function of the genes at any specific point on each chromosome is the same for all chromosomes of that type. Thus not only chromosomes but also genes exist in pairs. In any pair of genes there may be two contrasting forms or states of the gene, known as *alleles.* Some genes have multiple alleles; there are three alleles for blood type — A, B, and O. If an individual has similar alleles for a given trait, he is said to be homozygous for the particular gene. He may, for example, have two alleles for A-type blood, designated AA. When alleles differ, the individual is heterozygous, such as the man with AB blood. In heterozygous combinations, one allele, the *dominant* allele, may manifest itself in the *phenotype* (visible characteristic), while the other allele, which is *recessive,* is not apparent. Only when the zygote receives two recessive alleles will recessive traits be expressed. Examples of the inheritance of dominant and recessive traits are found on pages 24–27.

Twenty-two of man's 23 pairs of chromosomes are *autosomes,* i.e., they are alike in both sexes. The sex chromosomes, designated XX in the female and XY in the male, are the remaining pair. In egg cells the sex chromosome is always X. Half of the sperm cells carry the X chromosome, the other half the Y chromosome. The sperm cell as it unites with the egg to form the zygote determines the sex of the new organism, a sperm cell with an X chromosome producing a female (XX) and a sperm with a Y chromosome producing a male (XY). In addition to determining sex, the sex chromosomes also carry genes for a number of other traits, the *X-linked* characteristics. Hemophilia and red-green color blindness are two examples of X-linked traits.

Human chromosomes have been classified on the basis of size and the position of the centromere (the point at which the chromatids [or strands] of the chromosome are joined). Since it is often difficult to identify all 23 pairs of chromosomes in an individual sample, it has become an accepted practice to organize them into seven groups, identified by the letters A through G in order of decreasing length. A systematically arranged set of chromosomes is called a *karyotype* (Fig. 1–18). Cells for karyotyping may be white blood cells (since red blood cells have no nucleus they have no chromosomes) or tissue cells obtained in biopsy. Amniotic fluid is used to study fetal chromo-

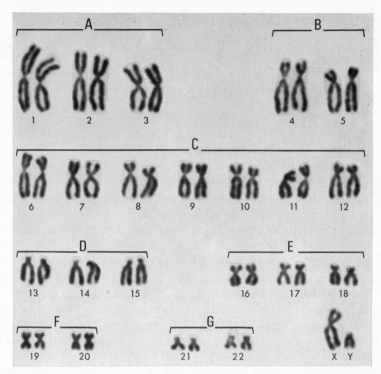

Figure 1-18. A karyotype of human chromosomes. (Courtesy of D. H. Carr *In* Thompson and Thompson: *Genetics in Medicine.* W. B. Saunders, 1966.)

somes. The cells are cultured and treated chemically; slides are made for examination and photography. Individual chromosomes are then cut from the photograph, matched in pairs and mounted according to the standard classification, usually called the Denver classification because of its adoption at a meeting in Denver, Colorado in 1960.

CELL DIVISION

Two different processes of cell division keep the number of chromosomes in both gametes and other cells constant. *Mitosis is* the process by which all the cells, other than those which produce the gametes, divide. Just prior to division each chromosome duplicates to form two identical chromosomes. Both daughter cells are identical with each other and with the parent cell (Fig. 1-19).

Gametes alone are produced by *meiosis,* rather than mitosis, in order that the number of chromosomes will always be halved in these germ cells. The zygote, formed when sperm and egg unite, will then

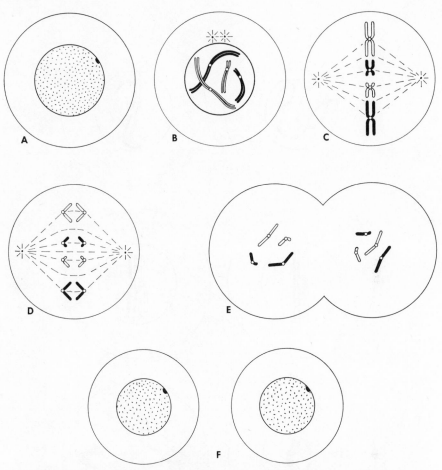

Figure 1-19. The stages of mitosis showing two of the 23 pairs of chromosomes. A, Before mitosis (interphase). B, Chromosomes have duplicated and become visible (prophase). C, Chromosomes line up at the equatorial plane of the cell (metaphase). D, Division (anaphase). E, Chromosomes arrive at the poles of the cells; the division of cytoplasm begins (telophase). Eventually a complete membrane is formed across the cell, producing two new daughter cells. F, Two daughter cells, identical with the former single cell. (From Thompson and Thompson: *Genetics in Medicine.* W. B. Saunders, 1966.)

contain the correct number of chromosomes for each species. Unlike the daughter cells produced by mitosis, the daughter cells of meiosis are not identical with each other or with the parent cell, each containing only half the genetic material of the mother cell. For instance, if the mother cell contained one allele for blue eye color and one allele for brown eye color, each gamete would contain only one of these alleles.

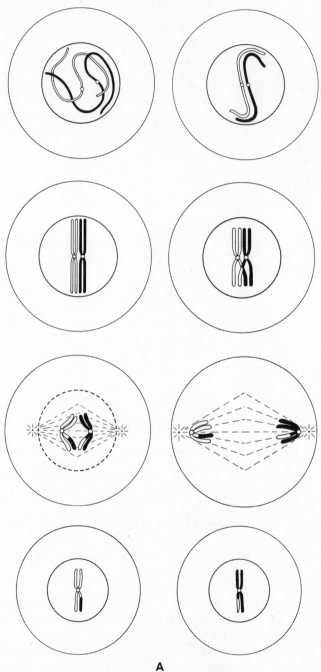

A

Figure 1–20. A, The first meiotic division.

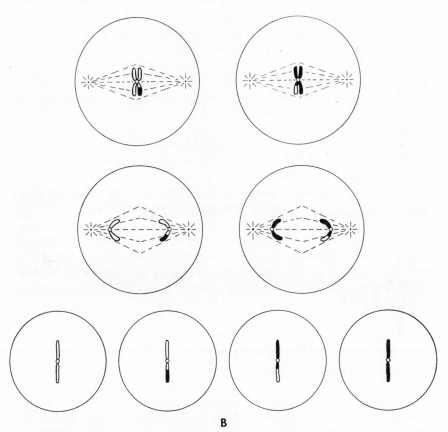

B

Figure 1–20 (Continued). B, The second meiotic division. (From Thompson and Thompson: *Genetics in Medicine.* W. B. Saunders, 1966.)

In the process of meiosis, chromosomes join in pairs, one chromosome of each pair having come from each parent cell. Each chromosome then duplicates, forming four similar strands, called tetrads. The mother cell divides into two daughter cells, each of which divides again, so that each of the resulting four daughter cells contains one strand from the tetrad (Fig. 1–20).

Since each gene contributes 23 chromosomes to the zygote, inheritance from each parent is equal. Moreover, of the 46 available chromosomes possessed by each parent, only 23 actually will be available to the new individual. Genetically there is no "chip off the old block" in the sense that no child can be just like either parent. Two children of the same parents may resemble each other closely in genotype (total gene content) or in phenotype, or they may be very different, depending on the genes they have received (and discounting the fact that the environment of each will also vary). The real surprise is not that some children fail to resemble either parent very closely, considering the tremendous number of potential combinations between two people, but that rather frequently strong similarities can be seen in even more distant relatives.

Twins may or may not have the same genotype. Dizygotic (fraternal) twins result when two separate ova are fertilized by two separate sperm. Their genotype, including their sex, is no more likely to be alike than is the genotype of any other brother and sister. Monozygotic (identical) twins result when one egg and one sperm unite to form a single zygote and then split at an early stage of zygote development. These twins have the same genotype and must, of course, be of the same sex.

THE GENETIC INHERITANCE OF CHARACTERISTICS

As genetic counseling becomes increasingly prevalent, it seems important that nurses be aware of some of the basic genetic principles governing inheritance. Many of these principles can be applied in very practical ways to help answer some of the questions about unborn and newborn infants and about future pregnancies that are of great concern to parents. Often questions revolve around characteristics that are debilitating or deforming. Both normal and pathological traits may be inherited through alleles of a gene that are dominant, recessive, X-linked, or polygenic.

Dominant inheritance. Hyperphalangy (an extra phalanx) of the thumb, one type of achondroplasia (Fig. 1–21), and Huntington's chorea, a degenerative disease of the central nervous system which usually affects young adults, are examples of hereditary malformations caused by dominant alleles.

If "A" is used to represent the allele for achondroplasia and "a" the non-achondroplastic form of the gene, the possible situations in which achondroplasia is inherited can be demonstrated. Since the dominant allele will be expressed in the phenotype, any combination of alleles which include "A" will result in an achondroplastic dwarf:

1. If one parent is of normal stature (genotype aa) and the other parent has achondroplasia (genotype Aa) there are four possible combinations of alleles. (Remember that because of meiosis the egg cell and the sperm cell will each contain only one of the parent's two alleles.)

	A	a
a	Aa	aa
a	Aa	aa

The children who inherit the genotype aa will be normal with respect to achondroplasia; the children who inherit the genotype Aa will be achondroplastic dwarfs. The probability is that half of the children of one achondroplastic parent and one non-achondroplastic parent would inherit the disorder.

2. If neither parent has achondroplasia, the child cannot inherit the condition from his parents. However, achondroplastic dwarfs are born to normal parents. Mørch, reviewing 94,075 births in a Danish hospital, found ten achondroplastic dwarfs. Two of these children had one parent who was achondroplastic and thus inherited the condition from the parent. The other eight, however, were born into families in which neither parent was achondroplastic. In these cases the gene may have been a new mutant, or the child may have been homozygous for a recessive gene carried by each parent for Ellis van Creveld syndrome, which includes achondroplasia as well as other symptoms.

Recessive inheritance. Cystic fibrosis and phenylketonuria (PKU) are examples of traits inherited through recessive genes. Unlike dominant alleles which may appear in every generation in the phenotype, recessive alleles may be carried for many generations without being manifest; it is only when two recessive alleles for the same trait are present in a single genotype that the trait is expressed.

PKU will be used to illustrate the inheritance of recessive alleles. The allele for PKU, since it is recessive, is designate "p;" the normal, dominant allele as "P." In order to have PKU, the infant must have the genotype "pp", i.e., two recessive alleles:

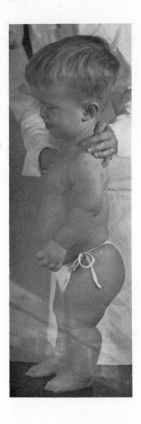

Figure 1-21. A child with achondroplasia, a cartilage disorder which leads to a specific kind of dwarfism. Because the long bones are most severely affected, body disproportion becomes increasingly obvious with growth. One type of achondroplasia is governed by a dominant gene. Another syndrome, Ellis van Creveld, which is autosomal recessive, leads to congenital achondroplasia plus other symptoms. (From Warkany and Kirkpatrick, Jr. *In* Nelson, Vaughan, and McKay (eds.): *Textbook of Pediatrics.* 9th Edition, W. B. Saunders, 1969.)

1. If neither parent carries an allele for PKU, neither the condition nor any allele for the condition can be transferred to the infant.

2. One parent may carry the recessive allele for PKU. Since the allele is recessive and will not appear in any outward characteristic, the individual will probably be unaware of its presence. He will differ in genotype but not in phenotype. If the other parent does not carry the recessive allele "p" none of the children will have PKU, but the odds are that half of them will carry the recessive allele. It is in this manner that a recessive allele may be carried for many generations before finding expression in the phenotype.

	P	P
P	PP	PP
p	Pp	Pp

3. If both parents carry the recessive allele for PKU, while they will display no outward evidence of the condition, the possibility now exists for a child with PKU, i.e., a child with the genotype "pp."

	P	p
P	PP	Pp
p	Pp	pp

The odds are that one child in four will have PKU, that two children in four will have the recessive allele but not the condition, and that one child in four will not have the condition or carry the recessive allele.

Theoretically, then, there is one chance in four that when both parents carry a recessive gene for any trait their offspring will be affected in phenotype as well as in genotype. It is important in applying this theoretical ratio to a specific family situation that the family understand as much as possible about the genetic principles involved lest they misunderstand the meaning of this ratio. It *does not* mean that if they have three normal children the fourth child will automatically have PKU. It *does not* mean that if one child has PKU the next three children will not. Because of the way in which genes segregate in meiosis and recombine at fertilization, there is the possibility that recessive alleles will combine at every fertilization, just as there is always the possibility that the recessive alleles will not be passed to any given zygote. Thus it is genetically possible that every child may have the genotype "pp" and have PKU, that every child could have the genotype "Pp" and be a carrier, or that every child could have the genotype "PP" and be neither affected nor a carrier.

Moreover, no matter how many children of whatever genotype have been produced by the parent, each succeeding child has exactly the same probability situation as the first child. The possibilities are analogous to the toss of a coin. If the coin is tossed a large number of times, one expects an approximately equal number of heads and tails. But if a person happens to throw 50 heads in a row, the odds are still even on the 51 toss. So too does chance determine which alleles will be present in a particular zygote.

Once a child with PKU is born to phenotypically normal parents, the genotypes of the parents in relation to PKU are known; both must carry the recessive allele. All future children should be observed carefully from the time of their birth and appropriate treatment instituted when necessary.

Three additional combinations of phenotypes exist, although because of the severe mental retardation which accompanies untreated PKU they have been rare in the past. But as children treated for PKU begin to reach adulthood, these other combinations may occur.

X-linked characteristics. The majority of genes are carried by the 22 pairs of autosomal chromosomes, and it makes no difference

whether the alleles causing a specific condition are inherited from the
mother or from the father. It has already been mentioned, however,
that sex chromosomes, in addition to determining sex, carry other
genes as well. These are termed sex-linked genes. Virtually all sex-
linked characteristics are carried by the X chromosome; a common
type of sex-linked characteristic is termed X-linked. Hemophilia is
one of the best known of the X-linked characteristics. If the symbol
"H" represents the X gene which transmits hemophilia and "h"
represents the X gene which does not, we have the following possible
combinations of genes:

> HY:hemophiliac male
> hY:normal male
> HH:hemophiliac female
> Hh:carrier female
> hh:normal female

Consider the possible combinations:

1. If the mother carries no gene for hemophilia (hh) but the father
is a hemophiliac (HY), all of the daughters will be carriers but the
sons will neither have the disease nor will they be carriers. The
daughters are carriers rather than hemophiliacs because one X
chromosome, the one inherited from their mother, has the normal
gene which is dominant over the allele for hemophilia inherited from
their father.

	Mother: h	h
Father:		
H	Hh	Hh
Y	hY	hY

2. If the mother carries the hemophiliac allele (Hh) but the father
is not a hemophiliac (hY), the odds are that half of the daughters would
be carriers and half of the sons would be hemophiliacs, the other
children having received the normal allele.

	Mother: H	h
Father:		
h	Hh	hh
Y	HY	hY

3. Should a woman who carries the recessive allele (Hh) marry a
man with hemophilia (HY), their daughters would all be either
carriers or hemophiliacs, but there is a probability of half their sons
being normal:

	Mother:	H	h
Father:			
H		HH	Hh
Y		HY	hY

Variations in genetic inheritance. Unfortunately, at least from the standpoint of unraveling genetic puzzles, not all traits are inherited in such a straightforward manner as has been described. Many traits are influenced by more than one gene (*polygenic*). Other genes are *incompletely penetrant;* that is, their phenotypic effects can be modified by environment. Birth weight, for example, is related to both genetic factors and to such environmental factors as the mother's diet during pregnancy and the mother's physiological state, such as diabetes which affects maternal metabolism. Some geneticists believe that cleft lip and palate represent a genetic trait which can be modified by environment, which would explain why the tendency for cleft lip recurs in families but does not follow classic patterns of inheritance. Gout, spina bifida, and pernicious anemia are other examples of pathological conditions which appear to be governed by genes and are expressed under some conditions of environment but not under others.

Summary. Genes, which direct the growth and differentiation of the infant-to-be, can cause abnormal development if they themselves are abnormal. Mutant (abnormal) genes may be passed from generation to generation through decades and even centuries, or they may be newly developed in the infant's parents. Dobzhansky (1962) has estimated that perhaps as much as 20 per cent of the population carries mutant genes which arose for the first time in the generation immediately preceding. Some mutants arise because of environmental influence; others seem to occur spontaneously for reasons that are not clear at this time, though it is known that radiation and certain drugs increase the probability of mutation. In the case of X-ray, the probability of increase may be double the natural rate (Papazian, 1967).

CHROMOSOMAL ABNORMALITIES

Abnormalities can occur in chromosomes as well as in genes, with consequent abnormalities in the infant. Because of the large number of genes located on each chromosome, it might be expected that any chromosomal change would produce not just one but a constellation of irregularities. It seems that it is the total effect of the imbalance of genetic material that is responsible for the changes.

Several types of chromosomal abnormalities can occur, involving either the autosomes or the sex chromosomes. The most common is *nondisjunction.* If, during the meiotic process (page 22), a chromosome pair fails to separate as it should, one gamete will contain not one but two of a given chromosome (Fig. 1–22). If the two-chromosome gamete then unites with a normal gamete to form a zygote, the zygote will then have three of the particular chromosome, hence the term trisomy (Fig. 1–23). During the same meiotic division, one gamete will receive no chromosome, but gametes lacking an autosome do not seem to form a viable zygote. Nondisjunction can also occur during mitosis, after the zygote has been formed.

Down's syndrome, which most often results from trisomy of the twenty-first chromosome (Fig. 1–24), is usually a result of nondisjunction. Occasionally Down's syndrome is due to a second type of abnormality, *translocation,* in which a piece of one chromosome breaks off and then attaches itself to another. In Down's syndrome of this origin it is the long arm of the twenty-first chromosome which breaks off and subsequently attaches itself to either a chromosome of the D group (13-15) or another chromosome of the G group (21-22) (Fig. 1–25).

One might well wonder whether these seemingly highly technical differences are merely medical curiosities. It should be stressed

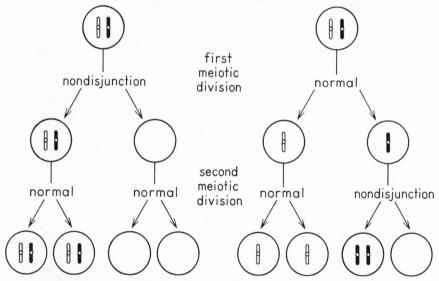

Figure 1–22. Nondisjunction can occur during either the first or second meiotic division, although it is believed to occur more frequently at meiosis I. (From Thompson and Thompson: *Genetics in Medicine.* W. B. Saunders, 1966.)

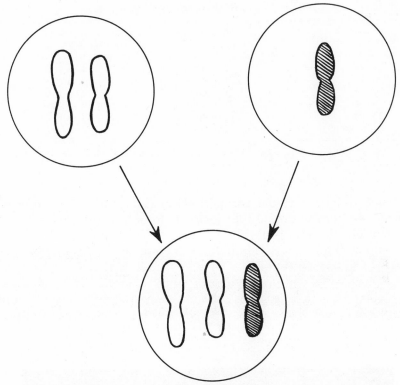

Figure 1-23. When a two-chromosome gamete unites with a normal gamete the zygote exhibits trisomy.

that they do have some value in genetic counseling. When the basis of Down's syndrome in an individual child is determined (by obtaining family history related to Down's syndrome, by karyotyping the infant, and sometimes by karyotyping parents as well), the likelihood that the syndrome may be repeated in future children can be evaluated more accurately. In the case of trisomy 21, the risk of having another affected child is considered to be two to three times the risk for the normal mother in the same age group, the risk rising with the age of the mother (Table 1-4).

Approximately 5 per cent of infants with Down's syndrome are a result of translocation rather than trisomy 21; about 2 per cent of these babies have inherited the translocation from a parent. The risk of another affected baby is very high if the mother is a translocation carrier, but lower if the father is the carrier—hence the need to karyotype all three individuals—mother, father, and infant.

In addition to trisomy 21, trisomy 18 (E syndrome) (Fig. 1-26) and trisomy D also result from nondisjunction, the letters in both

TABLE 1-4.   *Risk of Down's Syndrome*

AGE OF MOTHER	RISK OF DOWN'S SYNDROME IN CHILD	
	At Any Pregnancy°	*After the Birth of a Mongol*
-29	1 in 3000	1 in 1000
30–34	1 in 600	1 in 200
35–39	1 in 280	1 in 100
40–44	1 in 70	1 in 25
45–49	1 in 40	1 in 15
All mothers	1 in 665	1 in 200

°After Motulsky (1964); based upon the data of Carter and McCarthy (1951).

instances referring to the group of chromosomes involved. Affected infants are born with multiple severe deformities and usually die in the first months after birth.

Other chromosomal aberrations include *deletion,* in which a piece of chromosome breaks off and is lost; *duplication,* with an extra piece of chromosome either in the chromosome itself, attached to another chromosome (translocation), or existing as a separate unit; the development of *isochromosomes* because of an abnormal splitting;

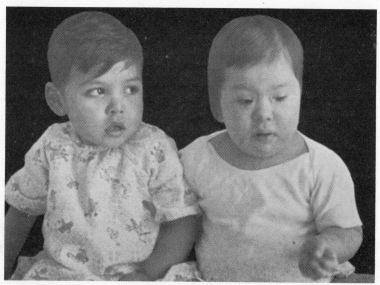

Figure 1-24. A 3-year-old Canadian Indian girl with trisomy 21 (Down's syndrome) and a normal Canadian Indian boy of the same age. Although Canadian Indians are of Mongolian origin, the trisomy 21 or "mongolism" phenotype is quite different from that of a normal Indian child. (From Thompson and Thompson: *Genetics in Medicine.* W. B. Saunders, 1966.)

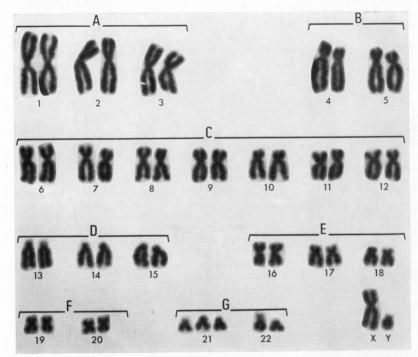

Figure 1-25. Trisomy 21 karyotype. Note that in the G group there are three 21 chromosomes. Compare this karyotype with Figure 1-18. (From Walker, Carr, Sergovich, Barr, and Soltan: *J. Ment. Defic. Res.*, 7:150–163, 1963.)

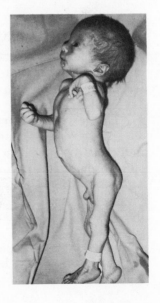

Figure 1-26. A 4-day-old male with trisomy 18 (E syndrome). Note the prominent occiput, micrognathia, low set ears, short sternum, narrow pelvis. (Courtesy of Robert E. Carrel from Wright *In* Nelson, Vaughan, and McKay (eds.): *Textbook of Pediatrics.* 9th Edition. W. B. Saunders, 1969.)

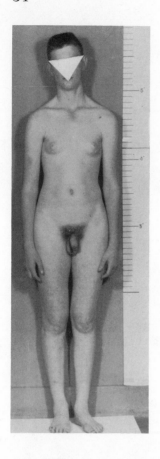

Figure 1–27. A boy with Klinefelter's syndrome, showing small testes and gynecomastia (female development of the breasts), the latter not always being present. Many affected males are mentally retarded. (Courtesy of M. L. Barr *In* Thompson and Thompson: *Genetics in Medicine.* W. B. Saunders, 1966.)

and *chromosomal mosaicism* in which an individual has at least two different cell lines with different chromosome compliments. Mosaicism always occurs after fertilization during the process of mitosis, leaving cells with two different types of chromosomes to develop.

The sex chromosomes and abnormalities. A number of anomalies are a result of abnormalities of the sex chromosomes with the individual possessing a number of possible combinations of X and Y chromosomes other than the normal female XX or the normal male XY. The XXY (Klinefelter's syndrome) occurring once in 400 male births (Fig. 1–27) and XO (Turner's syndrome) occurring once in 3000 live births (Fig. 1–28) are two of the more common abnormal combinations.

In general, those persons with unusual genotypes will be phenotypically male if they have a Y chromosome (e.g., XXY) and phenotypically female if they do not (e.g., XO). The higher the number of

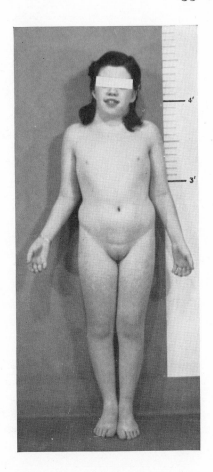

Figure 1-28. A girl with Turner's syndrome. Note the short stature, low set ears, mature facial appearance, the wide chest with broadly spaced nipples, poorly developed breasts, juvenile external genitalia. The ovary is usually only a streak of connective tissue. (From Barr: *American J. Hum. Genet.,* 12:118–127, 1960.)

extra chromosomes, the greater the likelihood of abnormality in the phenotype.

One example of nondisjunction in a single ovum illustrates how some unusual combinations can arise. Nondisjunction can take place in the sperm as well.

In the normal process of meiosis the XX chromosomes of the normal female would be divided:

XX

First meiotic division

X   X

Second meiotic division

X   X   X   X

Nondisjunction can occur at either the first or the second meiotic division. For the sake of example, assume that it occurs at the first.

XX
First meiotic division
XX   O
Second meiotic division
XX   XX   O   O

The potential combinations following fertilization with a normal sperm (XY) would then be:

	XX	O
X	XXX	XO
Y	XXY	YO

XO represents Turner's syndrome and XXY represents Klinefelter's syndrome. YO would be inviable. Females with the XXX pattern have been frequently found in surveys of hospitals for the retarded and among women in infertility clinics. They may be relatively common in the general population as well.

Causes of chromosomal breaks. What causes chromosomal breaks? Like genetic mutations some appear to arise spontaneously. Radiation is a factor in certain deletions and translocations. Maternal age correlates with nondisjunction (Fig. 1–25). Since viruses can produce fragmentation of chromosomes, they may play a role in resultant abnormalities. LSD has recently been suspect in relation to chromosomal breakage, but a final verdict awaits further research.

The Role of Fetal Environment

Chromosomes and genes constantly interact with the embryonic-fetal environment. Any part of that environment, chemical or physical, which affects the unborn infant adversely, is known as a *teratogen*. It seems likely in the light of discoveries in recent years about the effects of previously unsuspected teratogens that still other substances may be potentially dangerous to the developing child.

Before considering the specific varieties of environmental teratogens there are three general principles to be recognized. First, either too much or too little of almost any physical or chemical agent can have a teratogenic effect on some species of mammals. However, not every agent which affects one species or even one subspecies will necessarily affect another species in the same way or even in a way which is harmful. The practical implication of this is that there are limits to what animal research can tell us about the way in which a specific agent will affect humans. The experience with thalidomide, which did not show the characteristic effects in animal tests that it was to show in humans, is an example of this.

Second, the timing of the insult is of great importance. A teratogen introduced between the third and eighth week of embryonic life when the principle body systems are being established is likely to do far more harm than one introduced in the eighth or ninth month of pregnancy, because the nutritional and energy requirements of differentiating tissue are so much greater than those of tissue either before or after differentiation. Metabolic and nutritional disturbances which can be tolerated by tissues which are less active may be disastrous for tissues that are actively undergoing differentiation. This does not mean that the fetus is free from environmental hazard after the first trimester; environmental agents can cause difficulty late in pregnancy. For example, syphilis and toxoplasmosis in the late months can cause malformations in organs which were originally normal.

In addition to timing, it seems that some teratogens have a predilection for a specific system or area within the embryo. Thalidomide, for example, affects the limbs. However, with other agents, a broad range of deformities is possible.

Fetal tissues may respond to teratogens in several ways. They may hypertrophy or they may atrophy. Structures may split where they should have remained one, or they may fuse. Or there may be a general inhibition of normal growth and development. Underlying these more obvious responses may be failure of induction, that is, the failure of the tissue or organ to transmit the appropriate stimulus which leads to the development of a neighboring tissue, or failure of competence, in which the inductive stimulus is normal but the adjacent tissue is unable to respond normally. In both instances these initial failures may lead to still more change.

External environmental factors which have, or are suspected of having the potential to affect the embryo or fetus include: (1) maternal infection, both viral and bacterial, (2) medication and drugs, (3) maternal nutrition, (4) smoking, (5) lead, (6) pica, and (7) radiation.

MATERNAL INFECTION

Certain viral and bacterial infections, whether or not they are experienced by the mother herself, can affect her developing baby. The best known of the teratogenic viral infections, and the one which alerted researchers to the idea that there could be an environmental source of congenital deformities affecting the baby after conception, is rubella. The discovery followed rubella epidemics in Australia in

1939 and 1940. Because there had been no major rubella outbreak in Australia in the previous 17 years, the vast majority of young, pregnant women had no immunity and contracted rubella in large numbers, with a subsequent high incidence of what are now recognized as the classic sequellae in their newborn infants: cardiac defects (particularly patent ductus and pulmonary stenosis), cataracts, deafness, mental and motor retardation, dental and facial defects, retarded intrauterine growth, enlarged livers and spleens, encephalitis, thrombocytopenia, and thrombocytopenic purpura.

In United States population it has been estimated that of those mothers exposed to rubella during the first trimester, 82.5 per cent will already be immune. About 3 per cent will actually contract rubella, but another 6 per cent will have subclinical infections which can also harm the fetus (Katz, 1968).

Through what mechanism the rubella virus affects development remains a mystery. It is known that the virus enters the fetus through the placenta where it persists in the tissues of the embryo for as long as 6 to 12 months after birth. Thus a newborn with evidence of congenital rubella may himself be a source of infection to susceptible hospital personnel and should be isolated.

In 1970 a massive campaign was undertaken in the United States to vaccinate children under the age of 12 against rubella in order to curtail the spread of the virus to pregnant women. It was suspected that if previous patterns were followed, 1971 would be a year in which there would be a major outbreak of rubella, which seemed to appear in seven-year cycles. The rubella vaccine was not recommended for teen-age girls and women of childbearing age because of the risk that they might become pregnant shortly afterward with possible hazard to the fetus. At the time of this writing, there has not been time to evaluate the success of this campaign in terms of the reduction of birth defects. Should this reduction prove to be significant, it will rank as a major accomplishment of preventive medicine.

In addition to rubella a number of other viruses, some of which are widespread in the general population, have also been investigated in relation to congenital defects. Goldenberg (1969) cites the rubeola virus, the salivary gland virus, and the Coxsackie virus as probably associated with defects, and the viruses causing mumps, smallpox, and viral hepatitis as being possibly related. Infection with the virus of herpes simplex has been found in newborns, but since most adults have immunity to this very prevalent organism, which is the source of cold sores as well as a number of other lesions, it is believed that the baby contracts the virus during delivery. Cesarean section is recommended for mothers with herpes infection of the genital tract. Recently South (1969) has suggested that herpes simplex may also cross the placental barrier and affect the infant in utero.

In one disease of viral origin, cytomegalic inclusion disease, it has been assumed that because the disease is present in the newborn it was contracted in utero, even though there has been no history of the disease in the mother. A number of kinds of brain damage such as microcephaly, spasticity, hydrocephalus, optic atrophy, and chorioretinitis can result from this infection.

From the standpoint of congenital malformation the two most important nonviral infections are syphilis, which can cause fetal death, congenital deafness, and mental retardation, and toxoplasmosis which may cause hydrocephalus, microcephaly, and microphthalmos.

MEDICATION, DRUGS, AND HORMONES AS TERATOGENS

Several drugs have proven to be teratogenic in humans. The reason why these drugs interfere with normal development and the mechanism by which they do so is not clear.

Thalidomide causes either total or partial absence of extremities (amelia and phocomelia). Aminopterin and the related amethopterin, both folic acid antagonists, can cause malformation and, in higher doses, abortion. Aminopterin is used to induce therapeutic abortion in some instances.

Synthetic progestins, used in some pregnancies to control abortion, have produced masculinization of the female lower genital tract. The same virilization can occur following the administration of steroids or the presence of an ovarian tumor during pregnancy.

There have been reports of cleft palate in infants whose mothers have received ACTH or cortisone during pregnancy. Since these mothers would have had some pathological condition for which they received these hormones it is difficult to determine which might have been the cause of deformity. That steroid therapy may lead to the suppression of fetal ACTH and subsequent hormonal imbalance has also been suggested but the possibility is considered to be slight (Cleveland, 1970).

Propylthiouracil, given to the mother, can cause congenital goiter in the infant. The infestion of iodides can also lead to enlargement of the fetal thyroid which can in turn put pressure on the trachea and cause respiratory difficulty. Since many expectorants and cough suppressants sold over the counter contain iodides, additional emphasis is given to the plea that a pregnant woman take no medicine that is not specifically prescribed for her by a physician who is aware of her pregnancy.

The increased use of hallucinogenic drugs and narcotics such as heroin by teen-agers and young adults has heightened concern about the effect these drugs may have on infants in utero. The possible role of LSD in chromosomal breakage has already been mentioned (page 36). When the mother is addicted to narcotics, the baby in utero will also be dependent on the drug and will exhibit withdrawal symptoms shortly after birth (page 180).

Several drugs are suspected but have not yet been proven to be harmful to human infants. High doses of synthetic vitamin K given to the mother prior to delivery may cause hemolysis and hyperbilirubinemia in premature infants. Streptomycin, dihydrostreptomycin, and chloroquine, given to the mother during pregnancy, have been implicated in deafness in the newborn. Quinine is also suspect as a cause of congenital deafness. Reserpine, given for the treatment of hypertension during pregnancy, has been associated with nasal discharge, respiratory distress, lethargy, and anorexia in infants born to mothers receiving the drug.

Other drugs have demonstrated teratogenicity in animal studies but have not yet proven harmful to human infants. They include Dicumarol and its derivative Coumadin, which has produced fetal hemorrhage in many animal species; and tetracycline, which has inhibited the growth of long bones in animal studies. Tetracycline, given during the period when teeth are developing, causes staining of the tooth enamel in both human and animal fetuses.

MATERNAL NUTRITION AND THE DEVELOPING FETUS

Animal experimentation has produced a variety of malformations from deficiencies of nutritional elements such as vitamin A, riboflavin, zinc, and manganese. The only proven congenital malformation related to a specific dietary deficiency in humans is cretinism, which is related to a lack of iodine in the diet. Cretinism and the adult form of iodine deficiency is prevalent in several areas of the world where soil and water do not contain sufficient iodine. Recently there have been reports that goiter is increasing in some parts of the United States because of a decrease in the use of iodized salt. Since mountainous and inland areas are most likely to be affected, pregnant women in these sections should use iodized salt.

A general level of malnutrition has been correlated with low birth-weight babies who are less likely to thrive after birth and have a considerably higher incidence of infant mortality. There are two general sources of fetal malnourishment. The mother may be adequately nourished but because of pathology at the point of placental transfer, due, for example, to faulty implantation, the fetus is not adequately nourished. Or the mother herself may be so inadequately nourished that the fetus is affected. Physiological and cultural factors interact in maternal malnutrition. Changes in maternal metabolism, the expansion of maternal blood volume with the associated reduction in the concentration of hemoglobin and plasma albumin, pulmonary and cardiovascular adjustments—all put increased demands on the mother's nutritional status. On the cultural side, diet patterns, particularly those of teen-age and economically poor mothers, and the rather common tendency of medical professionals to limit calories in order to reduce the possibility of toxemia and produce a smaller infant so that delivery will be easier, have contributed to the incidence of low birth-weight babies. The Committee on Maternal Nutrition of the National Research Council in a new report, *Maternal Nutrition and the Course of Human Pregnancy,* recommends a weight gain of 24 pounds for the mother, in contrast to the 18 to 20 or 22 pounds once considered ideal. Iron and folate supplementation is also recommended as well as the use of iodized salt in those areas deficient in iodine.

SMOKING AND THE FETUS

Repeated studies support the finding that there are a greater number of low birth-weight babies in women who smoke during their pregnancy than in women who do not. This decrease in weight has been shown to be proportional to the number of cigarettes smoked during the pregnancy.

A British report indicates that the effects of smoking in pregnancy extend beyond infancy. In a study of 17,000 children, the children of heavy smokers (defined as women smoking 10 or more cigarettes a day after the fourth month of pregnancy) were found to have poorer physical and social development than the children of light smokers or nonsmokers (*OB Gyn News,* June 15, 1970).

Just why smoking should reduce birth weight and affect later development has not yet been determined, although it has been postulated that the fetal supply of oxygen and nutrients are affected in some way.

LEAD AS A TERATOGEN

Around the beginning of the century it was recognized that women employed in the lead trades often produced live-born infants who were small, weak, and neurologically damaged. It was discovered that lead crossed the placental barrier, resulting in retarded intra-uterine growth and postnatal failure to thrive. Industrial exposure is now controlled, but lead poisoning can result from the ingestion of moonshine liquor, which is still fairly common in the southeastern United States. In a 16-month period at the University of Alabama Medical Center 26 adult women, none of whom happened to be pregnant at the time, were admitted for various forms of lead poisoning related to drinking moonshine. Not all moonshine contains lead—only that produced in stills which use lead pipes or vats—but the buyer has no way of telling how the moonshine was produced.

PICA

Pica, the ingestion of unusual substances such as clay, starch, and flour, is a cultural practice fairly widespread among Negroes living in the southeastern United States and those who have migrated from these areas to northern cities. Counseling a mother about the dangers of clay eating is much like counseling about smoking hazards; it may not cause her to stop. In the case of clay eating, her traditions suggest that she is helping her baby. The anemia which results from clay eating cannot be relieved by oral iron preparations because the clay interferes with the absorption of iron from the gastrointestinal tract. Parenteral iron is essential.

Starch eating is even more common than clay eating because the starch is both inexpensive and easily available at the grocers. The starch comes in small chunks and is eaten as a snack, often with a soft drink, like pretzels or potato chips. Unlike clay, starch does not interfere with iron metabolism but it does add "empty calories" to the diet and gives a full feeling which may keep the mother from eating the food she and her baby need. (See also page 242.)

RADIATION

For many years it has been known that radiation is a direct cause for a number of congenital malformations. The specific organs affected depend upon the stage of fetal development at the time of exposure. The chance of defect is associated with the dose, but the safe limits are not known. Until they are it is recommended that fertile women be exposed to x-ray only in the first ten days after a menstrual period except in emergency.

Stewart and Kneale (1970) suggest that x-ray during pregnancy may increase the risk of cancer in children under the age of ten. After a statistical analysis of 15,000 children they felt that "among one million children exposed shortly before birth to one rad of ionizing radiations there would be an extra 300 to 800 deaths before the age of ten due to radiation induced cancer."

The role of radiation in causing spontaneous genetic mutations which would in turn lead to congenital malformation has been postulated but not yet proven.

The Mother's Body as Fetal Environment

Most of the environmental teratogens discussed so far enter the mother's body and then the body of the fetus through the placenta. Sometimes conditions exist in the mother's body itself which either alone or in interaction with the fetus becomes a source of danger to the unborn child.

MATERNAL DIABETES

Maternal diabetes is an example of a condition which exists in the mother and can affect the fetus. The perinatal mortality of infants of diabetic mothers continues to be six to ten times that of infants in general, even in the best of nurseries. Some researchers have also found a slightly higher rate of major malformation in these infants; others report no difference in this respect.

The infants of diabetic mothers share similar characteristics, often being obese and plethoric. The heart, liver, spleen, or umbilical cord may be enlarged. They are prone to excessive mucus in the respiratory tract, to hyperbilirubinemia, and to low blood levels of sugar and calcium. They may have respiratory distress syndrome, because, although they are large babies, they may actually be premature in terms of gestational age.

Controlling the mother's diabetes is believed helpful to the fetus (it is certainly helpful to the mother), but will not always control the size of the baby. Extraordinarily large babies are also born to mothers who later develop diabetes but do not have symptoms at the time of their pregnancy. There is also evidence that factors intrinsic to the fetus, i.e., genetic factors, may play a role in the way in which the mother's diabetes will affect the fetus. For example, on occasion fraternal twins have been born to diabetic mothers with one resembling the textbook picture of an infant of a diabetic mother while the other appears normal.

BLOOD GROUP INCOMPATIBILITIES

Blood group incompatibilities which may lead to erythroblastosis are another example of fetal-maternal interaction. The two most common types are incompatibility of the Rh_d factors and blood group (ABO) incompatibility. Occasionally rare blood groups are involved.

Rh_d incompatibility. It has been estimated that 90 per cent of the time severe erythroblastosis is due to Rh_d incompatibility (Odell, 1968). Each individual has a double set of Rhesus genes, the most common ones being represented by the letters C,c, D,d, E,e. The d gene determines whether one is considered Rh positive (genotype DD or Dd) or Rh negative (genotype dd). Two different patterns of inheritance are possible if the mother is Rh negative. If the father is homozygous (genotype DD) and the mother is negative, all of the children will be Rh_d positive and the potential for sensitization will exist at every pregnancy with the possibility of erythroblastosis at every pregnancy after the first, or even during the first if the mother has been previously transfused with Rh positive blood.

	Mother	
Father	d	d
D	Dd	Dd
D	Dd	Dd

However, if the father is heterozygous Rh_d positive (genotype Dd) the chances are that only half of his children will be Rh positive. Thus the possibility of erythroblastosis becomes considerably less in this instance.

	Mother	
Father	d	d
D	Dd	Dd
d	dd	dd

The mechanism of sensitization of the mother is the same as in ABO incompatibility, i.e., the mother becomes sensitized to the D positive erythrocytes crossing the placenta into her body and forms anti-D antibodies that then enter fetal circulation and become attached to the D positive fetal erythrocytes. The reticuloendothelial system of the fetus rapidly destroys the antibody-coated red blood cells. If the rate of destruction is so rapid that the infant cannot replace the destroyed cells, he becomes anemic. The more severe his anemia becomes, the more marked will be his other symptoms. The anemia reduces the oxygen-carrying capacity of the blood and leads to progressive hypoxia with subsequent cardiac failure, generalized edema, and finally, in many instances, intrauterine death. *Hydrops fetalis* describes an infant with severe hemolytic disease in utero; he is often stillborn with massive edema, ascites, and anemia.

Until relatively recently the chief help medicine had to offer these infants was early delivery when the maternal antibody titer rose sharply, with the risks of prematurity weighed against the risk of hydrops fetalis. Today the increasing use of amniocentesis (see page 52), which offers more precise diagnosis, and intrauterine transfusion have increased the survival chances for these babies. The use of antibodies (Rho-Gam) to destroy fetal cells in the maternal circulation, is expected to sharply reduce the incidence of erythroblastosis fetalis.

ABO incompatibility. In terms of prevalence in the population ABO incompatibility is found more frequently than are Rh problems. It exists when the mother has type O blood and the infant either type A or type B. Type A or B erythrocytes from the infant cross the placenta; anti-A or anti-B antibodies form in the mother's blood and then recross the placenta to enter fetal circulation. Fortunately, however, hemolytic disease occurs in only a very small proportion of the infants who have ABO incompatibility, being found in about 1 out of 50 instances where anti-A and anti-B are found in the maternal blood or in about 1 out of every 200 pregnancies. ABO incompatibility is rarely associated with the severe anemia and intrauterine death that marks Rh_d reactions. Postnatally, anemia is rare, but hyperbilirubinemia and the associated jaundice may be severe.

MATERNAL OBSTETRICAL CONDITIONS AFFECTING THE FETUS

Placenta previa. Placenta previa is a condition in which the placenta is attached low in the uterus (Fig. 1–29) in contrast to its normal high position. The mother has painless vaginal bleeding generally beginning after the thirty-second week of gestation because of the physiological changes which begin to occur in the uterus in preparation for labor. As the cervix shortens and dilatation begins there is a partial separation of the placenta from the uterus. The bleeding which occurs is strictly maternal.

Prior to 1945, pregnancy was terminated at the first indication of placenta previa, with a resulting fetal mortality of 50 per cent due chiefly to prematurity. Today, in the absence of continuous or severe hemorrhage the kind of treatment is determined largely by the age of the fetus. Before the thirty-sixth week of gestation the obstetrician will try to minimize the risk of prematurity by allowing the mother to

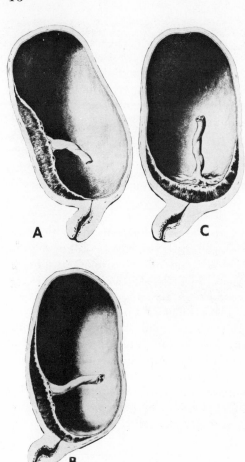

Figure 1-29. Some variations of placenta previa: *A*,
low implantation of the placenta; *B*, total placenta previa;
C, total and central placenta
previa. (From Danforth: *Textbook of Obstetrics and Gynecology.* Hoeber Medical Division, Harper & Row.)

rest and by correcting any deficiency brought about by bleeding. All vaginal examinations are avoided.

After 36 weeks, vaginal examination may be performed in an operating room which is completely prepared both for vaginal delivery and for cesarean section. With the exception of multiparas with low-lying partial placenta previa, most deliveries will be abdominal. Perinatal mortality from placenta previa remains near 25 per cent.

Abruptio placentae. The incidence of abruptio placentae (the premature separation of a normally implanted placenta) remains high. When the separation is sudden and severe, fetal mortality is close to 100 per cent, the fetus dying of intrauterine asphyxia and shock.

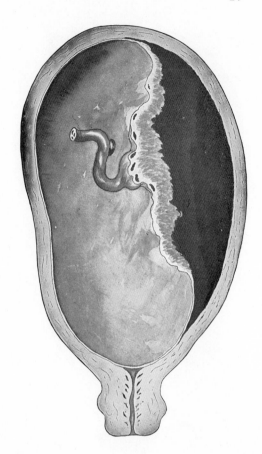

Figure 1–30. Abruptio placentae with internal or concealed hemorrhage. (From Greenhill: *Obstetrics.* 13th Edition. W. B. Saunders, 1965.)

Reports on the incidence of abruptio vary from 1 in 85 to 1 in 200 pregnancies. Reducing the high mortality from abruptio depends upon both prevention and prompt diagnosis and treatment.

Total prevention is probably not possible, but since in approximately 40 per cent of the cases abruptio is associated with either toxemia or hypertension, early recognition and treatment of these conditions should reduce the incidence and subsequent perinatal death rate from abruptio.

Prompt treatment which may save the baby is dependent on swift diagnosis. Uterine tenderness and pain bring the mother to the hospital. There is uterine bleeding but it may be concealed (Figs. 1–30 and 1–31). When the detachment is severe fetal mortality is almost inevitable. Usually a fetal heart beat cannot be detected when the mother reaches the hospital. But in mild to moderate cases immediate delivery, either vaginal or abdominal depending upon the condition of the cervix, may save the baby. Unlike placenta previa, where watch-

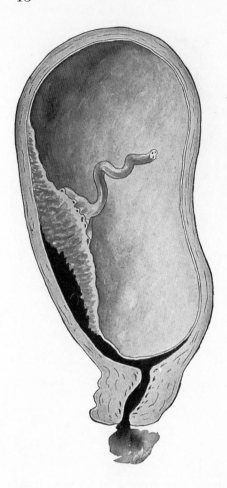

Figure 1–31. Abruptio placentae with external hemorrhage. (From Greenhill: *Obstetrics.* 13th Edition. W. B. Saunders, 1965.)

ful waiting is often indicated, immediate delivery is essential in abruptio placentae before additional separation further limits the baby's oxygen.

Toxemia. Toxemia is another significant cause of perinatal mortality, due in part to intrauterine asphyxia, which follows the disturbances in uteroplacental circulation, and in part to the prematurity of the baby. Prematurity, in turn, may be due either to spontaneous premature labor or to an early termination of pregnancy because of the mother's health. However, it is not felt that trying to postpone delivery serves any useful purpose; there is no evidence that the baby grows once the mother develops eclampsia and he may lose weight.

Even in pre-eclampsia, perinatal mortality is a danger in nearly 10 per cent of the cases. The figure rises to nearly 25 per cent when the mother develops eclampsia, because the mother then becomes the primary consideration. When the mother has both chronic hypertensive vascular disease and acute toxemia, perinatal mortality is as high as 50 per cent.

In most studies there is a correlation between the incidence of toxemia and the extent of prenatal care, although the exact factors in prenatal care which would prevent toxemia have not been identified altogether. Certainly the detection and correction of early symptoms of pre-eclampsia would seem to be important.

Anemia. When the mother is anemic during pregnancy the hazard to the developing fetus is one of chronic intrauterine asphyxia. One of the real values of early prenatal care is the prompt recognition and subsequent treatment of anemia. Not only is iron deficiency anemia prevalent, particularly in mothers from lower socioeconomic classes and in teen-aged mothers, but megaloblastic anemia due to folic acid deficiency has been recognized in 10 to 20 per cent of pregnancies. Some researchers feel that there may be a connection between folic acid deficiency and abruptio placentae (Hubbard, 1963).

The anemia of pregnancy differs from anemia occurring at other periods of life in that it is due not to a decrease in the number of red blood cells but to an increase in plasma volume which affects the relative proportion of red blood cells to plasma. For the woman whose iron stores are borderline, because of teen-age growth needs, marginal nutrition, or frequent pregnancies, this increase in blood volume lowers hemoglobin levels below acceptable limits. Iron therapy (or folic acid therapy in the instance of megaloblastic anemia) can help increase production of red blood cells. Unfortunately many of those mothers most in danger of marked anemia—the very young and the very poor—are also those least likely to have early prenatal care and long-term supplementation.

It must be added that while all the available knowledge points to the theoretical conclusion that iron supplementation improves the oxygen supply of the fetus there is no direct clinical evidence that this is so.

MATERNAL STRESS: A TERATOGEN?

Anxiety produces a variety of physiological changes in mammals due to the response of the sympathetic division of the autonomic nervous system: changes in heart rate, the constriction of blood vessels, dilation of coronary vessels, decrease in gastrointestinal motility, and so on. Generally the greater the anxiety, the more severe the response. In addition, anxiety also affects the adrenal cortical hormonal system as indicated in the following flow chart:

STRESS
activates
HYPOTHALAMUS
which stimulates
ANTERIOR LOBE OF PITUITARY
to produce
ACTH (ADRENOCORTICOTROPIC HORMONE)
which activates
ADRENAL CORTEX
to produce
CORTISONE
which enters
MATERNAL BLOOD STREAM

It has been known for sometime that hormones such as cortisone can cross the placental barrier and possibly affect the fetus.

Animal studies indicate that stress-producing situations do tend to affect the fetus. In a study subjecting one group of rat mothers to stress and then observing the behavior of their offspring as compared to the behavior of the offspring of a control group at 30 to 40 days and at 130 to 140 days, a definite behavior difference was noted in the two groups (Thompson, 1957).

Similar studies have demonstrated that changes in emotional states as well as in learning activity levels can be produced in rat offspring by exposing mothers to such stimuli as intense sound, x-ray, and anxiety-causing conditions during pregnancy. Even when offspring were immediately removed from their anxious mothers after birth to eliminate the possibility that the mothers would transmit anxiety postnatally, the young of stressed mothers responded differently from controls in that they were more timid and "unforthcoming" when placed in strange environments (Dubos, 1965).

Still other research has demonstrated that when mice are intensely crowded during pregnancy, behavioral abnormalities are evident in their offspring as compared to the young of uncrowded mothers. Crowding apparently leads to changes in hormonal secretion which is then reflected in behavior.

As was true of drugs and nutritional deficiencies, these studies cannot be considered directly analogous to human pregnancy, but they can suggest possible directions for research. Stott (1957) did find some indication that maternal illness or stress during pregnancy affected young children. Seventy-six per cent of the children of mothers stressed during pregnancy had nonepidemic illness in their first three years compared with 29 per cent of the children of mothers with no trouble in pregnancy. The association was statistically significant at the .001 level; that is, the probability that these findings could have occurred by chance if there was no relationship between the two factors in the population was less than 1 in 1000. Moreover, when variables, such as social class, premature and abnormal births, and possible neglect by mothers in a state of physical or nervous breakdown, were controlled, the statistical significance held. An analysis of the types of stress to which the mothers were subjected showed that matrimonial difficulties, illness or death of the husband or of another child, difficulties with relatives, eviction, and similar psychological stresses predominated.

Biological, Cultural, and Environmental Interaction

One final example illustrates the complex interaction of biological, cultural, and environmental factors in the effect on the fetus. Temperature is one factor in the maternal environment which affects genetic expression. Himalayan rabbits, for example, have black hair at cold temperatures and white hair at warm temperatures. It is considered likely that certain enzymes which are important in chemical changes leading to the development of black pigment are inactive at higher temperatures.

Can temperature affect the human embryo in a less direct manner? At least two studies (Peterson, 1934; Knoblock and Pasamanic, 1968) indicate that more mentally retarded children are born in the late winter and early spring months, having been conceived the previous spring and summer. The critical period for the organization of the cerebral cortex is the eighth through the twelfth week of pregnancy. Stress during those weeks may very possibly lead to damage in intellectual capacity. If a pregnant woman lowers her dietary intake, and particularly her intake of protein, during very hot weather, this could affect the central nervous system of her baby. If this hypothesis is correct, it would seem that more mentally retarded babies should be born in winters that follow very hot summers than in winters that follow cooler summers. This was found to be true at the .001 level (Knoblock and Pasamanic, 1968).

Monitoring the Fetus in Utero

During the decade of the 60's a number of techniques were developed or used with increasing frequency to make it easier to determine the status of the fetus. In conditions such as galactosemia or andrenogenital syndrome, early detection can be lifesaving. In

other instances early detection can help in the selection of an optimum delivery date for a baby who is beginning to have difficulty,
such as the baby with erythroblastosis, or it can reduce morbidity
such as the mental retardation of PKU.

Amniocentesis. Amniocentesis, the most widely used of these
procedures, has served as a diagnostic aid since the 1930's. It can be
performed as an office procedure with minimal risk to the fetus and
only slight discomfort to the mother. The amniotic fluid that is aspirated during this procedure can be subjected to several types of
tests depending on the information that is desired.

The procedure itself consists of having the mother void and then
lie supine on the examining table, draped so that her abdomen is
exposed. The position of the fetus is determined by palpation, and the
fetal heart rate is ascertained and recorded. After the abdomen is
prepped with antiseptic solution and draped and the skin is infiltrated
with local anesthesia, a #20 gauge spinal needle is inserted trans-
abdominally into the amniotic cavity over the fetal small parts or into
the space just posterior to the fetal neck. The amniotic fluid that is
withdrawn must be shielded from light to prevent the bilirubinoid
pigments from breaking down into other compounds. It must also be
centrifuged immediately to remove blood and other particles that
interfere with analysis.

Amniocentesis is frequently used to determine the status of an
infant with an Rh-sensitized mother. On the basis of the analysis of
the bilirubinoid pigment, the fetus can be grouped into one of three
classifications according to the severity of hemolytic disease. The first
group would include those fetuses who, like their mothers, are Rh
negative, and those whose bilirubin level shows them to be only
mildly affected. A second group consists of fetuses who show moderate hemolytic disease for whom premature delivery may then be considered. Fetuses with severe hemolytic disease are in a third group;
they may be possible candidates for intrauterine transfusion, particularly if their early gestational age rules out premature delivery.
Decisions about the best way to treat these fetuses are usually based
on more than one amniocentesis repeated at intervals of one to four
weeks, depending on the bilirubin level (Horger, 1969).

It has been proposed that amniocentesis, aimed at detecting elevations in bilirubin, be done in any Rh_d negative pregnant woman
who has previously delivered an infant with hemolytic disease or
who has an antibody titer of 1:8 or greater as indicated by indirect
Coombs test.

Amniotic fluid may also be examined for the presence of meconium, a sign of fetal distress. Normally the fetus does not pass mecon-

ium until after birth, but in the presence of anoxia the anal sphincter relaxes and meconium can escape into the amniotic fluid.

Through the measurement of the 17-keto-steroids and pregnane-triol in amniotic fluid, adrenogenital syndrome has been diagnosed in utero.

Other studies suggest that a decrease or absence of several substances in the amniotic fluid may be related to respiratory distress syndrome at birth.

Maternal conditions such as toxemia and maternal diabetes are often indications for the termination of pregnancy before term. Amniotic fluid analysis, together with physical examination, careful history, and x-ray, can aid in the selection of optimum time for delivery. The value of amniotic fluid in such circumstances stems from the fact that the fluid changes in chemical composition as pregnancy proceeds.

Amniocentesis can provide information on the chromatin bodies which can serve as a basis for determining fetal sex. When the mother is known to be a carrier of a sex-linked recessive disorder, such as hemophilia or some types of muscular dystrophy, which has a 50 per cent probability of being expressed in her male children but not in her female children, information about the sex of the fetus may be helpful in determining the possible desirability of therapeutic abortion where this is legal.

Amniotic fluid cells grown in culture have been used in the detection of abnormal fetal karyotypes (page 29). In a study reported by Nadler at the 1969 International Congress on Congenital Malformations, 14 of 150 women undergoing amniocentesis on the fourteenth or fifteenth week of pregnancy were found to have fetuses with chromosomal abnormalities. Thirteen of the mothers were aborted at their request; in every instance the fetus was abnormal. The fourteenth mother decided against abortion and delivered an infant with Down's syndrome. The remaining 136 mothers delivered normal healthy infants with no indications of abnormality.

Not every study of amniocentesis has resulted in such accurate prediction. Nadler suggests that the timing of the test at the fourteen to fifteenth week, a period during which 90 per cent of the amniotic fluid cells can be successfully grown in culture, may be a factor in the extremely accurate prediction in this study.

Cultured cells from amniotic fluid are also being used to detect the presence or absence of some enzymes which lead to the diagnosis of inborn errors in metabolism, such as galactosemia, prior to birth.

Amniography. Amniography is a second technique of monitoring the fetus in utero and like amniocentesis, involves penetrating the amniotic sac. In amniography a radiopaque contrast medium is introduced into the amniotic cavity. The fetus, who is constantly in-

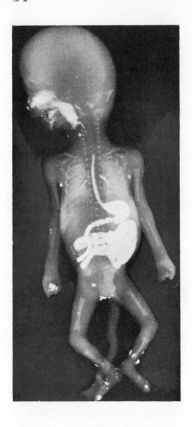

Figure 1–32. A radiopaque substance has been introduced into the amniotic cavity and swallowed by a 10-week-old, 38-gm. fetus. Not only is the gastrointestinal tract visible, but the lungs are visible as well, indicating respiratory movement quite early in fetal life. (From Davis and Rubin: *DeLee's Obstetrics for Nurses.* 18th Edition. W. B. Saunders, 1966.)

gesting amniotic fluid, swallows the contrast medium, so that the gastrointestinal tract subsequently becomes opaque (Fig. 1–32). In the x-ray studies that follow, skeleton, soft tissues and placenta can be observed. Anomalies of the uterus, abnormalities of fetal position, and the soft tissue edema characteristic of hydrops fetalis become evident. The condition of the fetus can also be determined because a fetus who is too moribund to swallow amniotic fluid will not show opacity of the gastrointestinal tract.

Currently amniography is used most frequently as an aid to fetal transfusion, since it indicates a more direct target for the transfusion needle.

Techniques which do not penetrate the amniotic sac. Study techniques which leave the amniotic sac intact include sonar, amnioscopy, and the analysis of maternal steroids. *Sonar,* or ultrasonic echo sounding, employs intermittent sound waves of very high frequency which are projected toward the uterus and then "bounce back" to be displayed on a screen and photographed. Because the waves bounce differently from junctions between tissues of different physical properties, a two-dimensional picture is built on the screen and the size of the fetus can be determined.

Sonar is used chiefly when there is a previous history of an under-developed fetus and when the mother has some condition known to interfere with intrauterine development such as hypertension, chronic renal disease, diabetes, or pre-eclamptic toxemia. Like several of the other newer diagnostic measures, sonar can help the obstetrician decide the extent of risk in early termination of pregnancy. Sonar has the advantage of presenting no known risk to the fetus and no discomfort to the mother other than the slight inconvenience of a contact medium which is smeared on the abdominal skin.

Amnioscopy involves inserting a conical speculum through the cervical canal and inspecting the amniotic fluid through intact transparent fetal membranes during the last trimester. Abnormal fluid pigmentation, such as that caused by meconium can readily be detected.

Excretion of Steroids. The analysis of steroids in the mother's urine can also give some indication of the fetus's well being. The steroid, estriol, produced by the fetus and the placenta functioning as a unit, is normally excreted in the maternal urine at levels of from 10 to 40 mg. per day during late pregnancy. When estriol levels fall much below that margin the fetus may be in trouble. Estriol levels below 1 mg. per day are usually evidence of a dead fetus; urinary estriol between 1 and 4 mg. indicates a fetus in danger of dying. Persistently low levels between 4 and 12 mg. per day are associated with intrauterine growth retardation. A rapidly falling level suggests failing fetal health. Urinary estriol levels are often low in mothers with toxemia, diabetes, or pyelitis. Knowledge of maternal estriol level, if it is available, should be one of the factors in the mother's obstetrical history that is known to the nurse who cares for the baby. These babies need especially careful observation for breathing difficulties, problems in temperature regulation, hypocalcemia, and hypoglycemia.

The Treatment of Fetal Abnormalities

At this time our ability to treat fetal problems is more limited than our ability to detect them. In general there are three options available when fetal difficulties are encountered: therapeutic abortion, when there is good evidence that the fetus is seriously defective; early termination of pregnancy when the chances of survival seem less in utero than after delivery; and intrauterine transfusion.

Intrauterine transfusion is reserved for those infants who are severely affected with hemolytic disease — those who would probably have no chance of survival without it. The chances of survival even with transfusions are not high. Following amniography a needle is inserted into the fetal abdominal cavity. If a series of transfusions is to be given, the catheter attached to the needle may be left in place and antibiotics given via the catheter to combat any possible infection.

The success of intrauterine transfusion is related both to the severity of the hemolytic process and the gestational age of the infant at the time of the first transfusion. If the hemolytic process is so severe that the infant has hydrops fetalis before the first transfusion, the prognosis is generally poor. The later the first transfusion is given in the course of pregnancy, the better the chance of the infant's survival.

SOME LEGAL AND MORAL ASPECTS OF FETAL MEDICINE

Technological advances can at times raise moral and legal questions; recent developments in fetal medicine are no exception. The desirability of abortion based on knowledge of a defective fetus and the right of a fetus to prenatal treatment are two current controversial issues.

The concept of therapeutic abortion when there is strong evidence that the fetus is defective, either because of known exposure to a teratogen such as rubella, or because of abnormal chromosome findings in the amniotic fluid, is intertwined with religious and philosophical beliefs as well as medical and cultural values. The current trend in the United States undoubtedly points toward acceptance of abortion under these circumstances even by individuals who would not accept legalized therapeutic abortion for other reasons.

The legal rights of the unborn infant were considered at a conference held at the National Institute of Child Health and Human Development in 1969. Legal consensus seems to support the idea that life, and therefore the right of the fetus to protection, begins at five to six months after conception, based on the assumption that at this age the fetus could conceivably exist on its own outside the uterus. Many court decisions have rejected the concept that a fetus is living before this time.

The question of legal rights becomes more direct when intrauterine transfusion is considered in the face of parental objection, such as may arise with members of a religious sect such as Jehovah's Witnesses who believe that no foreign blood should enter the body. In such instances the physician or hospital administrator may go to court to have the guardianship of the unborn child temporarily removed from the parent and assigned to himself. After the transfusion takes place the child is then returned to the legal guardianship of the parents. One consequential problem in this sort of procedure, as pointed out by Professor Sanford Katz of the Boston College Law School, is the future attitude of parents toward a child "hexed" by foreign blood. Would he really be welcomed into the family?

The long range implications of these procedures are likely to pose many questions for which we have no answers as yet. And as our technological ability to care for the fetus increases, these problems will surely multiply as well.

Bibliography

Alexander, G. G., Gold, G. M., Miles, B. E., and Alexander, R. B.: Lysergic Acid Diethylamide Intake in Pregnancy: Fetal Damage in Rats. *The Journal of Pharmacology and Experimental Therapeutics, 173*:48, 1970.

Amniocentesis Found 100% Accurate in Prediction of Certain Defects. *Journal of the American Medical Association, 209*:1990, 1969.

Andrews, B. F.: Amniotic Fluid Studies to Determine Maturity. *Pediatric Clinics of North America, 17*:49, 1970.

Arey, L.: *Developmental Anatomy.* 7th Edition. Philadelphia, W. B. Saunders, 1965.

Asimov, I.: *The Genetic Code.* New York, The Orion Press, 1962.

Berrill, N. J.: *The Person in the Womb.* New York, Dodd, Mead and Company, 1968.

Blattner, R. J., Robertson, G. G., and Williamson, A. P.: Principles of Teratology *In* Cooke, R. E. (ed.): *The Biologic Basis of Pediatric Practice.* New York, McGraw-Hill, 1968.

Blattner, R. J.: German Measles *In* Nelson, W. E., Vaughan, V. C. III, and McKay, R. J. (eds.): *Textbook of Pediatrics.* 9th Edition. Philadelphia, W. B. Saunders, 1969.

Blechschmidt, E.: *The Stages of Human Development Before Birth.* Philadelphia, W. B. Saunders, 1961.

Borek, E.: *The Code of Life.* New York, Columbia University Press, 1965.

Carswell, F., Kerr, M. M., and Hutchinson, J.: Congenital Goiter and Hypothyroidism Produced by Maternal Ingestion of Iodides. *Lancet, 1*:1241, 1970.

Cleveland, W. W.: Maternal-Fetal Hormone Relationships. *Pediatric Clinics of North America. 17*:273, 1970.

Cohen, M. M., Hirschhorn, K., and Frosch, W. A.: In Vivo and In Vitro Chromosomal Damage Induced by LSD-25. *New England Journal of Medicine, 277*:1043, 1967.

Danger of Iodides in Pregnancy. *Lancet, 1*:1273, 1970.

Dargassies, S. Saint-Anne: Neurological Maturation of the Premature Infant of 28 to 41 Weeks' Gestational Age *In,* Falkner, F. (ed.): *Human Development.* Philadelphia: W. B. Saunders, 1966.

Desmond, M. M., Rogers, S. F., Lindley, J. E., and Mayer, J. H.: Management of Toxemia of Pregnancy with Reserpine. II. The Newborn Infant. *Obstetrics and Gynecology, 10*:140, 1957.

Dobzhansky, T.: *Mankind Evolving.* New Haven, Yale University Press, 1962.

Donald, I.: Sonar as a Method of Studying Prenatal Development. *Journal of Pediatrics, 75*:326, 1969.

Dubos, R.: *Man Adapting.* New Haven, Yale University Press, 1965.

Effects of Nicotine on the Unborn. *The Stethoscope 24*:1, 1969.

Falkner, F.: *Key Issues in Infant Mortality.* Bethesda, Maryland, National Institute of Child Health and Human Development, 1969.

Fong, Susie W., Margolis, A. J., Westberg, J. A., and Johnson, P.: Intrauterine Transfusion: Fetal Outcome and Complications. *Pediatrics, 45*:576, 1970.

Goldenberg, R. L.: Viral Infections During Pregnancy. *Bulletin of the Sloane Hospital for Women.* XV, 4:135, 1969.

Gravida's Smoking Seen Handicap to Offspring. *Ob. Gyn News, 5,12*:16, 1970.

Hamilton, W. J., Boyd, J. D., and Mossman, H. W.: *Human Embryology.* Baltimore, Williams and Wilkins, 1962.

Horger, E. O., and Hutchinson, D. L.: Diagnostic Use of Amniotic Fluid. *Journal of Pediatrics,* 75:503, 1969.

Hubbard, B. M., and Hubbard, E. D.: Aetiological Factors in Abruptio Placentae. *British Medical Journal,* 2:1430, 1963.

Knoblock, H., and Pasamanic, B.: Seasonal Variation in the Births of the Mentally Deficient. *In* Bresler, J. B. (ed.): *Environments of Man.* Reading, Massachusetts, Addison-Wesley Publishing Company, 1968.

Knudson, A. G., Jr.: Heredity. *In* Cooke, R. E. (ed.): *The Biologic Basis of Pediatric Practice.* New York, McGraw-Hill, 1968.

Langman, J.: *Medical Embryology.* Baltimore, Williams and Wilkins, 1963.

Little, W. A.: Drugs in Pregnancy. *American Journal of Nursing,* 66:1303, 1966.

McKusick, V. A.: *Human Genetics.* Englewood Cliffs, New Jersey, Prentice Hall, 1964.

Medovy, H.: Outlook for the Infant of the Diabetic Mother. *Journal of Pediatrics,* 76: 988, 1970.

Monie, I. W.: Influence of the Environment on the Unborn. *In* Bressler, J. B. (ed.): *Environments of Man.* Reading, Massachusetts, Addison-Wesley Publishing Company, 1968.

Mørch, E. T.: Chondrodystrophic Dwarfs in Denmark. *Opera ex Domo Biol. Hered. Hum. Univ. Hafniensis,* 3:1, 1941.

Murphy, G.: *Personality: A Biosocial Approach to Origins and Structure.* New York, Harper and Brothers, 1947.

Nadler, H. L.: Antenatal Detection of Hereditary Disorders. *Pediatrics,* 42:912, 1968.

Nadler, H. L.: Perinatal Detection of Genetic Defects. *Journal of Pediatrics,* 74:132, 1969.

Odell, G. B.: Historical Data and Alerting Signs in the Newborn (Including Multiple Births). *In* Cooke, R. E. (ed.): *The Biologic Basis of Pediatric Practice.* New York, McGraw Hill, 1968.

Palmisano, P. A., Sneed, R., and Cassady, G.: Untaxed Whiskey and Fetal Lead Exposure. *Journal of Pediatrics,* 75:869, 1969.

Papazian, H. P.: *Modern Genetics.* New York, W. W. Norton, 1967.

Peterson, W. F.: *The Patient and the Weather.* Volume III. Mental and Nervous Diseases. Ann Arbor, Edwards Brothers, 1934.

Reynolds, J. W.: Assessment of Fetal Health by Analysis of Maternal Steroids. *Journal of Pediatrics,* 76:464, 1970.

Shank, R. E.: A Chink in Our Armor. *Nutrition Today,* 5,2:2 (Summer), 1970.

South, M. A., Tompkins, W. A., Morris, C. R., and Rawls, W. E.: Congenital Malformation of the Central Nervous System Associated with Genital Type (Type 2) Herpesvirus. *Journal of Pediatrics,* 75:13, 1969.

Stewart, A., and Kneale, G. W.: Radiation Dose Effects in Relation to Obstetric X-Rays and Childhood Cancers. *The Lancet,* 1:1185, 1970.

Stott, D. H.: Physical and Mental Handicaps Following a Disturbed Pregnancy. *The Lancet,* 272:1006, 1957.

Thompson, J., and Thompson, M.: *Genetics in Medicine.* Philadelphia, W. B. Saunders, 1966.

Thompson, W. R. Influence of Prenatal Maternal Anxiety on Emotionality in Young Rats. *Science, 125*:698, 1957.

Ursprung, H.: Developmental Genetics. *In* Cooke, R. E. (ed.): *The Biological Basis of Pediatric Practice.* New York, McGraw-Hill, 1968.

Wilson, J. G.: Physiology of Development. *In* Cooke, R. E. (ed.): *The Biological Basis of Pediatric Practice.* New York, McGraw-Hill, 1968.

Wright, S. W.: Chromosomal Abnormalities in Man: The Autosomes. *In* Nelson, W. E., Vaughan, V. C., and McKay, R. J. (eds.): *Textbook of Pediatrics.* 9th Edition. Philadelphia, W. B. Saunders, 1969.

CHAPTER 2

Transition: The Newborn During Labor and Delivery

"Every delivery is an emergency until the baby is safely born and breathing easily"

(ABRAMSON, 1966)

Just as the well being of the fetus is intimately related to the health of his mother, so too during labor and delivery will this interrelationship continue. The factors which initiate labor are still not completely understood, but it is very likely that there are several or even many interacting reasons rather than a single cause.

As visible changes occur in the mother—contractions, effacement, dilatation of the cervix—the baby begins to descend through the vaginal canal. Figure 2–1 illustrates the changes in position which the baby normally undergoes in the process of birth. The nurse in the labor room, while she cares for the mother, is also caring for the baby by monitoring and evaluating his condition throughout the period of labor. Everything she is able to do for the mother, e.g., relieving the mother's anxiety so that only a minimum amount of analgesia and anesthesia will be needed, is also a boon to the baby.

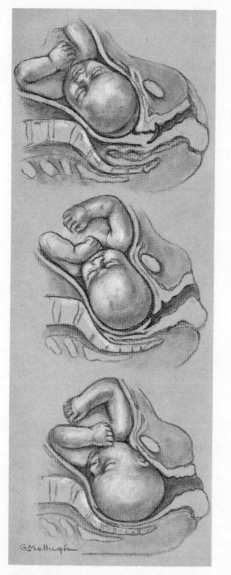

A

B

C

Figure 2–1. The baby undergoes a number of changes in position in the process of birth: *A*, engagement; *B*, descent; *C*, flexion.

Figure 2-1 (Continued). D, completion of internal anterior rotation; *E,* extension; *F,* external rotation. (From Davis and Rubin: *DeLee's Obstetrics for Nurses.* 18th Edition. W. B. Saunders, 1966.

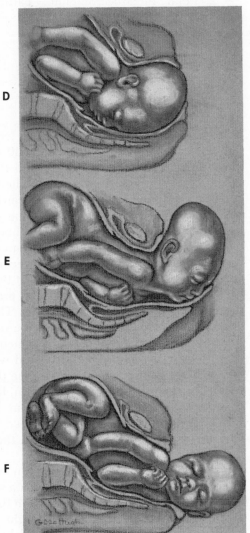

Monitoring the Fetus

There are a number of ways in which the fetus can be monitored during labor:

1. Observation of fetal heart rate
2. Fetal electrocardiogram, particularly in connection with amniotic fluid pressure
3. The presence of meconium
4. Fetal movement
5. Analysis of fetal capillary blood for pH or oxygen concentration.

FETAL HEART RATE

The average fetal heart rate is 140 beats per minute, the normal range encompassing rates from 120 to 160. This rate may drop at the height of a contraction, so that if the heart rate is being monitored by auscultation rather than fetal electrocardiogram it should be counted between contractions. For while some studies have shown no significant change during contractions, others have noted a drop in heart rate to 110 to 120 beats per minute and even to 100, with the rate returning to normal within 15 to 20 seconds before the contraction is completed. It has been theorized that this "physiologic" bradycardia is the result of increased intracranial pressure due to the pressure of the cervical ring on the skull bones. This idea is supported by evidence that "physiologic" bradycardia occurs most frequently when the cervix is dilated 4 to 8 cm., at which time the head is passing the cervical ring; it is infrequently noted when dilatation is less than 4 cm. or more than 8 cm., at which time the skull is pressing against a relatively smooth surface. In addition, fetal bradycardia is not found in breech presentation, unless there are cord complications (see page 72). Bradycardia can also be produced by applying pressure to the fetal head with forceps or a pessary, thereby increasing intracranial pressure.

Pathological fetal bradycardia, in contrast, is almost always an indication of fetal anoxia and is thus a serious sign which, if persistent, will require medical intervention in the labor process to prevent death or subtle brain damage brought about by periods of anoxia.

How can the two types of fetal bradycardia be differentiated? Pathological bradycardia has a late onset in relation to the beginning of the contraction, with the drop in rate beginning at about 25 to 30 seconds after the contraction begins and possibly falling below the rate of 100 as late as 50 seconds after the beginning of the contraction. In these instances bradycardia often persists beyond the end of the

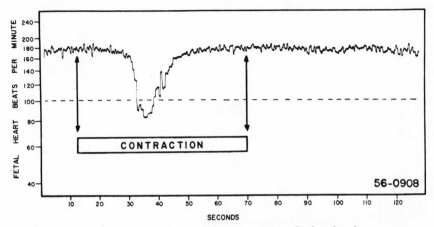

Figure 2-2. "Physiologic" bradycardia occurring at the height of a uterine contraction. The pattern tends to be V-shaped. (From Hon: *American J. Obstet. Gyn., 77*: 1084, 1959.)

contraction. When low heart rates last for more than a minute after the contraction is completed, the baby will be severely depressed at the time of birth (Brady and James, 1962). Should the fetal heart rate at any time fall to less than 60 beats per minute, there must be intervention in the pregnancy if the baby is to survive (Behrman, 1969).

Brief periods of fetal *tachycardia* (rates above 160) are sometimes observed in healthy newborns during the final stages of labor. But tachycardia during early labor and particularly between contractions nearly always is a sign of fetal respiratory embarrassment. In one series every infant with a heart rate of more than 160 between contractions required active resuscitation because of severe neonatal depression (Brady and James, 1963).

FETAL ELECTROCARDIOGRAM

While fetal heart rates can be periodically and even frequently monitored by auscultation, far more precise, continuous measurement is obtained through the use of a fetal electrocardiogram. For the EKG by recording different patterns of heart beat, as well as measuring heart rate, makes it possible to differentiate types of bradycardia (Figs. 2-2, 2-3, 2-4).

Initially, fetal EKG's were obtained by placing the electrodes on the mother's abdomen (Fig. 2-5). Now in many institutions a small electrode is placed on the presenting part of the fetus in utero. At

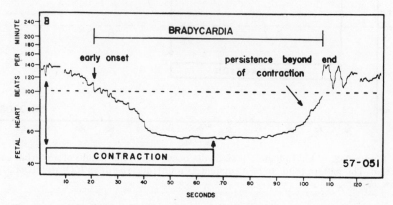

Figure 2-3. Pathologic bradycardia, with early onset and persistence beyond the end of the contraction. The infant was a double footling breech with prolapsed cord. The pattern is U-shaped. (From Hon: *American J. Obstet. Gyn., 77*:1084, 1959.)

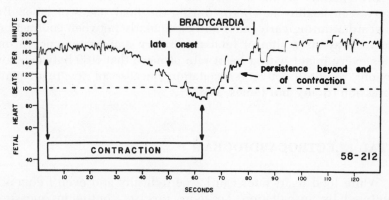

Figure 2-4. Pathologic bradycardia with late onset and persistence beyond the end of the contraction. This type of bradycardia often accompanies frequent and very strong uterine contractions. The pattern is U-shaped. (From Hon: *American J. Obstet. Gyn., 77*:1084, 1959.)

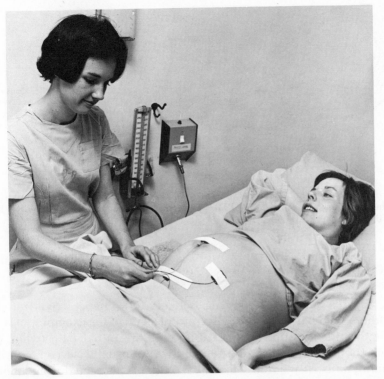

Figure 2-5. Fetal electrocardiography through electrodes placed on the mother's abdomen. (From Davis and Rubin: *DeLee's Obstetrics for Nurses,* 18th Edition. W. B. Saunders, 1966.)

the same time a thin polyethylene catheter, which will measure amniotic fluid pressure, is inserted into the vagina, the membranes having been artificially ruptured if they had not already ruptured spontaneously (Fig. 2-6). The resulting record will demonstrate the relationship between fetal heart rate and contractions.

Fetal electrocardiography can also be used during the prenatal period to determine whether or not the fetus is alive, to diagnose multiple gestation, and to indicate whether the presentation will be vertex or breech (Fig. 2-7).

MECONIUM IN THE AMNIOTIC FLUID

Even before the time of our Civil War, a German physician, Schwartz, had recognized that meconium in the amniotic fluid indicated a distressed fetus. A baby with both bradycardia and meconium in the amniotic fluid has, at best, a guarded prognosis.

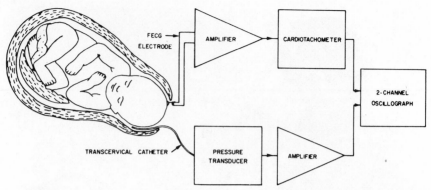

Figure 2-6. The placement of an electrode on the fetal scalp and a transcervical catheter to measure amniotic fluid pressure. (From Willis: *The Canadian Nurse*, Dec. 1970, p. 28.)

FETAL MOVEMENT

A fetus deprived of oxygen is likely to be hyperactive initially. Mothers who have a severe abruptio placentae, for example, may report that for a period of time following the initial pain (when the placenta became detached) the baby was unusually active before becoming unusually quiet. Unusual activity of this type during labor or the mother's report of strenuous activity should be noted, and the mother even more carefully observed for other signs of fetal distress.

ANALYSIS OF FETAL CAPILLARY BLOOD

Amnioscopy can be used during labor as well as during the prenatal period to visualize amniotic fluid. If the fluid is green, indicating that it contains meconium, or yellow, because of the presence of bile pigments, the membranes can be ruptured and capillary blood obtained from the fetal scalp for analysis of pH and blood gases.

The technique of obtaining scalp blood is as follows: the fetal scalp is exposed with a sterile speculum, vaginal retractors, or a conical amnioscope and a small incision is made (Fig. 2–8). Blood is collected in microtubes which are immediately clamped at both ends to keep the blood anaerobic. The blood is placed on ice and analysis is done immediately.

Following scalp sampling the incised area is observed for bleeding during at least one contraction. Usually the site bleeds very little after initial blood collection.

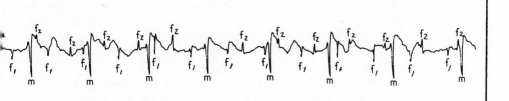

Figure 2–7. An electrocardiographic tracing showing the maternal tracing (m) and two fetal tracings (f_1 and f_2). This indicates a twin gestation, with one twin (f_1) in a breech presentation and one twin (f_2) in a vertex presentation. (From Davis and Rubin: *DeLee's Obstetrics for Nurses.* 18th Edition. W. B. Saunders, 1966.)

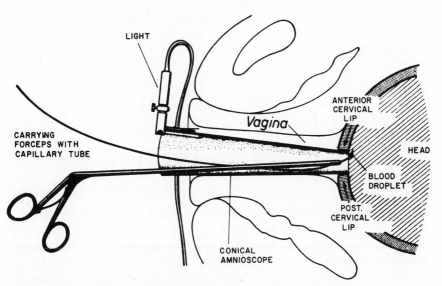

Figure 2–8. Diagram showing method of obtaining a fetal blood sample. (From Willis: *The Canadian Nurse,* Dec. 1970, p. 28.)

Monitoring the Mother

It is neither practical nor necessary for every mother to have intensive monitoring. Auscultation of fetal heart rate together with close observation still provides the most adequate means of monitoring in the majority of deliveries. However, when a mother is classified as a high risk before delivery (i.e., the mother with diabetes or the very young mother) or when careful observation suggests that the fetus is having difficulty, more extensive monitoring can serve a very useful purpose.

There is some discomfort to the mother, and some anxiety as well. Clear explanations concerning the equipment used and the reasons for monitoring, with stress being placed on how this will help the baby to be delivered in the safest manner possible, should help to make the temporary inconvenience more acceptable. If a potentially high risk mother is to be induced, these techniques, as well as other aspects of labor and delivery, can be discussed with her on the evening before the procedure is done. Willis (1970) reports that at the Royal Victoria Hospital in Montreal the same nurses talk with the mother on the previous day, care for her during labor and delivery, and visit her again on the postpartal hall. Patient reaction to this kind of nursing is excellent. Many mothers say their confidence is increased and they are better able to relax during labor. There is also considerable satisfaction for the nurses who are able to give this kind of care.

Special Hazards of Labor and Delivery

OBSTETRICAL ANALGESIA AND ANESTHESIA AND THE NEWBORN

Because analgesia or anesthesia is used in the majority of deliveries in the United States (more so than in many other nations; see page 263) it is important to understand how each type of drug affects the fetus. It is believed that all drugs used during labor and delivery for the relief of apprehension and pain can pass through the placenta and affect the infant. Moreover, animal studies suggest that the fetus is far more sensitive to depressant drugs than an adult would be.

Barbiturates.   Barbiturates, once widely used to relieve apprehension during early labor, tend to depress the newborn, particularly in the following circumstances:

1. If the drug was used in large doses in a mistaken attempt to relieve pain (barbiturates will only relieve pain in overdosage);

2. If the drug was used in combination with a general anesthetic; or

3. If the baby was unusually asphyxiated for some other reason.

The better the mother's preparation for delivery during the prenatal period and the better her care in the labor room, the less apprehensive she will be, thereby eliminating the need for barbiturates. Since there is no reliable barbiturate antidote, the baby depressed from these drugs will have to be resuscitated (page 80).

Tranquilizers. Tranquilizers, such as chlorpromazine (25 mg.), promethazine (50 mg.), and promazine (50 mg.), given I.M., are also used to alleviate apprehension and, like barbiturates, tend to depress the baby, particularly if they are combined with narcotics or sedatives.

Morphine and meperidine. Morphine and meperidine (Demerol) are the two narcotics most often used to relieve pain during labor. Again the possibility of respiratory depression exists. However, Shnider and Moya (1964) report that if Demerol is given to the mother within one hour of delivery, rather than one to three hours before delivery, there is no significant depression. Giving larger than usual dosage (generally 50 mg.) or giving the drug intravenously or in combination with a barbiturate, decreases this "margin of safety" and increases the chance that the newborn will be depressed.

Unlike depression caused by barbiturates, much of the depression due to morphine and Demerol can be overcome through the use of narcotic antagonists, the two in most frequent use being nalorphine (Nalline) and levallorphan (Lorfan). These antagonists act through the mechanism of drug competition, probably replacing the narcotic itself in the medulla and to a certain extent in the higher areas of the brain because of a greater affinity for receptor sites. They are not central nervous system stimulants and are of no value to the baby who is depressed for any reason other than narcotics.

Nalline and Lorfan are currently being used in the delivery room in three different ways:

1. The antagonist (Nalline, 10 mg. or Lorfan, 1 mg.) is given to the mother intravenously 5 to 15 minutes prior to delivery.

2. The antagonist is used in combination with the narcotic during labor with the hope of providing analgesia without depression.

3. Nalline 0.2 mg. or Lorfan .05 mg. is injected directly into the infant's umbilical vein or given by deep intramuscular injection, the site being well massaged afterward. These drugs should be given to the baby only after a clear airway and adequate ventilation have been established.

Regional anesthesia. In regional anesthesia the chief hazard to the infant is the possibility of hypotension which will, in turn, interfere with uterine blood flow and hence with fetal oxygenation. Prevention of hypotension includes the rapid infusion of intravenous fluids at the time the anesthesia is being given and positioning the mother on her side for five minutes or more after the drug has been injected to take the pressure of the heavy uterus off the inferior vena cava, which in itself will cause hypotension. Frequent checks of maternal blood pressure should detect hypotension promptly.

One additional danger in the use of caudal anesthesia is the accidental penetration of the fetal scalp, thereby introducing the anesthetic directly into the fetus with resultant severe bradycardia and generalized convulsions. The treatment in this case is gastric lavage combined with prompt exchange transfusion.

General anesthesia. General anesthesia for the mother in labor involves several problems which reflect the anatomical and physiological changes that differentiate her from the nonpregnant adult. Her residual lung volume is decreased because of her enlarged uterus, which means that she will quickly build up higher alveolar concentrations of anesthetic (there is less air to dilute it). Because of a tendency toward hyperventilation in labor she will become anesthetized more quickly — in three minutes as compared to ten to twelve minutes for nonpregnant women. The emptying time of the stomach is delayed during labor; once labor has begun, no solid foods can pass through the stomach. Moreover, pressure on the fundus can cause her to aspirate even if she has been NPO for many hours. Thus if the mother has eaten within six hours of the onset of labor, general anesthesia will be avoided if at all possible.

All of these factors can affect the baby. "The depression produced in the baby is directly related to the depth and the duration of the mother's anesthesia" (Abramson, 1958). It takes only about two minutes for gases to reach the baby. Since the mother will be anesthetized very quickly, so will the infant. The shorter and lighter the anesthesia, the better. There should always be at least 25% oxygen in any gaseous mixture given for delivery.

Aspiration is the chief hazard to the mother when general anesthesia is used for delivery and obviously any such serious problem in the mother is a potential danger to the baby as well.

Long-range effects of anesthesia and analgesia. Most early research which evaluated the depressant effect of drugs on infants used Apgar scores at one and five minutes (see page 75) but rarely followed the infant beyond this period. There are now several studies involving observation of the baby during the first four days of life.

1. In a test of visual attentiveness of 20 term infants between the second and fourth days of life there was a significant relationship indicating that "the more drugs administered closer to delivery, the less attentive is the infant likely to be" (Stechler, 1964).

2. Behavioral impairment, defined as failure to have sustained movement after stimulation, and EEG changes were found more frequently at 36 hours in a group of babies whose mothers received medication during labor than in a control group whose mothers were not medicated (Borgstedt, 1968).

3. Infants born to mothers who were sedated during labor consistently demonstrated depressed sucking activity during the first four days of life (Kron, 1966).

None of these studies indicates any long-range change due to drug-induced depression; this is an area in which there would seem to be a real need for further research.

ABNORMAL POSITION OF THE FETUS IN UTERO

Breech position. In about 2 or 3 per cent of all deliveries the baby is in a breech position (Fig. 2–9), either complete or frank (incomplete) breech (Fig. 2–10). While there is no clear reason why the baby assumes or maintains this position at birth, several theories exist. At 30 weeks gestation about one fetus in four will be in a breech position; thus the incidence of breech delivery is considerably higher in premature than in term deliveries. At approximately 34 weeks most infants will shift position and will present head-first at the time

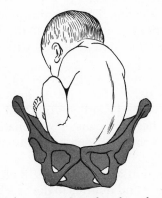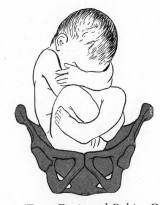

Figure 2–9. Complete breech presentations. (From Davis and Rubin: *DeLee's Obstetrics for Nurses.* 18th Edition. W. B. Saunders, 1966.)

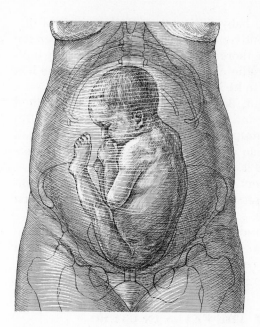

Figure 2-10. One type of incomplete breech presentation. The legs are extended. (From Davis and Rubin: *DeLee's Obstetrics for Nurses.* 18th Edition. W. B. Saunders, 1966.)

of delivery. But if the fetus's legs are extended and for some reason cannot be flexed, the fetus will be unable to turn. At the time of delivery the baby's body will emerge first, and difficulties may arise if the head is delivered either too quickly or too slowly. In the first instance, that of too rapid delivery, intracranial hemorrhage may result from a tear in the tentorium cerebelli and lead to the infant's death. Considering how many hours it takes the head to pass through the pelvis in a normal vertex delivery and how quickly it must pass the pelvis in a breech delivery (usually ten minutes or less) it is not difficult to see why this problem can develop. The pressure on the head tends to pull the cranium away from the base of the skull, thus pulling the falx cerebri away from the tentorium cerebelli with the resultant tear and hemorrhage.

If delivery is too slow the danger is one of asphyxia rather than hemorrhage. Once the head enters the pelvis, the cord is squeezed between the unborn head and the bony pelvis and cervix. Until the nose and mouth are delivered the baby has no means of oxygenation. However, this is much less frequently a cause of death than hemorrhage.

Babies presenting in a breech position are also more likely to have fractures of the clavicle or long bones and injuries to the brachial plexus or the sternocleidomastoid muscle. Injuries to the spinal cord may result from forceful traction on the feet during extraction.

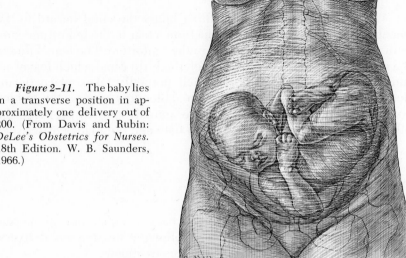

Figure 2–11. The baby lies in a transverse position in approximately one delivery out of 200. (From Davis and Rubin: *DeLee's Obstetrics for Nurses.* 18th Edition. W. B. Saunders, 1966.)

Transverse position. In one delivery out of 200 the baby lies in a transverse position in the uterus (Fig. 2–11). If vaginal delivery is attempted in this situation perinatal mortality is approximately 30 per cent. Early diagnosis and abdominal delivery reduce the rate of mortality.

Face and brow presentation. There is usually no difficulty when there is an anterior-face and brow presentation; babies with a posterior-face and brow presentation are generally delivered by cesarean section.

MULTIPLE GESTATION

Perinatal mortality in multiple gestation is double that of single births because of the following reasons:
1. the increased frequency of toxemia
2. the increased frequency of prematurity (80 per cent of all twin deliveries are premature)
3. hazards to the second twin during delivery. Perinatal loss of the second twin is 100 per cent greater than that of the first twin; both breech delivery and version of the fetus in breech position carry a high rate of loss.

DELIVERY FOLLOWING RAPID LABOR

When labor lasts less than three hours the chief hazard to the infant is that of subdural hematoma from a tear in the tentorium cerebelli which in turn ruptures veins in the tentorium. The tear is due to the rapid descent of the head through the birth canal which leaves no time for the gradual molding which normally takes place during delivery. Less frequently there is cranial bleeding because the sudden compression of the skull causes one cranial bone to over-ride the other, catching veins as if they were between the blades of scissors.

DELIVERY USING FORCEPS

Occasionally the baby is found to have a cephalohematoma (see page 111) or a linear skull fracture following low-forceps delivery. Neither condition is serious nor requires treatment.

However, mid- to high-forceps delivery is associated with an increased incidence of both perinatal mortality and neonatal morbidity. This is due in part to the conditions which cause the use of mid- to high-forceps, such as prolonged labor or uterine inertia. Among the hazards of forceps delivery are depressed skull fracture, intracranial hemorrhage, and brachial plexus injuries.

Care Immediately Following Delivery

CLEARING THE RESPIRATORY TRACT

The classic picture of a physician holding a newborn head-down following delivery illustrates a real essential of immediate newborn care. Unless the head is lower than the body, mucus and sometimes blood clots and meconium will be drawn into the respiratory tract, causing serious respiratory obstruction and even death.

There are differences of opinion as to the value of suctioning the respiratory tract immediately after the head has been delivered but before delivery is complete. Proponents of suctioning obviously consider it important to clear the airway immediately. However, opponents of suctioning before complete delivery argue that (1) the act of suctioning may stimulate the infant to breathe before he is delivered, (2) when the secretions are watery the procedure is unnecessary and will only delay birth, and (3) it is virtually impossible to adequately suction a partially delivered infant while the mother is in a lithotomy position (Abramson, 1966).

Once delivery is complete, gentle aspiration of mucus with the baby in a head-down position is all that is necessary for the baby who is in good condition. Spontaneous respirations should begin within a few seconds to a minute after birth. If they do not, the delivery-room staff must take immediate steps to initiate respirations (see page 80); there is no time to hope that the baby will eventually begin to breathe on his own.

IMMEDIATE EVALUATION OF THE INFANT

In evaluating the newborn it is advisable to note and record the time at which the baby first gasped and cried and then was able to sustain respiration. A system for recording this kind of information was devised by Dr. Virginia Apgar and is now widely used in the evaluation of the newborn (Table 2–1). The first recording is made at one minute after delivery, this time having been chosen because in a large series of observations it was found to be the point at which the lowest score was likely to be obtained. A second Apgar evaluation is then made at five minutes past delivery.

Although each item scored—heart rate, respiratory effort, muscle tone, reflex irritability, and color—is numerically equivalent, some signs are actually more significant than others. For example, an Apgar 9 newborn who is scored 2 in every area with the exception of color is in less distress than an Apgar 9 infant who is scored 2 in every area but heart rate or respiratory effort. However, it is likely that an infant with cardiac or respiratory distress would also have a low score on other items. Only about 15 per cent of infants will score 2 in color at one minute after delivery.

*TABLE 2–1. The Apgar Scoring Method**

SIGN	0	1	2
Heart rate	Absent	Below 100	Over 100
Respiratory effort	Absent	Minimal; weak cry	Good; strong cry
Muscle tone	Limp	Some flexion of extremities	Active motion; extremities well flexed
Reflex irritability (response to stimulation on sole of foot)	No response	Grimace	Cry
Color	Blue or pale	Body pink; extremities blue	Pink

*From Apgar: *Anesthesia and Analgesia*, 32:260, 1953. Apgar, et al.: *J. American Med. Ass.*, 168:1985, 1958.

Statistically significant correlations have been found between mortality and low Apgar scores at one minute and even more significant correlations with low five-minute scores. The incidence of neurologic defects is also high in infants with low five-minute Apgar scores.

PROVIDING WARMTH FOR THE NEWBORN

A most crucial need of the infant during the first minutes and hours after birth is warmth. Chilling increases the baby's need for oxygen and aggravates the metabolic acidosis which is present to some extent in all infants during the first hour of life. In addition recent evidence indicates that hypothermia may increase the possibility of hyperbilirubinemia in newborns.

In the average delivery room there is a 15-degree difference between room temperature and the temperature of the intrauterine environment from which the baby has been delivered. A wet, small newborn loses up to 200 calories per kilogram per minute in the delivery room, through evaporation, convection, and radiation. Realizing that an adult at full compensation generates only about 90 calories per kilogram per minute makes it easier to appreciate the severity of this heat loss.

The conservation of heat is directly related to the several processes of heat loss. Loss by evaporation is due to the fact that the baby is wet; the single act of drying him immediately cuts heat loss in half. Convective heat loss, due to air blowing across the baby, causes a transfer of heat from baby to environment. We deliberately use cool air to cool ourselves on a hot day or to reduce temperature in a febrile patient. But no newborn should be accidentally cooled by a current of air blowing across his body.

A third mechanism of heat loss is radiation. The baby will radiate heat to the nearest object. If he is swaddled in a blanket, he will radiate to the blanket and his environment will be warm. If he is left uncovered and unclothed he will radiate heat in an attempt to raise the temperature of the entire delivery room — rather like trying to raise the temperature of an entire house by means of a single fireplace.

To counterbalance heat loss, the newborn has mechanisms through which he strives to retain heat (vasoconstriction and insulation) and to produce heat.

Vasoconstriction is the most important of the mechanisms of heat retention. However, if the mother has been treated with magnesium sulfate for toxemia, the baby's vasoconstrictive mechanisms may not function at peak capacity. Insulation is a second way in which the body conserves heat. But even the term infant in this regard is at a relative disadvantage in comparison with older children and adults because of his limited amount of fat. The baby weighing less than 2500 gm. has almost no subcutaneous fat and will thus have difficulty conserving heat. The third way in which the baby conserves heat is by assuming a position similar to his position in utero.

Besides conserving heat, the baby will also produce heat. While older individuals do this predominately by shivering, newborns rely primarily on nonshivering thermogenesis; they raise their temperature by an increase in their rate of metabolism. This increases oxygen consumption, but if for some reason the baby has difficulty delivering oxygen to his cells, he will be unable to increase his metabolic rate and nonshivering thermogenesis will be compromised.

If all the preceding principles are implemented in the nursing care of the baby it will not be too difficult to keep the full-term, apparently healthy newborn warm; he can be dried, swaddled, and placed in a warm crib. The problem comes when a baby having difficulties needs resuscitation or other medical attention which requires exposure. Yet this baby, who may be of low birth weight and who is probably not oxygenating adequately, is even more in need of warmth than the healthy newborn who lies bundled and warm in his crib. The best available solution to this dilemma at present is an overhead warmer which utilizes radiant heat to keep the baby warm yet allows free access for resuscitation (see page 147). If possible, the baby's extremities can be covered to further minimize heat loss.

Several points need to be kept in mind in relation to these warmers:

1. Hyperthermia, as well as hypothermia, is a stress, leading to increased oxygen consumption. When the baby is under a warmer for more than a few minutes, his temperature should be monitored. The temperature on most warmers can be easily adjusted to more than one level.

2. Burns are a possibility though they are infrequent.

3. The warmer should be turned on before the baby is delivered; in this way the blankets will be warm and the baby will not have to be placed on a cold surface on which he will immediately lose heat.

IDENTIFYING THE INFANT AND ADMINISTERING PROPHYLACTIC EYE DROPS

The administration of prophylactic eye drops and the identification of the infant also should be carried out in the delivery room before the baby is taken to the nursery. Occasionally because of severe illness a baby may not be footprinted nor given eye drops in the delivery suite. The nurse in the nursery must always be aware of this so she can complete these tasks as soon as it is possible.

Identification. Identification bands for mother and child, with matching numbers as well as names and showing the sex of the baby, are one way in which mother and baby can be identified. These bands should be checked each time the baby is removed from his crib or taken to his mother, as well as at the time of discharge.

Footprinting, another widely used means of identification, has been subject to much criticism. In a study by the Chicago Board of Health, policemen who were accustomed to interpreting finger-prints found that 98 per cent of footprints submitted by most of the Chicago hospitals were valueless and could not serve as a means of identification. However, two minutes of instruction to the hospital personnel responsible for taking the footprints, produced prints from which positive identification could be made in 99 per cent of the cases (Gleason, 1969).

To produce reliable and meaningful prints Gleason suggests the following procedure for footprinting:

1. Proper equipment should be used, preferably a disposable footprinter ink plate and a smooth, high gloss type of paper.

2. Immediately after the baby is received from the physician and wrapped in a warm blanket his foot should be wiped so that the vernix will not dry on it. This will make it easier to clean the foot when the actual footprinting is done.

3. At footprinting time, immediately before the baby is to be taken from the delivery room, the following technique is used:

a. The foot is cleaned thoroughly but gently. Scrubbing it too hard will make the baby's skin peel.

b. The foot is dried thoroughly.

c. The baby's knee is flexed so that his legs are close to his body; his ankle is grasped between the thumb and middle finger; the nurse's index finger is pressed on the upper surface of the foot just behind the baby's toes to prevent his toes from curling.

d. The footprinter is pushed gently to the baby's foot.

e. The baby's foot is gently touched to the footprint chart; the chart should be attached to a hard surface such as a clip board.

f. The heel is placed on the chart first; then the baby's foot is walked gently onto the chart with a heel to toe motion. The foot should not be rolled back and forth either on the inking pad or on the foot-print chart.

The footprint should be checked to see if the ridges are dis-cernible. Any excess ink can then be wiped from the baby's foot. Commonly the mother's fingerprints are placed on the same sheet as the baby's footprint.

Aside from the whole controversy as to how accurate footprints are, there has been some question about chilling the baby during the process of footprinting. An alternative means of identification has been suggested by Shepard (1968, 1969) which involves writing a name or code on the infant's chest with a 4% solution of silver nitrate, using a specially treated fountain pen or a felt pencil containing a 7% solution of silver nitrate. This method is rapid and can easily be done under a warming cradle. The silver nitrate leaves an indelible tattoo which lasts for three or four weeks and eventually disappears completely.

Prophylactic eye care. The instillation of 1% silver nitrate drops in the eyes of the newborn as a protection against gonorrheal infection is still the only lawful method of prophylaxis in many areas. Saline irrigations immediately afterward reduce the incidence of conjunctivitis without affecting efficacy of the treatment. Where it is legally permissible, tetracycline or penicillin is sometimes used because they cause less irritation, and appear to be just as effective.

Caring for the Baby Who Does Not Breathe Spontaneously

A nurse working in the delivery room plays a central role in preventing death or permanent brain damage in the baby who does not breathe spontaneously and immediately after birth. Even if she does not actively participate in resuscitation, it is she who makes sure that both personnel and equipment are ready for emergency use at every delivery.

In relation to personnel, the ideal situation is to have a pediatrician or pediatric house officer present who is able to devote full attention to the baby so that the obstetrician can continue to care for the mother. The need for a pediatrician can be anticipated in certain instances, when the possibility exists that the baby will be depressed, such as in those situations in which the mother has (1) illness such as toxemia, diabetes, severe anemia, cardiorespiratory disease, and low blood pressure, (2) abnormal uterine contractions, (3) premature rupture of the membranes, which may lead to sepsis or pneumonia in the baby, (4) has received a large amount of analgesia, or (5) had antepartum hemorrhage from an abruptio placenta, a placenta previa, or some other source.

Cesarean section, premature delivery, and the possibility of cord compression as in a breech delivery or in cord prolapse are still other indications for alerting the pediatrician.

Should a pediatrician not be available either because of the size of the hospital or because no difficulty was expected, the anesthesiologist may be the one who cares for the infant in distress. However, statistics indicate that only about one-third of vaginal deliveries in the United States are attended by either an anesthesiologist or a nurse anesthetist. In the remaining two-thirds, either the obstetrician or some other person—a nurse or a medical student, for example,—administers the anesthesia.

Often, then, in some hospitals or some situations, resuscitation or assistance in resuscitation becomes the responsiblity of the nurse. Before discussing the routine of resuscitation, let us note that the following equipment should be available for every delivery:

1. a bulb syringe for suctioning
2. suction equipment and suction catheters; suction should be checked prior to each delivery to be sure it is in working order
3. oxygen
4. mask and bag
5. De Lee glass bulb with catheter for aspiration of mucus
6. laryngoscope
7. small endotracheal tubes
8. drugs and syringes: narcotic antagonists (see page 69); sodium bicarbonate; glucose for injection
9. umbilical artery catheter

ROUTINE FOR RESUSCITATION

1. The airway must be cleared. This is done by gentle suctioning and, particularly if the baby is flaccid, by inserting a small airway to keep the tongue from obstructing the passage of air.

2. Flicking the heel lightly may initiate respiration. More vigorous stimulation, such as spanking, back slapping, compressing the anterior chest, and immersing the baby in cold water is considered more dangerous than helpful and should never be used.

3. If the depression is believed to be due to narcotics given to the mother during labor, narcotic antagonists are given (see page 69).

4. Once the airway is clear, one of several techniques may be used. Oxygen may be given by funnel or by bag and mask. By watching the chest wall and listening to the lungs with a stethoscope it will become evident whether the lungs are becoming inflated when a bag and mask are used. Pressure on the bag must be light to avoid overexpansion of the lungs. Mouth-to-mouth breathing, with the breather taking a breath before blowing and blowing only the amount of air in his mouth (not the amount in his lungs) is another possibility. Oxygen may flow from a tube into the operator's mouth during

mouth-to-mouth breathing to increase the oxygen concentration of the air blown into the baby's lungs.

5. If all of the preceding measures have been taken and the baby still fails to breathe, the infant's head is hyperextended and a laryngoscope is inserted by someone experienced in its use. Any mucus or blood clots in the trachea are aspirated and an endotracheal tube inserted. Mouth-to-endotracheal tube inflation may now initiate respiration, using the same principles as in mouth-to-mouth resuscitation. While both mouth-to-mouth ventilation and mouth-to-tube ventilation risk pulmonary infection, they decrease the risk of pneumothorax that could occur from too vigorous a use of mechanical ventilators.

6. If the heart rate remains below 70 beats per minute in spite of these measures, closed chest cardiac massage at the rate of two compressions per second for three to four seconds is begun, alternating with lung inflation.

7. Further treatment, if necessary, may include the insertion of an umbilical catheter, the administration of sodium bicarbonate and glucose, and the withdrawal of blood for blood gas determination.

It is emphasized again that during all of these procedures the baby must be kept warm, as any chilling only further compounds his problem. The baby who has undergone extensive resuscitation must be carefully observed in the days that follow.

The Transition to Extrauterine Life

From the moment of birth throughout the first hours of life the newborn adapts to a new way of life. Under normal circumstances both his internal changes and his behavior are characteristic.

Arnold and her associates (1965) have described the behavior of a "standard baby," i.e. a baby delivered vaginally with a vertex presentation, weighing 2500 gm. or more and having an Apgar score of 7 or higher. The babies they studied were observed constantly for the first 15 minutes of life, and then at 15-minute intervals for periods of 6 to 48 hours.

At the time of birth the baby was intensely active. The mean peak heart rate at three minutes was 180 beats per minute, dropping to rates between 120 and 140 at 30 minutes. The mean peak respiratory rate of 82 per minute came at one hour of age. Transient flaring of the nasal alae, retractions, and grunting were not unusual during this period in apparently healthy babies.

Following this initial outburst of activity the baby was quiet and relatively unresponsive to external and internal stimuli. On the

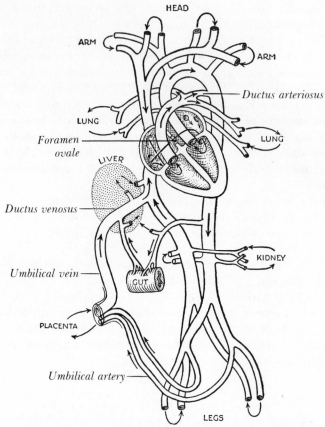

HEAD

ARM

ARM

Ductus arteriosus

LUNG

Foramen ovale

LUNG

LIVER

Ductus venosus

KIDNEY

Umbilical vein

GUT

PLACENTA

Umbilical artery

LEGS

Figure 2-12.   Human circulation before birth. (Partly after Dodds *In* Arey: *Developmental Anatomy.* 7th Edition. W. B. Saunders, 1965.)

average he slept first at around two hours of age, the period of sleep lasting from a few minutes to two to four hours. When he first awakened the infant was temporarily hyper-responsive with an increased heart rate, change in color, and, in some babies, a considerable amount of oral mucus. After this second period of reactivity the baby remained relatively stable with good sucking and swallowing co-ordination.

INTERNAL CHANGES

The best known internal change is the transition from fetal to neonatal circulation. Fetal circulation is diagrammed in Figure 2–12. Fetal circulation differs from neonatal and later circulation in several respects:

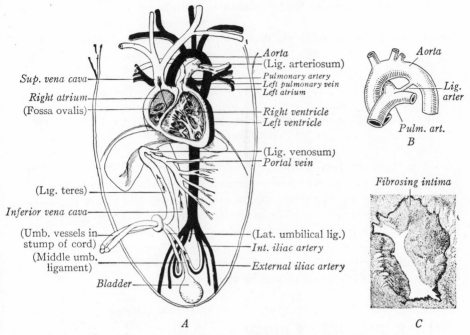

Labels on figure A:
Aorta
(Lig. arteriosum)
Pulmonary artery
Left pulmonary vein
Left atrium
Sup. vena cava
Right atrium
(Fossa ovalis)
Right ventricle
Left ventricle
(Lig. venosum)
Portal vein
(Lig. teres)
Inferior vena cava
(Umb. vessels in stump of cord)
(Middle umb. ligament)
(Lat. umbilical lig.)
Int. iliac artery
External iliac artery
Bladder

Labels on figure B:
Aorta
Lig. arter.
Pulm. art.

Labels on figure C:
Fibrosing intima

A   *C*

Figure 2–13. Changes in the human circulation after birth. A, Plan of circulation, in ventral view; obliterated fetal passages are designated by Roman type within parentheses (Heisler). B, Ligamentum arteriosum, at three months. C, Transverse section of the interior of the obliterating ductus arteriosus, at one month after birth (after Schaffer). (From Arey: *Developmental Anatomy*. 7th Edition. W. B. Saunders, 1965.)

1. The umbilical vein carries oxygenated blood from the placenta through the liver and the ductus venosus to the inferior vena cava and then to the right atrium of the heart.

2. Most of the blood entering the right atrium is shunted through the foramen ovale into the left atrium. Pressure is relatively low in the left atrium because of the small pulmonary circulation in fetal life: the blood flow from left atrium to left ventricle and then to the body.

3. The ductus arteriosus shunts most of the blood from the right ventricle to the descending aorta and thence to the body, rather than to the lungs as it will after birth.

4. The umbilical arteries carry blood with low-oxygen content from the fetal body to the placenta.

Changes in circulation at the time of birth are directly influenced by the initiation and maintenance of good ventilation. When the alveoli expand at birth, there is a decrease in the resistance of the pulmonary vessels which in turn brings about the changes characteristic to newborn circulation (Fig. 2–13). Thus the following diagram:

Decrease in the resistance of pulmonary vessels
↓
Decrease in pressure in right atrium due to increased flow of blood to the lungs
↓
and
↓
Increase of pressure in left atrium because of increased blood flow from the lungs

At the same time muscular contraction closes the ductus arteriosus, perhaps in response to the increased oxygen in the blood. Shortly afterward, the umbilical arteries and then the umbilical vein contract.

Generally these functional changes are sudden and complete. Anatomical changes, such as the fibrosis of the fetal blood vessel no longer in use, proceed slowly through the postnatal months. By comparing similar structures in Figures 2–12 and 2–13 with Table 2–2, these changes in structure can be recognized.

OTHER CHANGES AT BIRTH

Even under the best conditions of labor and delivery, the infant will be slightly acidotic immediately after birth, but if his ventilation is good he will "blow off" excess carbon dioxide in the first one to two hours. Changes in hepatic and renal function, the passage of meconium, and a reorganization of the body's metabolic processes are also part of the transition period.

TABLE 2–2.   *Structural Changes from Fetal to Infant Circulation*

STRUCTURES IN FETAL CIRCULATION	APPROX. TIME OF ANATOMICAL OBLITERATION	RESULTING STRUCTURES
Foramen ovale	1 year	Fossa ovalis
Ductus arteriosus	1 month	Ligamentum arteriosum
Ductus venosus	2 months	Ligamentum venosum of the liver
Umbilical arteries	2–3 months	Distal portion: lateral umbilical ligaments
		Proximal portion: Internal iliac arteries, which function throughout life
Umbilical vein	2–3 months	Ligamentum teres of the liver

Bibliography

Abramson, H. (ed.): *Resuscitation of the Newborn Infant.* 2nd Edition. St. Louis; C. V. Mosby, 1966.

Apgar, V.: Proposal for a New Method of Evaluation of the Newborn Infant. *Anesthesia and Analgesia, 32*:260, 1953.

Apgar, V., Holaday, D. A., James, L. S., Weisbrot, I. M., and Berrien, C.: Evaluation of the Newborn Infant: Second Report. *Journal of the American Medical Association, 168*:1985, 1958.

Arey, L.: *Developmental Anatomy.* 7th Edition. Philadelphia, W. B. Saunders, 1965.

Arnold, H. W., Putnam, N., Barnard, B. L., Desmond, M., and Rudolph, A. J.: Transition to Extra-Uterine Life. *American Journal of Nursing, 65*:77 (October), 1965.

Behrman, R. E.: Acid-base Monitoring of the Fetus During Labor with Blood Obtained From the Scalp. *Journal of Pediatrics, 74*:804, 1969a.

Behrman, R. E.: Treatment of the Asphyxiated Newborn Infant. *Journal of Pediatrics, 74*:981, 1969b.

Borgstedt, A. D., and Rosen, M. G.: Medication During Labor Correlated with Behavior and EEG of the Newborn. *American Journal of Diseases of Children, 115*:21, 1968.

Brady, J., James, L. S., and Baker, M. A.: Heart Rate Changes in the Fetus and Newborn During Labor, Delivery and the Immediate Postnatal Period. *American Journal of Obstetrics and Gynecology, 84*:1, 1962.

Brady, J., and James, L. S.: Fetal Electrocardiographic Studies; Tachycardia as a Sign of Fetal Distress. *American Journal of Obstetrics and Gynecology, 86*:785, 1963.

Cohen, S. N., and Olson, W. A.: Drugs that Depress the Newborn Infant. *Pediatric Clinics of North America, 17*:835, 1970.

Davis, M. E., and Rubin, R.: *DeLee's Obstetrics for Nurses.* 18th Edition. Philadelphia, W. B. Saunders, 1966.

Donald, I.: *Practical Obstetric Problems.* Philadelphia, J. B. Lippincott, 1969.

Du, J. H. N., and Oliver, T. K., Jr.: The Baby in the Delivery Room. *Journal of the American Medical Association, 207*:1502, 1969.

Garland, G. W.: Breech Presentation. *In* Donald, I. (ed.): *Practical Obstetric Problems.* Philadelphia, J. B. Lippincott, 1969.

Gleason, D.: Footprinting for Identification of Infants. *Pediatrics, 44*:302, 1969.

Hon, E. H.: The Electronic Evaluation of Fetal Heart Rate: Preliminary Report. *American Journal of Obstetrics and Gynecology, 75*:1215, 1958.

Hon, E. H.: Observations on Pathological Fetal Bradycardia. *American Journal of Obstetrics and Gynecology, 77*:1084, 1959.

Kron, R. E., Stein, M., and Goddard, K. E.: Newborn Sucking Behavior Affected by Obstetric Sedation. *Pediatrics, 37*:1012, 1966.

Miller, D. L., and Oliver, T. K., Jr.: Body Temperature in the Immediate Neonatal Period; the Effect of Reducing Thermal Losses. *American Journal of Obstetrics and Gynecology, 94*:964, 1966.

Resuscitation of the Newborn Infant. Evanston, Illinois, 1958. American Academy of Pediatrics,

Schaffer, A.: Disorders Related to the Birth Process. *In* Cooke, R. E. (ed.): *The Biologic Basis of Pediatric Process.* New York, McGraw-Hill, 1968.

Shepard, K. S.: *Care of the Well Baby.* Philadelphia, J. B. Lippincott, 1968.

Shepard, K. S.: Further on Footprinting. *Pediatrics, 43*:639, 1969.

Shnider, S. M., and Moya, F.: Effects of Meperidine on the Newborn Infant. *American Journal of Obstetrics and Gynecology, 89*:1009, 1964.

Silverman, W. A., and Parke, P. C.: The Newborn: Keep Him Warm. *American Journal of Nursing, 65*:81 (October), 1965.

Sinclair, J. C.: Heat Production and Thermoregulation in the Small-for-Date Infant. *Pediatric Clinics of North America, 17*:147, 1970.

Smith, C. A.: *The Physiology of the Newborn Infant.* Springfield, Illinois, Charles C Thomas, 1953.

Smith, R. M.: Temperature Monitoring and Regulation. *Pediatric Clinics of North America, 16*:643, 1969.

Stechler, G.: Newborn Attention as Affected by Medication During Labor. *Science,*
    144:315, 1964.
Wierschem, J.: Know Them by Their Feet. Medical Record News. *Journal of the Ameri-*
    can Association of Medical Record Librarians, 1965.
Willis, T.: Monitoring the Mother and Fetus During Labor. *The Canadian Nurse,*
    December: 28, 1970.

CHAPTER 3

The Apparently Healthy Newborn: His Characteristics and Needs

Baby J, a seven-pound six-ounce apparently healthy male, arrived at the term nursery at 2:37 P.M. The nursery staff had been alerted to expect him and a bassinet was ready. Together the nursery and delivery room nurses checked his identification, the number of umbilical vessels, and the charted record of maternal history and performance during labor and delivery.

The baby, still wrapped in the warm delivery room blanket, was placed in the bassinet on his side to facilitate the draining of mucus. Hot water bottles were filled and wrapped to be placed on either side of him, a clamp was applied to the cord which had been tied in the delivery room, and a sterile bulb syringe was put beside him.* During the next one or two hours he would remain closely observed but undisturbed unless an emergency arose.

In a large metropolitan hospital this scene may be played, with minor variations, any number of times during each 24-hour period. The procedure may become so routine that the steps are taken for granted, yet each step is highly important in giving the best of nursing care to every infant.

---

*Vitamin K_1, 1.0 mg., was given intramuscularly.

Nursing care for newborns includes:
1. Meeting the baby's physical and psychological needs
2. Protecting him from hazards in the environment
3. Recognizing any signs of illness at the earliest possible stage
4. Teaching the mother how she can best care for her baby

Meeting the Physical Needs of the Newborn

THE IMPORTANCE OF ALERTING
THE NURSERY STAFF

Since infants arrive at every hour, often at times when nursery personnel are intensely busy, a call from the delivery suite to the nursery means that someone should be free to give the infant immediate attention on his arrival. On a day when the nursery is particularly full, the failure to give advance warning may mean that a delivery room nurse will have to stand with babe in arms as a spare bassinet is brought from a back room and made up. Such a call will also indicate whether any special preparations will have to be made for the baby—a warmed bed, perhaps, or isolation because the baby is meconium-stained or the product of a delivery in which the mother's membranes have been ruptured for more than 24 hours (see page 90).

CHECKING THE BABY'S IDENTIFICATION

Some means of identification should be attached to the baby before he leaves the delivery room; identification should be rechecked in the nursery before the delivery room nurse leaves and checked again with the mother's identification each time the baby is brought to his mother for feeding. Of course, it should also be checked at the time of discharge.

THE SIGNIFICANCE OF THE NUMBER
OF UMBILICAL VESSELS

The umbilical cord normally contains three vessels: a single vein, the largest of the vessels, and two arteries. In about 0.5 per cent of all deliveries (3.5 per cent of twin deliveries) there is a single umbilical artery rather than two. One-third of the time this single umbilical artery is associated with one or more congenital anomalies, which are not always readily observed by just looking at the baby. The existence of a single umbilical artery must be noted on the baby's chart and the baby observed with even more care than he would ordinarily be.

THE IMPORTANCE OF MATERNAL HISTORY

Since a newborn has no history but the mother's history, the nurse receiving the baby into the nursery needs to know as much as possible about his mother and the course of her pregnancy, labor, and delivery. For while any mother can give birth to a baby who may become ill or may have a congenital defect, the chances are significantly higher for some mothers, as revealed by their history. Conditions occurring during pregnancy and these factors associated with labor and delivery which increase neonatal risk are discussed in Chapters 1 and 2.

The nursery-room nurse should also know the baby's Apgar score, as recorded at one and five minutes (see page 75), and whether the mother has had a previous child who was stillborn or had a congenital anomaly or some other illness in the newborn period. The latter is significant not only because of the genetic inheritance of some conditions but also because a mother who has had one sick or malformed baby is likely to be more anxious about this new infant. She needs and may unconsciously demand extra reassurance. If a previous baby has had a clubfoot, for example, she may check this infant's feet and legs repeatedly, asking if they seem to be all right. Human beings that we are, we can better help her if we understand the reasons for her over concern.

ADMINISTRATION OF VITAMIN K

The administration of 1.0 mg. of water-soluble vitamin K to the baby shortly after birth has virtually eliminated hemorrhagic disease in the newborn by preventing a decrease in plasma prothrombin level that usually occurs in the neonatal period. Larger amounts of the vitamin do not carry a greater therapeutic value; in fact they predispose the baby to hyperbilirubinemia and kernicterus. Although Vitamin K has been given to the mother while she is in labor this method has generally been found to be less dependable than giving the medication directly to the baby.

Placed in a bassinet, the baby now needs WRS: warmth, rest, and security. If any major abnormalities exist, they will have been noted in the delivery room, and special plans will have been made for the baby. In the newborn who seems to be healthy more detailed examination will be deferred until his temperature has stabilized.

THE NEED FOR WARMTH

The baby's need for warmth from the moment of birth has already been discussed on page 76. Meeting this need is a nursing responsibility which can be met in a number of different ways depending upon the baby's general condition. The full-term infant who has had no difficulty during labor and delivery will probably be able to maintain body temperature with the use of blankets and hot water bottles. The latter should be filled halfway, and excess air eliminated so as not to restrict the baby in any way. Water temperature should be 105° to 110° F. The bottle should be completely covered and placed outside the blanket in which the baby is wrapped.

PROTECTION FROM INFECTION

Infection is one of the major hazards affecting newborns; both the prevention of infection and the early recognition of its presence, which is absolutely essential to cure, are basically nursing responsibilities.

Why are newborns more prone to infection? A complete answer to this question is not yet available. Considerations that seem to play a role are the baby's relatively poor immunity to most bacteria, a diminished capacity to produce the immunoglobins IgG and IgM, and difficulty in localizing infection so that what begins at one site quickly becomes systemic.

Moreover, there are several portals of entry which exist in the newborn but which disappear shortly: the vessels of the umbilical stump, circumcisions, and breaks in the skin due to forceps delivery. In addition, delicate infant skin is easily irritated and broken down.

An increased risk of infection is inherent in certain anomalies: esophageal atresia, exstrophy of the bladder, omphalocele, congenital diaphragmatic hernia, imperforate anus with rectourinary fistula, meningomyelocele, and those anomalies which require bowel resection. Babies who receive repeated exchange transfusions or fluids or who have frequent blood sampling through the umbilical vein are at heightened risk as are babies who must be mechanically resuscitated. In one respect infants in isolettes are protected against certain infections, but an isolette that has not been thoroughly cleaned can in itself be a reservoir of pathogenic bacteria.

Maternal factors which increase the likelihood that the baby will be infected include:

1. rupture of membranes more than 24 hours before delivery
2. fever or infection in the mother during the last week of pregnancy

3. foul smelling or purulent amniotic fluid
4. prolonged labor
5. excessive manipulation during labor
6. maternal infectious disease such as syphilis, gonorrhea, tuberculosis, residual rubella, vaccinia, polio, and salmonellosis.

Preventing infection in the nursery. It has been said often, but it is worth repeating, that thorough handwashing with a hexachlorophene solution is an absolute essential in the prevention of nursery infection. This means a scrub up to the elbows for two to three minutes before entering the nursery and repeated handwashing after caring for each infant. Not only must each member of the nursing staff carry out the proper techniques of handwashing but so must everyone else who enters the nursery, from cleaning personnel, to aides, to medical students, to physicians.

For nearly a decade the use of hexachlorophene soap for the bathing of newborns has been a recommended practice. Gluck (1963) stated that if all of the infants in the nursery were bathed with a hexachlorophene preparation each day, the rate of staph infection could virtually be eliminated. In late 1971, however, warnings were issued by the Food and Drug Administration about the use of products containing hexachlorophene, because of demonstrated absorption into the blood stream in both animal and human studies. For most nurseries the decision about bathing infants remains unresolved at the time this is written. One point does seem clear. If used, the soap should be thoroughly rinsed from the baby's skin and not left as a barrier to infection as has been previously suggested by some authors.[8]

Another source of infection is contaminated or improperly cleaned equipment. The water reservoirs in incubators, water taps, nebulizers, and equipment used in resuscitation, all may contribute to infection if they are not frequently and thoroughly cleaned. If it is at all possible, each infant confined to an incubator should be moved to a clean bed every four days, certainly weekly. The dirty incubator should then be washed with antiseptic solution, and every movable part removed and cleaned separately. Just wiping or soaking with solution is not sufficient. If there are plugs of dirt or dust in corners or around screws the solution may eliminate the top layer of bacteria but colonies of bacteria can continue to flourish beneath this layer. After the incubator or isolette is washed, it is advisable to run it in a dry condition for 24 hours to provide a further interruption of the cycle of bacterial growth.

Silver nitrate (0.5 ml. of a 1:10,000 solution) can be added to each liter of water in the incubator. Distilled water must always be used in solution with silver nitrate because the chlorine in tap water will precipitate the silver out of solution and it will no longer be bacteriacidal. Since silver nitrate disappears rapidly from metal pans, plastic humidification pans should be used (Baker, 1969). Some institutions object to the use of silver nitrate because it is hard on isolettes; an alternative is the use of acetic acid (vinegar) to rinse water reservoirs each time the incubator is cleaned.

The physical set-up of the nursery can be a factor in the prevalence of infection. The ideal set-up would be small, multiple nurseries of four to six infants, to which no new infants are admitted until all previous babies are discharged and the nursery thoroughly cleaned. Unfortunately such a set-up is not always possible. But in every nursery each unit can be thoroughly cleaned (including the inside of drawers, shelves, walls of the cubicle) before another baby is admitted. Daily dusting of each unit with a towel dampened in an antiseptic solution is also a part of the nursing care in the control of infection. Whether the actual cleaning is done by nurses or supervised by them, there is no underestimating its importance.

Any individual with diarrhea, upper respiratory infection, or skin infection must be excluded from the nursery. Not only medical and nursing personnel but the housekeeping staff as well must observe this precaution.

Rarely do term babies spend all of their time in the nursery. Most of them are taken to their mothers for feeding from one to several times a day. To eliminate these visits to the mother in the interest of preventing infection would overlook the very important need of both mother and baby to be together. The risk of infection can be minimized by close cooperation between the nurses who care for the mothers and those in the nursery.

There should be no visitors on the obstetrical floor during the hours when babies are with their mothers. At other times, visitors should be limited not only in terms of the number of visitors at any one time but also in terms of total number. Besides providing protection from infection, strict visiting regulations—stricter than most hospitals seem willing to enforce—give the mother a chance for much needed rest, especially for the multipara who will be going home to care for other small children in addition to caring for this new infant round the clock.

Before the baby is taken to his mother for the first time, a nurse needs to spend a few minutes talking with her about the ways in which she can help protect him from infection while he is in the hospital. She should know approximately when he will be brought to her so she can wash her hands thoroughly in preparation. A clean diaper can be brought with the baby at each feeding to be placed between her bedding and the baby. She needs to know that visitors should never be allowed to sit on her bed and that coats or packages should never be placed on it. While the baby will be wrapped in a blanket when taken to his mother it is perfectly natural for her to want to unwrap and inspect him closely (see p. 127). She can do this easily without completely removing him from the blanket. When explanations are made in advance, the majority of mothers will be willing to comply. They are, after all, interested in doing what is best for their babies. For the few mothers who seem to be unwilling or unable to cooperate, a change of clothing when the baby returns to the nursery may be the only alternative.

If the mother has symptoms of infection, such as an elevated temperature, a sore throat or upper respiratory infection, or has been vomiting or has diarrhea, she should not feed her baby. But neither should she be forgotten by the nursery nurse. The baby can be taken to the door of her room so that she can see him at least once during the day, and she can be given reports of his progress.

As important as it is to prevent infection it is equally important that the agent used in prevention is not in itself deleterious. Boric acid was at one time widely used in newborn nurseries until evidence indicated that its use as a wet dressing or as an ointment for diaper rash could result in infant mortality rates as high as 70 per cent.

The agents and procedures used in the laundering of infant linen and clothing can also constitute a hazard. Armstrong (1969) reports an instance in which severe illness and death in newborns was traced to a bactericide compound, pentachlophenol, used in the laundry. The chemical was subsequently absorbed through the infant's skin after the baby was repeatedly exposed to linen laundered with this compound. The babies in this particular group were in a maternity hospital for unwed mothers and thus stayed in the hospital longer than many newborns. However, their stay was probably shorter than that of a tiny premature baby or a baby with a congenital defect. Even one such finding emphasizes how important it is that we know what kinds of procedures are being used in other areas of the hospital, such as the laundry. Nyhan (1969) feels that only plain water should be used as a terminal rinse for infant clothing and bedding.

Recognizing infection in the baby. Rarely are there dramatic signs of infection in newborns such as the sudden elevation of temperature often seen in older children. Even in sepsis severe enough to cause mortality there may never be fever; hypothermia or marked variations evidencing the infant's ability to control his temperature is often present.

Infection should be suspected when a baby is inactive and does not eat well. Jaundice, beginning after the third day, is frequently a sign of infection. Or the skin may have a mottled appearance. Abdominal distention is a common manifestation of generalized sepsis and may be one of the first signs of infection. A full fontanel, a high-pitched cry, and irritability usually indicate infection of the central nervous system. Babies with diarrhea need to be isolated immediately, and their stools cultured. Vomiting, changes in respiratory pattern and skin lesions need to be evaluated for infection. Most of the time these changes will first be noticed by an observant nurse who will alert the physician to the possibility of sepsis so that necessary therapy can begin as soon as possible (see page 178).

> During the next hours, Baby J sleeps in his nursery bed, closely observed but not disturbed. He cries occasionally but seems generally content. When he was a little more than two hours old his temperature was taken rectally and registered 97°F. Since he has demonstrated no evidence of respiratory distress he is ready to be weighed and bathed and, at the same time, examined more closely for any evidence of abnormality.

MONITORING TEMPERATURE

In checking newborn temperature the choice lies between rectal and axillary methods. The intial rectal temperature taken shortly after birth enables the nurse to detect without delay the presence of an imperforate anus. Taking subsequent temperatures in the axilla eliminates the danger of perforating the rectum.

BATHING

Most hospital nurseries have routine procedures for bathing newborns when they are first taken to the nursery and then on the days that follow. These routines need to be examined frequently in the light of new knowledge. For example, for several years it was believed that the vernix caseosa—that sticky white covering on newborn skin—served to protect the baby from skin infection; thus it was not washed off soon after birth but was gradually wiped away over a period of several days. Now it appears that the vernix may actually encourage infection, especially in those areas where skin folds rub tegether, such as at the neckline or in the vaginal folds.

The controversy over hexachlorophene soap has already been discussed. Another long-standing nursery tradition, the use of alcohol to dry the umbilical stump, is felt by Gluck to interfere with the effectiveness of hexachlorophene if it is used.

Characteristics of the Newborn:
Normal Versus Abnormal

It has been said that newly born babies are beautiful only to their parents and the nurses who care for them. To the curious stranger passing the nursery they are a rather unusual assemblage—red-faced, oddly proportioned, inclined to be easily startled. They are different in a number of ways from the baby who is just a few weeks old. The nurse's task is to recognize which of these differences is within the normal range of appearance and behavior for a newborn, and which differences are indications of pathology.

Babies cannot tell us, verbally, when there is something wrong with them. Yet there are few patients who communicate as dramatically through nonverbal means. Their lack of speech seems very nearly compensated for once their signal system is understood—body posture, the pitch of a cry, the character of respirations, and a multitude of other signs. Because these signals change rapidly, it is the nurse, to a very large extent, who must catch any slight change in condition so that appropriate medical attention can be given as quickly as possible. Frequently a baby may appear quite normal when a physician examines it at 8 o'clock in the morning yet be in significant distress by 2 in the afternoon. An alert nurse in the newborn nursery can be a lifesaver in the fullest sense of the word.

Following is a guide to some of the major characteristics—both normal and pathological—of newborns. Very obvious defects, such as omphalocele, meningomyelocele and hare lip have been omitted since they are so readily recognized.

GENERAL CHARACTERISTICS

Normal	Abnormal
Strong flexor muscle tone	Floppy; lack of muscle tone Rigid
Symmetrical posture and movement	Weak, random movements Lack of movement on one or both sides Abnormal position or posture
Strong cry	Feeble cry or absence of cry High pitched, piercing cry
Edema of presenting parts	Edema of any other area
Moro reflex; grasp reflex	
Brief tremors or twitching	Prolonged tremors and convulsions
	Inability of examiner to abduct one thigh

Crying. A full-term infant cries vigorously for as much as two hours out of every 24. A high-pitched, shrill cry, excessive crying for which there does not seem to be a reason, and very little crying may be indications of intracranial injury or infection. A very hoarse cry suggests partial paralysis of the vocal cords.

Some babies seem supersensitive right from the start and cry more than usual during their first weeks. If the crying is from hunger, i.e., crying accompanied by rooting and sucking, feeding is the obvious answer. But babies also cry from what appears to be loneliness and a desire to be held. Nurses sometimes joke with mothers that they are spoiling their babies in the nursery by holding them when they cry; with some mothers such jokes may have unfortunate results if they take them seriously. There is no evidence to indicate that holding a small, fussy baby will in any way "spoil" him or make him more demanding as he grows older. In many societies babies are almost never out of contact with another human body — mother, grandmother, sister, aunt — during their first weeks. Most mothers have a strong desire to pick up a crying baby and hold him; they need to know that this is the right thing to do.

Edema. Edema of the part of the infant presenting during delivery is not unusual. Some premature babies are edematous for no apparent reason. This edema is transient, making the two- to three-day-old premature infant seem dehydrated by comparison, even when fluid intake is actually adequate. Infants of diabetic mothers also may appear edematous, but their excess weight is due largely to fat rather than to fluid.

Severe generalized edema at birth may be a sign of erythroblastosis, of heart failure due to congenital heart disease, or of electrolyte imbalance. It is not always easy to recognize this kind of edema. Pitting may or may not be present. But normally a baby should have fine wrinkles over the knuckles of his hands and feet. If these wrinkles are not evident, the area is very likely puffed with fluid.

Position. The position of a normal full-term newborn follows definite patterns. When lying prone, he turns his face to one side; he flexes his legs and draws his knees up under his abdomen, raising his pelvis off the mattress (Fig. 3–1). Placed on his back, he rolls to one side or the other. When he is lying on his side, his arms and legs are flexed. This strong flexor tone of the muscles, along with symmetry, is a significant postural indicator of normality. Certain exceptions, however, do not automatically indicate abnormality. An infant born in the breech position with legs extended is likely to keep his legs extended during the newborn period. An infant delivered by face presentation may appear, at first glance, to be assuming a position of

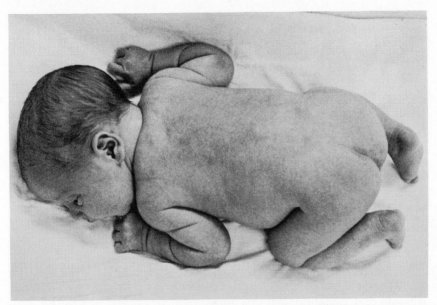

Figure 3-1. A term infant lies with his limbs flexed, pelvis raised, and knees usually drawn up under his abdomen. (Courtesy of Mead, Johnson, and Company.)

opisthotonos. But this baby will have normal muscle tone, as opposed to the hypertonia of true opisthotonos.

Conditions which produce asymmetry of posture include fractures of the clavicle or humerus, injury to the brachial plexus, and asymmetry of muscle tone.

Moro reflex. A normal newborn, startled by a sudden noise or the jaring of his bed, will first abduct and extend his arms and then adduct them as if to embrace (Fig. 3-2). This is the Moro reflex, the most commonly used of all reflexes to evaluate the neurological status of the new baby. As with asymmetry of posture, injuries to the brachial plexus, clavicle, or humerus will cause the baby to have an asymmetrical Moro reflex (Fig. 3-3). Consistent absence of the Moro reflex suggests the possibility of brain damage; there is, for example, no Moro reflex in babies with kernicterus. After the first weeks of life the Moro reflex disappears. Should it persist beyond three or four months there is some delay in the maturing of the central nervous system.

Grasp reflex. The grasp reflex of a normal newborn enables him to "hang on" for a moment when lifted. Premature babies will make the initial grasp but will open their grip when pressure is applied.

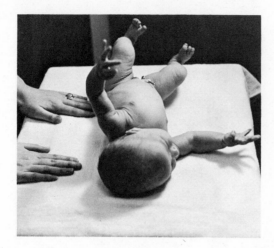

Figure 3-2. Moro response, showing symmetrical abduction and extension of the arms. (From Davis and Rubin: *DeLee's Obstetrics for Nurses.* 18th Edition. W. B. Saunders, 1966.)

Tremors, twitching, and convulsions. Brief, spontaneous tremors and twitching are not uncommon in normal newborns. Prolonged tremors and convulsion, however, may be due to hypoglycemia (page 177), to hypocalcemia, to neurological damage, or to infection. After the third day of life, convulsions are more likely to be due to infection than to trauma.

During a convulsion the baby should be watched for any signs of regurgitation. Charting of tremors or convulsions should include the duration of the seizure, the time at which it occurred, and the parts of the body involved. The baby's cry and his behavior before and after the convulsion should be noted.

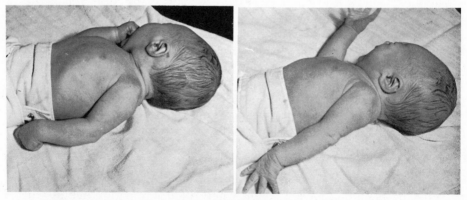

Figure 3-3. Injury to the brachial plexus is one cause of an asymmetrical Moro response. (From McKay; *In* Nelson, Vaughan, and McKay (eds.): *Textbook of Pediatrics.* 9th Edition. W. B. Saunders, 1969.)

EXTREMITIES

Normal	Abnormal
Extended legs in a baby born from a breech presentation	Inability to abduct thigh
	Abnormal position or posture of an extremity
	Webbed fingers or toes

The position of the extremities in the newborn has been discussed generally under position. The extended legs of a baby born with his legs extended is a normal variation from the semiflexed to flexed position usually found in newborns. Abnormal positioning of an arm may be due to injury of the brachial plexus, to a fractured clavicle, or, rarely, to a fracture of the humerus.

Inability to abduct one thigh. The inability to abduct one thigh is the primary indication of congenital dysplasia or dislocation of the hip (Fig. 3–4). With the baby lying on his back, his thighs are flexed, one at a time, outward and downward to the table or bed. When one

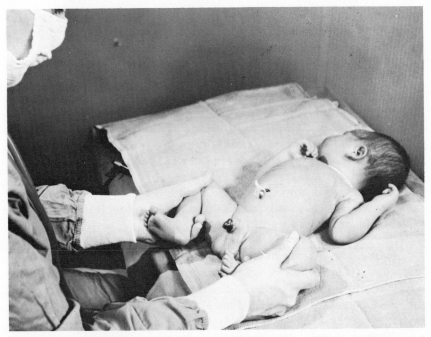

Figure 3–4. Inability to abduct one thigh is the primary indication of congenital dysplasia or dislocation of the hip. (Courtesy of Pfizer Laboratories, Brooklyn, New York.)

thigh does not abduct easily, the diagnosis is quite certain. Other indications of dysplasia or dislocation include a consistent sharp click heard on the affected side during abduction and higher or extra creases in the affected thigh. Spotting these babies in the nursery is most important, for the earlier treatment begins the more simple and successful it will be. Mild dysplasia will not need to be treated at all.

SKIN

Normal   **Abnormal**
Milia
Mongolian spots
Toxic erythema
                                                    Impetigo
                                                    Hemangiomas
                                                    Cracked or peeling skin

Milia.   Milia are tiny cysts which result from the obstruction of the sebaceous glands of the face, particularly those across the bridge of the nose. They disappear without treatment.

Mongolian spots.   Mongolian spots, sometimes called "Oriental patches," are at times mistakenly thought to be bruises. They are present in some Negro babies at the time of birth, usually in the area of the sacrum or buttocks. They also disappear of their own accord within a few weeks to months.

Erythema toxicum.   The most common skin disorder of infancy, erythema toxicum (also known as "flea-bite" rash though fleas are in no way involved) is found in 30 to 70 per cent of normal term infants. However, it is rare in prematurely born babies (Fig. 3–5). It usually occurs in the first four days of life but may appear at any time in the first two weeks. A common pattern is for the papule to appear one day, look worse on the second day, and be completely gone by the third, although it may disappear in as brief a time as two hours. Etiology is unknown and treatment is unnecessary, but the lesions must be differentiated from those of impetigo which must be treated.

Impetigo.   The vesicles of impetigo are pustular (Fig. 3–6), as occasionally are the vesicles of toxic erythema. In impetigo these vesicles rupture to produce thick, moist, yellow crusts which must be soaked off before the prescribed antibiotic ointment can be applied.

Hemangiomas.   Hemangiomas, even when they do not pose a threat to the baby's physical well being, are highly distressing to the baby's parents because they are so obvious. To the extent that they

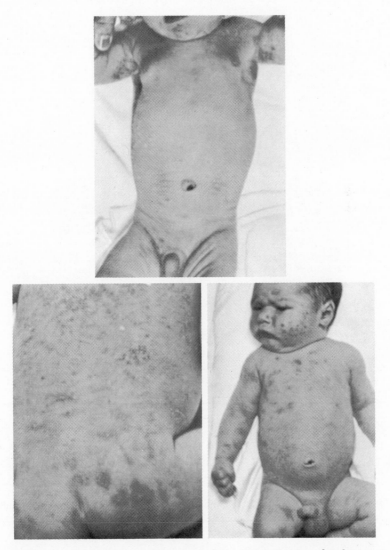

Figure 3–5. Noninfectious rash in a newborn. (From Davis and Rubin: *DeLee's Obstetrics for Nurses.* 18th Edition. W. B. Saunders, 1966.)

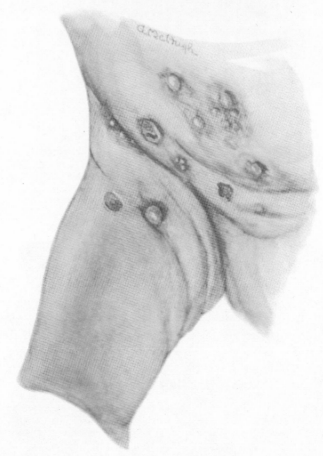

Figure 3–6. The vescicles of impetigo are pustular. (From Davis and Rubin: *DeLee's Obstetrics for Nurses.* 18th Edition. W. B. Saunders, 1966.)

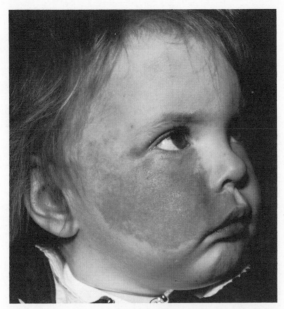

Figure 3–7. Port-wine stain, present from birth, does not usually fade but can be covered with a cosmetic preparation. (From Pillsbury, Shelley, and Kligman: *A Manual of Cutaneous Medicine.* W. B. Saunders, 1961.)

affect the way a mother feels about her baby and the way in which she treats him, they can have far reaching significance (see page 131).

A port wine stain (nevus flammeus) is a flat, purple or dark red lesion, consisting of mature capillaries, and is present at birth (Fig. 3–7). Those port wine hemangiomas located above the bridge of the nose tend to fade; others do not, but since they are level with the surface of the skin they can be covered with a cosmetic preparation (Covermark).

Strawberry hemangiomas (nevus vasculosus) are elevated areas consisting of immature capillaries and endothelial cells. They may be present at birth or appear in the first two weeks following birth, and continue to enlarge for six months to a year. After the first birthday they begin to be absorbed, the process of involution taking as long as ten years (Fig. 3–8). Half to three-fourths of strawberry hemangiomas disappear by the time the child is seven years old, leaving no evidence that they ever existed. The end result seems to be better if the hemangioma is untreated unless it interferes with normal functioning because of its location.

A third type, cavernous hemangioma, consists of dilated vascular spaces with thick walls which are lined with endothelium (Fig. 3–9). They do not regress spontaneously.

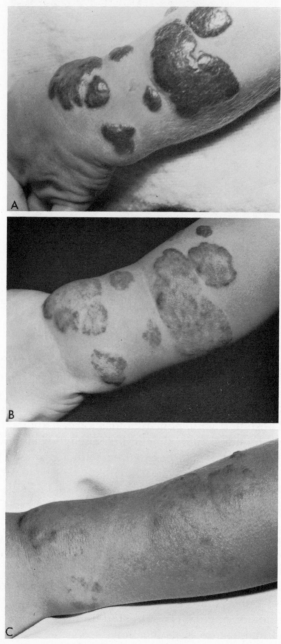

Figure 3–8. The spontaneous progressive involution of a strawberry hemangioma: *A,* age 6 weeks; *B,* age 8 months; *C,* age 2 years. (From Burgoon, Jr.: *In* Nelson, Vaughan, and McKay (eds.): *Textbook of Pediatrics.* 9th Edition. W. B. Saunders, 1969.)

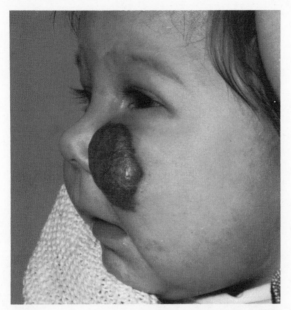

Figure 3–9. A cavernous hemangioma. (From Pillsbury, Shelley, and Kligman: *A Manual of Cutaneous Medicine.* W. B. Saunders, 1961.)

Cracked and peeling skin. This condition is often evidence of a small-for-date baby who has experienced intrauterine malnutrition (Fig. 3–10).

COLOR

Normal	Abnormal
Red	Pallor, gray color
Cyanosis of the lips, fingernails, toenails, hands, feet; cyanosis of the face in a baby born with facial or brow presentation	Generalized cyanosis
Jaundice after 36 to 48 hours	Jaundice in the first 24 hours
Harlequin sign	

The very red color of the newborn baby's skin is due both to the higher concentration of red blood cells in the vessels and the thin layer of subcutaneous fat which causes the blood vessels to be closer to the surface of the skin.

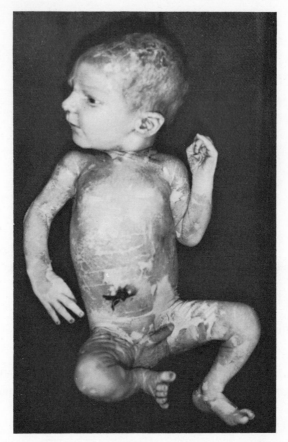

Figure 3–10. Cracked or peeling parchment-like skin often indicates intrauterine malnutrition. (From Clifford: *In* Levine (ed.): *Advances in Pediatrics,* Vol. 9. Yearbook Publishers, Inc., 1957.)

Cyanosis. In contrast to the localized cyanosis, which is due to immature peripheral circulation involving lips, hands and feet, and to stasis, in which the presenting parts are cyanotic, generalized cyanosis is a cause for concern. Sometimes generalized cyanosis is so slight that the baby must be compared with an infant who has obviously good respirations in order to detect its presence. The need for such a comparison is indicated when the baby is having other symptoms of respiratory distress and the possibility of cyanosis is raised. In babies with dark skin, cyanosis can often be best observed in the mucosal lining of the mouth.

The relationship between cyanosis and crying is an important observation. The baby may be cyanotic except when he cries vigorously and thereby raises his intake of oxygen as, for example, in the case of babies with atelectasis. Or he may be cyanotic only when he cries, which can be a warning of the later, more persistent cyanosis of some types of congenital heart disease.

Cyanosis related to apnea can usually be terminated by provoking the baby to cry, either by flicking the soles of his feet or his buttocks.

Babies with bilateral choanal atresia (occlusion of the posterior nares by either bone or membrane) will be cyanotic, for all infants are obligate nose breathers; they breathe through their mouths only with great difficulty. Diagnosis is made by holding a wisp of cotton in front of each nare; the air movements of respiration can then be easily observed.

Sudden cyanosis and apnea in a baby who has apparently been doing well may be related to excessive, thick mucus obstructing the upper respiratory tract. For this reason a bulb syringe should be in each baby's bed and a suction machine with a supply of catheters readily available for nasal suction. Once the obstructing mucus is removed the baby becomes pink and immediately resumes respirations.

Damage to the central nervous system, either because of congenital reasons or because of trauma during delivery, is another cause of cyanosis. The baby is likely to have very irregular breathing and may have some other signs of central nervous system damage—a high-pitched cry, either very rigid or very floppy muscle tone, or absence of a Moro reflex. As in the case of babies who are cyanotic because of respiratory distress, crying and oxygen tend to improve their color.

Babies who are cyanotic because of cardiac malformations are rarely helped by oxygen and generally appear worse when they cry. At first these babies may be only briefly pale or cyanotic such as during a gavage feeding or immediately after an injection.

Pallor. Pallor may be due to anemia, to hemorrhage, to the hemolysis of red blood cells, or to shock. Loss of blood may have occurred before the cord was clamped, because of fetal-maternal transfusion, or afterward. Sometimes when twins share a single placenta there is transfusion from one twin to the other. When there is no visible source of external hemorrhage, such as from the umbilical cord, a pale baby needs to be watched for signs of internal bleeding in vomitus or stool. Babies with intracranial damage are often pale due to shock. Gray color is also associated with infection and with chloramphenical intoxication.

Physiologic jaundice. About 40 to 60 per cent of term infants and even a higher per cent of premature infants are jaundiced on the second to third day of life. There is no discernible pathological reason for this, such as hemolytic anemia or sepsis. This jaundice is termed physiologic. The following points should be noted concerning physiologic jaundice:

1. It never occurs in the first 24 hours of life.
2. It does not have levels of indirect bilirubin above 10 to 12 mg. per cent.
3. It rarely lasts past the first week of life, the exception occasionally occurring in breast-fed infants.

The yellow color of jaundice is due to high levels of bilirubin; the source of the bilirubin is the breakdown of red blood cells which normally follows birth.

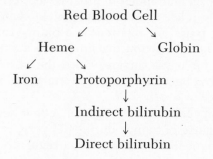

Both globin, which is a protein, and iron are re-used by the body. Indirect bilirubin, which is fat soluble and cannot be excreted by the kidneys, is converted to direct bilirubin (which is water soluble and can be excreted) by the hepatic enzyme glucuronyl transferase. In many term babies and most premature ones, liver function is immature; thus part of the bilirubin remains in the indirect, fat-soluble form.

As long as this bilirubin remains within the circulatory system no jaundice is visible because the red of the hemoglobin obscures the yellow of the bilirubin. But when the indirect level rises above 7 mg. per cent in term infants, bilirubin moves outside the vascular space and is then visible. It often takes higher bilirubin levels to bring about visible jaundice in low birth weight babies because the capillary bed lies closer to the skin surface due to a lack of subcutaneous fat. The red of the hemoglobin is thus reflected on the skin surface, obscuring the yellow of jaundice. Jaundice can be visualized, however, by blanching the skin with the thumb.

Some breast-fed infants have a longer lasting jaundice. This is believed to be due to the presence of pregnanediol in breast milk which depresses the action of the glucuronyl transferase enzyme. Most of the time these babies can continue to breast feed, with frequent checks of indirect bilirubin. Occasionally breast feedings are withheld for a brief period until the bilirubin level drops, after which breast feeding can usually be resumed with no further difficulty. During the interim, if the baby is fed by dropper and the mother's breasts pumped, breast feeding can be resumed with little difficulty.

Rarely is treatment necessary for physiologic jaundice. There is serious danger to an infant whose level of bilirubin rises to 20 mg. per cent or more, but in physiologic jaundice (by definition) bilirubin rarely exceeds 12 mg. per cent and is generally lower. Phototherapy is occasionally used to treat the term baby with physiologic jaundice, but since its chief use is with low birth weight babies it is discussed in Chapter 4 (see page 154).

Harlequin sign. Occasionally one will glance at a baby and see one side of the infant flushed, the line of demarcation between the flushed and unflushed side being very clear. This is a very transient phenomenon and is of no known pathological significance.

HEAD

Normal	**Abnormal**
Circumference: approximately 13–14 inches	
Molding	
Anterior fontanel open;	No anterior fontanel
Posterior fontanel may be closed	Sunken fontanel
	Bulging fontanel
Craniotabes	
Caput succedanum	
Cephalhematoma	

Molding. Molding, the process by which the bones of the head over-ride one another in order to facilitate delivery is so natural that nurses may scarcely notice that the baby's head is asymmetrical. But the mother is often concerned and needs to know that her infant's head will be normally rounded in a few days.

Closed anterior fontanel. While a closed anterior fontanel is of serious concern to the physicians and nurses who care for the baby (usually being related to microcephaly), rather ironically it is the open fontanel which may distress the new mother. Hopefully she can be reassured by knowing that:
1. the presence of an open fontanel helped to protect the baby's head during delivery;
2. the fontanel allowed his brain to grow before he was born and will continue to do so for the next 18 months;

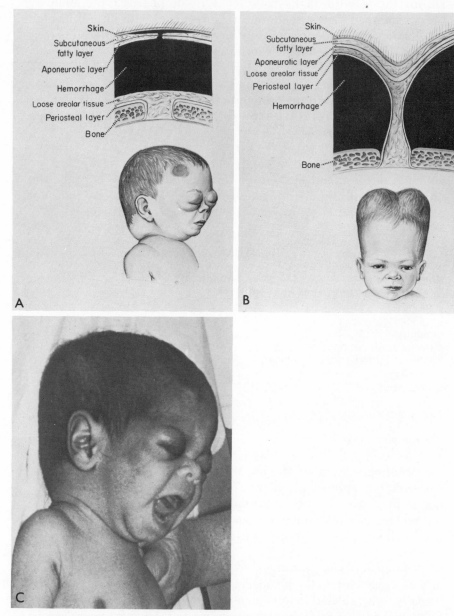

Figure 3–11. A, Edema and hemorrhage in caput succedaneum. B, Location of swelling in cephalhematoma; note that the swelling does not cross the suture lines. C, A baby with a large caput succedaneum. (Reprinted with permission of Daniel J. Pachman, M.D., of the University of Illinois Pediatric Department. A and C appeared in *Pediatrics,* Vol. 29, 1962.)

3. his brain is adequately protected by a tough membrane so there need be no fear of either handling him or washing his head which is a very necessary part of his care.

Both a bulging fontanel, which can indicate intracranial hemorrhage or infection, and a depressed fontanel, which indicates dehydration, are abnormal.

Craniotabes. Craniotabes is the softening of localized areas in the cranial bones. These areas seem sponge-like in that they are easily indented by the pressure of a fingertip, but they resume their shape when the pressure is removed. The cause of craniotabes is unknown. There is no treatment; although the condition may persist for months, it eventually disappears completely.

Caput succedaneum. This term refers to swelling of the superficial tissues over the bone of the part of the head presenting in delivery. It is seen immediately after birth and usually is absorbed within a few days (Fig. 3–11 A, C).

Cephalhematoma. In a cephalhematoma blood collects between a cranial bone and the overlying periosteum (Fig. 3–11, B). In contrast to caput succedaneum, it may be several weeks, even months, before it is completely absorbed. There is another difference between the two: the swelling of caput succedaneum may cross suture lines because only soft tissue is involved; a cephalhematoma is confined to one bone because it lies beneath the periosteum. This can be a help in differentiating between the two.

Treatment is not required for either condition, nor is the baby in any danger (unless the hemorrhage is massive). The mother, however, may need reassurance that her baby is in no distress and does not require special handling, particularly when the baby has a cephalohematoma which may last for several weeks. The fluid is never aspirated; to do so would risk infection.

EYES

Normal	Abnormal
Swelling, after administration of silver nitrate or after forceps delivery	Discharge from eyes
	Unusually large cornea
Subjunctival hemorrhage following long delivery	Opacity of pupil
Gray color	
"Crossed" eyes	

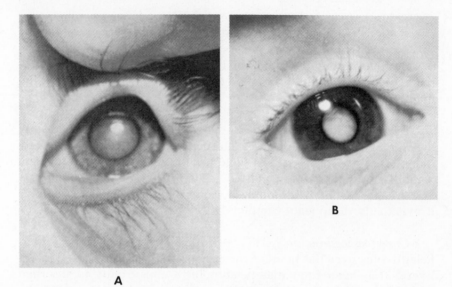

B

A

Figure 3–12.   The opaque pupil of a congenital cataract. (*A,* from the collection of Dr. Richard Hoover, Baltimore; *B,* from the collection of Dr. Arnall Patz, Baltimore: *In* Schaffer and Avery: *Diseases of the Newborn.* 3rd Edition. W. B. Saunders, 1971.)

Gray-blue in color, eyes may seem to be crossed at times in the newborn period because eye coordination is limited during the first month.

Swelling.   It is not unusual for swelling to develop around the eyes as a result of instillation of silver nitrate or following forceps delivery. It disappears in a few days.

Subconjunctival hemorrhage.   Subconjunctival hemorrhage may be seen as a small patch of red or as a red ring around the cornea. This absorbs in two to three weeks with no serious sequelae.

Opacity of pupil.   An opaque pupil, the evidence of *congenital cataract,* is rare; it most commonly occurs in babies with rubella syndrome, galactosemia, or cytomegalic inclusion disease (Fig. 3–12).

Large cornea.   A baby with an unusually large cornea is likely to have congenital glaucoma, which requires immediate treatment if the infant's vision is not to be permanently damaged (Fig. 3–13). The cornea may also be hazy or cloudy. Confirmation of the diagnosis of glaucoma is made by measuring intraocular tension. The treatment is immediate surgery.

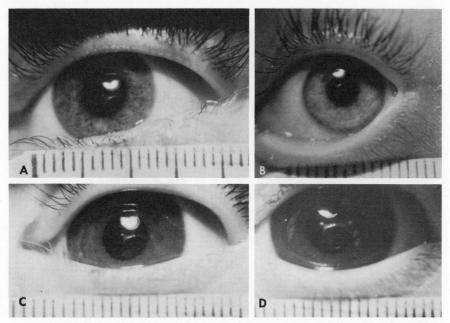

Figure 3-13. A, Normal eyeball with cornea of normal size. B, Small eyeball with microcornea. C, Early glaucoma without hazing of cornea or tearing of Descemet's membrane. D, Enlarged cornea of early glaucoma. (From the collection of Dr. Arnall Patz, Baltimore: *In* Schaffer and Avery: *Diseases of the Newborn*. 3rd Edition. W. B. Saunders, 1971.)

EARS

Normal
Upper part of ear should be on
   same plane as angle of eye

Abnormal
Low set ears

Low set ears. Low set ears are characteristic of some autosomal chromosomal abnormalities; they are also associated with some congenital renal disorders (Fig 3-14).

MOUTH

Normal
Epithelial pearls

"Sucking blisters"

Some mucus

Abnormal
Thrush

Corners of mouth which don't move
   when the baby cries

Cleft palate
Excessive frothy mucus; "blowing
   bubbles"

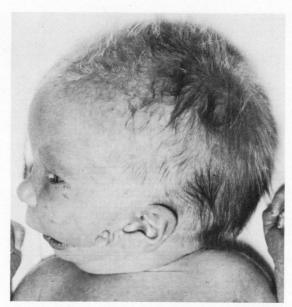

Figure 3–14. This infant has low-set malpositioned ears and extreme micrognathia. (From the files of Harriet Lane Home: *In* Schaffer and Avery: *Diseases of the Newborn*, 3rd Edition. W. B. Saunders, 1971.)

Thrush. Stimulating the baby to cry will make him open his mouth so that the inside of it can be checked for evidence of cleft palate (Fig. 3–15) and thrush (Fig. 3–16). Numerous small white and gray patches on the tongue and in the mouth are the indications of thrush, an infection by the fungus *Monilia albicans.* The differences between thrush and the epithelial pearls found on the hard palate need to be recognized. Milk curds are also occasionally mistaken for thrush.

Babies with thrush will usually be poor eaters. While there are many other much more serious reasons for failure to feed well – heart defects, infection, and central nervous system damage – any baby eating poorly should be given a thorough mouth examination. Babies receiving oral antibiotics are particularly good candidates. Most healthy newborns who acquire thrush do so in the delivery process, being infected by the Monilia in the mother's vagina.

Treatment usually includes the administration of a nystatin solution given orally every six hours. The solution should be administered slowly and gently so that it will be widely distributed throughout the oral cavity before it is swallowed. Individual lesions are sometimes painted with a 1% solution of aqueous gentian violet. An excess amount of gentian violet should be avoided because it may be irritating if it is swallowed. After gentian violet has been used, the baby should be placed face downward so that saliva containing the solution

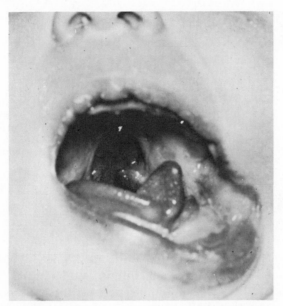

Figure 3–15. An open mouth reveals a large midline cleft in the posterior palate. (From the files of Harriet Lane Home: *In* Schaffer and Avery: *Diseases of the Newborn.* 3rd Edition. W. B. Saunders, 1971.)

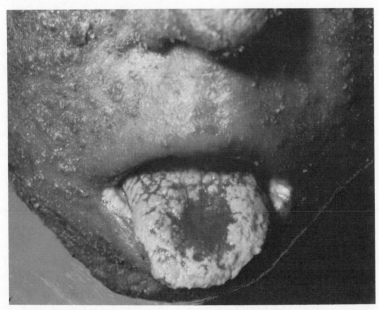

Figure 3–16. Numerous small white and gray patches on the tongue and palate are an indication of thrush. (From Pillsbury, Shelley, and Kligman: *A Manual of Cutaneous Medicine.* W. B. Saunders, 1961.)

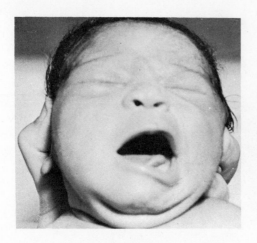

Figure 3-17. When there has been injury to the facial nerve there will be movement on only one side of the face. (From Davis and Rubin: *DeLee's Obstetrics for Nurses.* 18th Edition. W. B. Saunders, 1966.)

will drain outward. A paste of sodium bicarbonate can be used to remove gentian violet stains from clothing and bedding. Treatment is continued for at least three days after all visible evidence of thrush is gone to assure that the fungus itself is irradicated.

Movement on one side of face. When there has been injury to a facial nerve either because of pressure in utero or during labor or because of the use of forceps during delivery, there will be movement on only one side of the face when the baby cries, with the mouth drawn to that side (Fig. 3–17).

Excessive mucus. For a day or so after birth some babies have a fairly large amount of mucus, which can usually be aspirated with a bulb syringe. Continued excessive mucus that is frothy, as if the baby were "blowing bubbles," suggests a tracheo-esophageal fistula and calls for an immediate examination of the baby, whereby attempts are made to pass a catheter through his esophagus into his stomach. If the catheter curls up or will not pass, the baby must not be fed (see page 169).

JAW

Normal
Size in normal range

Abnormal
Micrognathia

Micrognathia. An abnormally small jaw, micrognathia (Fig. 3–14), can cause respiratory distress because the tongue falls back into the pharynx. This can partially be relieved by keeping the baby on his stomach so that the tongue falls forward. Sometimes the tongue is temporarily sutured in place until the jaw grows. Many babies with micrognathia have a cleft palate as well and may be more easily fed with a Breck feeder (page 216).

CHEST

Normal	Abnormal
Circumference: 12–13 inches Normal heart rate: 90 to 180 beats per minute	
Engorgement of breasts	Heart sounds on right side of chest
	Knot on clavicle

Breast engorgement. During pregnancy, maternal hormones cross the placental barrier and enter fetal circulation. When these hormones are withdrawn at the time of birth, the breasts enlarge and may even secrete fluid resembling colostrum or milk. The enlargement lasts from several days to as long as several weeks.

Mothers need to know that:

1. this is perfectly normal;
2. this is not a sign of infection;
3. the breasts should not be handled other than in routine bathing; no attempt should ever be made to express fluid from the breasts. To do so is to risk mastitis.

Heart sounds. Heart sounds on the right side of the chest may be due to dextrocardia, which in itself is not an immediate threat to the baby, or to a diaphragmatic hernia, a true surgical emergency which requires swift attention (see page 172).

Knot on clavicle. A "knot" is sometimes found on the clavicle on the third or fourth day after birth which was not evident at the time of delivery. It indicates a fractured clavicle which can occur in a seemingly normal delivery. The fracture heals without difficulty.

RESPIRATIONS

Normal	Abnormal

Average respiratory rate: 40 per
  minute
Range of normal: 30 to 60
  per minute	

Diaphragmatic and abdominal breathing	Intercostal retractions Retractions of the xyphoid
Obligate nose breather	
Transient tachypnea of the newborn	
	"Grunting" on expiration Flared nostrils

There is a considerable amount of variation in the "normal" respiratory patterns of newborns. Short periods of apnea, a Cheyne-Stokes type of respiration followed by several deep breaths, and irregular respiration are not uncommon in healthy babies. Various theories have been proposed as to why this is so, but no single answer has been universally accepted.

Rate. One of the most obvious differences between the respirations of all newborns and those of older children and adults is rate. The average rate is 40 per minute, but is often irregular. Rates of 30 to 60 per minute are considered within the range of normal. This increased rate is due to the newborn's metabolic need to move much more air per minute in proportion to his body weight because of his proportionately larger area of skin surface.

Muscle action. The character of neonatal breathing is diaphragmatic and abdominal. If intercostal muscles are being used to any extent there is likely to be some type of pulmonary pathology.

Transient tachypnea. Transient tachypnea of the newborn is one type of rapid breathing which does not indicate pathology. Transient tachypnea occurs in babies delivered by cesarean section or in breech position; it has been suggested that the fluid which is in the lungs in fetal life is not "squeezed out" as well under these circumstances as it is in a vertex delivery. The lungs, as a result, are somewhat less flexible, but air exchange is good and blood gases are normal. The condition usually lasts from 48 to 72 hours, although it may persist throughout the first week.

It can be difficult to feed babies with continued rapid respirations; they aspirate easily and must be fed with extra care and allowed frequent periods of rest. When respiratory rates are consistently faster than 60 per minute, alternate routes of feeding, such as gavage, should be considered.

ABDOMEN

Normal	Abnormal
Moderately protuberant	Scaphoid
	Distended
Bluish-white umbilical cord	Yellow discoloration of the cord at birth
Cutis navel	
Granulation tissue in the navel	Exudate or bleeding around the cord

Scaphoid abdomen. Normally the abdomen of a newborn is moderately distended. If it is small and scaphoid, it is very possible that the baby has a diaphragmatic hernia; part of the abdominal contents are in the thoracic cavity and the baby is likely to be dyspneic and cyanotic as well. Immediate surgery is essential to life (see page 172).

Distention. An overly distended abdomen is also abnormal and may be related to several conditions. An infant with a type of tracheoesophageal fistula in which there is an opening between trachea and stomach will become distended from the continual entry of air. Distention is also an early sign of infection. Congenital obstructions of the gastrointestinal tract and congenital megacolon are also among the conditions causing distention in newborns. It is important to know whether distention is increasing or decreasing. Marking the area of distention with a waxed pencil makes this easier to detect.

Pyloric stenosis. Peristaltic waves, most prominent during or immediately after feeding, and progressing from the upper left quadrant toward the pylorus, suggest pyloric stenosis. Babies with small bowel obstruction may also have visible peristaltic waves; these waves more commonly move from right to left. Peristaltic waves which are difficult to see may be visualized by focusing a light on the baby's abdomen while he is eating.

Umbilical cord. Bluish white at birth, the umbilical cord begins to dry shortly afterward and usually separates in six to eight days, the wound being healed by the time the baby is two weeks old. Yellow discoloration of the cord at the time of birth is an indication of hemolytic disease. Exudate around the cord usually signifies infection, although the baby may have an umbilical-cord infection serious enough to cause generalized sepsis without any localized sign. A weeping cord is cleaned with alcohol several times a day. Cord bleeding may be due to inadequate tying, or it may be a symptom of a bleeding disorder.

Cutis navel describes an umbilical cord that projects beyond the skin. It looks at first glance as if the baby might have an umbilical hernia, but a hernia can be returned to the abdomen while the cutis navel cannot. No special treatment is required; the navel will slowly invaginate.

Granulation tissue in the navel will also spontaneously disappear; until it does, the navel should be kept clean and dry.

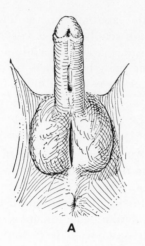

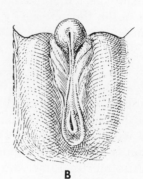

A   **B**

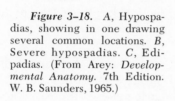

Figure 3–18. *A,* Hypospadias, showing in one drawing
several common locations. *B,*
Severe hypospadias. *C,* Edi-
padias. (From Arey: *Developmental Anatomy.* 7th Edition.
W. B. Saunders, 1965.)

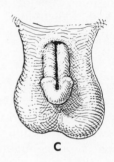

C

GENITALS

Normal	**Abnormal**
Red and swollen	
Vaginal discharge	
Vaginal bleeding	Excessive vaginal bleeding
Hymenal tag	
Swelling of the scrotum	Undescended testicles in a term baby
	Hypospadias; epispadias

Vaginal discharge. A vaginal discharge of thick, white mucus is
passed by all baby girls in the first week of life. Occasionally the
mucus is blood tinged about the third or fourth day, staining the
diaper. The cause of this "pseudo-menstruation," like that of breast
engorgement, is the withdrawal of maternal hormones. Excessive
vaginal bleeding, however, is not normal; it may be due to a blood
coagulation defect.

A hymenal or vaginal tag may be distressing to the mother, but it
will drop off in a few weeks.

Swelling of scrotum. Swelling of the scrotum is common in
newborns, and is especially noticeable in babies delivered from
breech. The edema disappears after a few days.

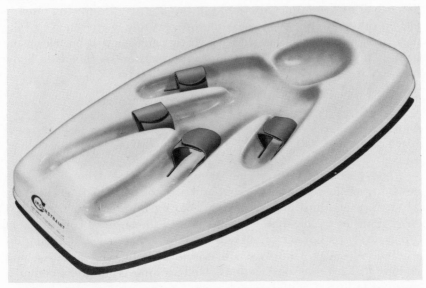

Figure 3-19. A circumcision board is a rapid and easy way to restrain a newborn not only for circumcision but for a number of other procedures. (Courtesy Olympic Surgical Co., Inc.).

Undescended testicles. Normally testicles descend into the scrotum in the eighth month of fetal life. It is possible that a baby boy with undescended testicles is of a younger gestational age than suspected.

Hypospadias. In about one out of every 300 births, the urethra open on the ventral surface of the penis (Fig. 3-18). The condition is termed hypospadias. Surgical correction is usually made by the time the boy is two years old and always before he starts to school so that he will be able to urinate in the same way as the other boys in his class. These babies should *not* be circumcised because the foreskin is used in the surgical repair.

Epispadias. Epispadias (Fig. 3-18), the opening of the urethra on the dorsal aspect of the penis, is far less common and is also corrected by surgery.

Circumcision. Circumcision in the newborn, as suggested elsewhere (page 124) is based primarily on cultural rather than medical consideration. A circumcision board (Fig. 3-19) provides an easy method for positioning and restraining the baby. Aftercare includes applying a Vaseline dressing or an ointment such as Vaseline to the raw area, with frequent checks to make sure there is no bleeding.

Some babies seem uncomfortable in the first days following circumcision; others do not even seem to notice. A newly circumcised baby may not like to lie on his stomach. If the mother will be taking the baby home within a day or so after circumcision she needs to know how to care for the area until it heals completely.

URINE

Normal   **Abnormal**
Peach colored crystals   Failure to void

The peach colored crystals which can discolor the diaper of a newborn are crystals of uric acid and are not pathologic at this age.

It is exceeding important that voiding be noted on the baby's chart. Failure by the baby to void is an indication of some type of urinary tract pathology which will need to be investigated. Examples are the absence of one or both kidneys, polycystic kidneys, and various urinary tract obstructions. Dehydration is the most common cause of failure to void in newborns.

It is common for an infant not to void in the first 12 hours after birth, and he may not void until the second or third day, depending to an extent, on his fluid intake and also on environmental temperature and the condition of his digestive and nervous systems. Failure to void within 48 hours should be reported to the physician in charge of the baby's care.

STOOLS

Normal   **Abnormal**
Meconium stools for 3 to 4 days;   No stool in 48 hours
  odorless, dark green to black, viscid

                                    Meconium stool but no feces
Transitional stools; greenish
  brown to yellow   Thick putty-like meconium

Breast-fed baby: golden to mustard,   Small putty-like stool
  from one to six in 24 hours

                                      Diarrhea
Bottle-fed baby: Pale yellow, more
  formed, more frequent and regular   Blood in stool
  than those of breast baby

Darkened stools when baby is
  receiving iron

Faint purple when baby is receiving
  gentian violet for thrush

Bright green stool when baby is being
  treated under bililight (see page 154)

The consistency, color, and odor of stools are all important in evaluating the baby's general condition. Because color changes can occur shortly after defecation, their evaluation has to be made right away if it is to have meaning.

Obstruction. If no stool is passed within 48 hours there is usually an intestinal obstruction (page 173). If meconium was passed initially, but then no feces are passed, the obstruction is in the ileum. Thick, putty-like meconium is the initial symptom of meconium ileus (page 173). A small, putty-like stool may be due to stenosis or atresia somewhere in the bowel.

Diarrhea. Diarrhea is a somewhat nonspecific symptom in newborns. It may be due to overfeeding. Some babies will have diarrhea from certain formulas that will have no effect on other infants. Gastroenteritis causes diarrhea in some babies and can spread quickly through the nursery if the baby is not quickly isolated. The degree of severity of diarrhea can be estimated by measuring the water margin around the stool if the baby has not voided in the diaper. Aside from the danger of sepsis, diarrhea is always serious in the newborn because of his extremely labile water balance (see Chapter 5).

Intestinal bleeding. Flecks of blood in the baby's stool may come from an anal fissure. Either bright red or old blood are signs of intestinal bleeding, just as they are at any age.

VOMITING

Mild regurgitation is not at all unusual in the newborn and is due in part to swallowed air and in part to a "temporary inability of the cardiac sphincter to completely prevent a flow of fluid from the stomach in a reverse direction" (Craig, 1969).

Vomiting is quite another matter. Occurring shortly after birth or within the first 24 hours, vomiting is likely to be due to obstruction of the upper digestive tract or to increased intracranial pressure. After the first day, vomiting may still be due to central nervous system or gastrointestinal problems, but it can also be a sign of a multitude of other conditions including septicemia, overfeeding, pyloric stenosis, milk allergy, and adrenal insufficiency.

Blood in the vomitus of a breast-fed baby, unless copious in amount, is very possibly due to fissures in the mother's nipples. Maternal blood swallowed during delivery is also a common cause of blood appearing in the vomitus in the first two to three days of life.

Dark green vomitus indicates an obstruction in the gastrointestinal tract (see page 173).

Whether or not vomiting is projectile is always a significant observation. Projectile vomiting in the first week is often related to intestinal obstruction; beginning in the second week, the cause may be pyloric stenosis.

Psychological Characteristics and Needs of the Newborn

At the beginning of this chapter it was suggested that nurses must understand both the physiological and psychological characteristics and needs of newborns. While certain questions about physiological areas remain unanswered, they are certainly both better understood and more frequently studied than the psychological aspects of the first days and weeks of life.

The main research interests of psychologists in relation to newborns has come from a desire to establish a baseline for understanding the baby's future development by discovering the attributes with which the human baby is born. They find that this new baby is an individual with intelligence, who differs from his fellows and is able to respond to a variety of sensory stimuli and to learn from his environment—a rather different picture from the unmolded lump of clay visualized by earlier philosophers.

His visual acuity is in the range of 20/150, a level considered adequate for binocular vision. Color vision is limited, but he can see form and motion. Even by the end of the first week some babies begin to show an interest in the human face.

Both sense of smell and hearing are present. The baby can discriminate between tones of varying frequencies and seems to have a preference for the human voice.

Sensitivity to pain increases each day. A week-old baby reacts to pain when his skin is irritated, a factor that probably needs to be considered in relation to circumcision. There seems little doubt that the baby feels pain from such a procedure; what we don't know is whether that pain is quickly forgotten or whether the baby's subconscious mind retains the memory. If the latter is true, should a local anesthetic be used in circumcision? Since for most babies the decision for circumcision is based on cultural rather than medical values, is the wholesale circumcision practiced in the United States really necessary? What does pain mean for the baby who must have repeated blood tests, injections, intravenous fluids, painful changes of dressings which cannot be explained to him and which he cannot possibly understand? Many of these procedures are absolutely essential to life and the baby's well being, yet to assume that they can in no way harm such a young infant seems unwarranted.

Aside from pain, babies show their displeasure at several other conditions by crying and fretting. Although there are individual differences in response, most newborns seem to dislike having their positions changed abruptly, having a cold or wet object placed next to their skin, and having their movement restrained. Sudden loud noises also appear to be unpleasant.

Mother-child interaction. On the other hand, pleasant, relaxed responses can be brought about by patting the baby, by holding him snugly wrapped in his blanket and rocking him, and by keeping him warm. Sucking appears to bring satisfaction quite apart from the nourishment it affords. Most of the behavior that elicits these pleasant responses comes from physical contact with the mother, a desire that is by no means confined to human babies. Harlow's experiments (1959) with newborn monkeys demonstrated that they, too, felt the need for more than physical nourishment. One group was fed from a bottle attached to a "mother" figure of wire mesh; the second group was fed from a terry-cloth mother. Yet when the baby monkeys were frightened, all clung to the terry-cloth mother, even those who had not been fed by her. Also, all of the baby monkeys were more adventurous in their exploration of their surroundings when they were near the terry-cloth mother.

But even the cloth mother had her limitations. In the long run the babies with the cloth mothers as well as those with wire mothers grew up to be unpleasantly aggressive, unable to make friends, and troubled by sexual problems. What apparently was lacking was the interaction between mother and baby—the all important response of the mother to her child.

The idea that interaction is important is hardly a new one. Perhaps one of the earliest experiments which pointed to the need for interaction between mother (or mother-substitute) and child was that attributed to Frederick II in the thirteenth century, an experiment which, like many since his time, brought far different results than were expected. It is said that Frederick wondered what language children would speak when they grew up if no one had ever spoken to them—Hebrew, perhaps, or Greek or Arabic, or would it be the language of their parents? The children were given to foster mothers who fed them and bathed them and gave them good physical care, but who were forbidden to ever talk to them, lest their language development be influenced. Frederick never found the answer to his original question; all of the children died.

So too do babies today appear apathetic and lethargic when they lack the stimulation that comes from interaction with another human who talks and sings to them and carries them about. Sometimes interaction is hard to find in an industrialized society. Under what we consider ideal conditions, baby has his own bed, often his own room, a car bed and a carriage for trips away from home—all of which can separate him from others. By contrast, in many (but not all) traditional societies babies may have continual contact with another human body—mother, grandmother, or a slightly older sibling—for many months after birth. We don't really know yet how significant this constant contact is in comparison with the baby who lacks continuous interaction but receives frequent stimulation from his mother. And we may never be able to make exacting comparisons since there is no way to hold a variety of other factors affecting the baby constant, including his own inherited individuality. Yet we do seem to be on firm ground when we emphasize that some interaction is needed beyond that required to meet physical needs. Without this early sensory stimulation the baby may fail to develop an interest in people and objects outside of himself.

Many things influence the way in which a woman will "mother," i.e., nurture and care for her infant. To a large extent, the practices of the mother's cultural group will play a role, yet obviously there are differences within cultural groups. The kind of care a mother has received from her own mother is a factor, as is the relationship between the mother and her husband. Important, too, are the experiences of previous pregnancies. Klaus and Kennell (1970) cite the previous loss of a newborn, miscarriage, induced abortion, and a previous newborn who was seriously ill as some of the factors which can lead to serious disturbances in the ability to "mother." The status of the current pregnancy—whether or not it was planned, whether it has been difficult or easy—is also significant.

If the mother is a primipara under the age of 17 or older than 38, if she has had difficulty in becoming pregnant, if she has had a medical problem which could possibly affect the baby such as toxemia or diabetes or Rh incompatibility, mothering may be impaired (Klaus and Kennell, 1970).

All of the aforementioned circumstances have been predetermined at the time of the baby's birth. It is too late to change them. But nurses who care for mothers and their babies can alter other variables that also affect mothering. How can we do this?

TEACHING THE MOTHER TO CARE FOR HER BABY

For the woman who is nurturable and feels secure about her own capabilities, we can provide an opportunity for her to come to know her baby in the first days of his life. Klaus and his associates (1970), observing the behavior of mothers toward their newborns, found their actions to follow very similar patterns, regardless of the socioeconomic, cultural, or ethnic groups to which they belonged. The mothers first explored their babies' arms and legs with their fingertips.

Within four to five minutes the mother had begun to explore the baby's trunk with her palm. Seventy-five per cent of the mothers awakened their babies so they could look into their eyes, several mentioning that once their babies had looked at them they felt closer to them.

Hospital routine. Hospital routine must help the mother, and not hinder her, in this exploratory behavior. If her baby is brought to her wrapped in a blanket she needs to feel free to unwrap and caress him. At least one visit before the baby's first feeding (depending, of course, on the time of first feeding) gives her a chance to begin to know him. At each feeding period there needs to be time allowed for visiting.

Ideally the father should have the same chance as the mother to touch his baby and begin to know him. We have conditioned so many fathers to be afraid to handle their own infants by our "hands off" attitude when the babies are new; it is not surprising that many of them see the baby as belonging to the mother — "her baby" — and even as competing with them for the mother's affection. While some institutions are outstanding exceptions in that they draw the father into the entire birth process, many still appear to see his role as the man who pays the bill. This is in conflict with current middle-class norms which expect him to be a partner in the care of his baby, not just a provider. A great many of us need to re-evaluate the routines of our own hospitals in relation to these norms.

Anxiety, and even just plain lack of information, is another factor interfering with happy, relaxed mother-baby relationships. At some time during each mother's hospitalization, an experienced nurse needs to find time to talk with her, particularly with those mothers who have no private physician to care for them. Hopefully this will happen more than once, but with hospital stays becoming constantly shorter, largely for economic reasons, there can be a tremendous gap between the ideal and reality.

Conferences. A mother-nurse conference might be on an individual basis, or it may be an informal, small-group conversation. Each has its advantages. Some mothers may be hesitant to speak out in a group but willing to voice their questions and concerns to the nurse in private. Others, seeing that most of the other women have queries similar to their own, are relieved that they are not the only ones who do not know all the answers.

Demonstrations. A baby-bath demonstration will bring many mothers, who might just come to talk, to a "conversation" level. In the past we have sometimes made the bathing of this little baby, like many other aspects of baby care, into something of a mystique. (Perhaps to make our own role seem somewhat more important?) But what we want to communicate to mothers is that baby care is not the mysterious, complicated task they may have feared, but a happy, fairly easy one. Baby doesn't need an elaborate bassinet, baby lotion, shampoo, powder, oil, or an extensive wardrobe. He is better off without most of the trimmings; baby powder, because of an ingredient in it to prevent it from caking, is drying to newborn skin; he is adequately clothed in a diaper and shirt; time spent doing laundry can be used to talk to him when he frets, as all babies will occasionally; he needs a bath, each day if possible, milk, and loving; he needs a mother and father who can relax and enjoy him.

Rooming-in. Possibly the best way in which the hospital can help both mother and father overcome initial anxiety is through the practice of rooming-in — the mother taking care of her baby in her room for at least part of the day under the guidance of a nurse who is readily available to help her. When babies spend 23 out of 24 hours in a central nursery, the mother usually does not even have a chance to change a diaper until after she returns home. And more than one mother has been somewhat upset by the first sight of her baby's partially dried umbilical cord. A bath demonstration is no substitute for a chance to bathe your own baby with a nurse standing by to answer questions.

Observations at Duke University Hospital support the concept that continual contact between mother and baby during the first days may facilitate mothering behavior. After rooming-in was made compulsory, McBryde (1951) noted that the incidence of breast feeding rose from 35 to 58.5 per cent while phone calls from anxious mothers during the first weeks after discharge decreased by 90 per cent.

Experiences in a number of hospitals have shown that rooming-in can be accomplished without any major change in the physical facilities of an obstetrical unit. The change that is necessary is an ideological one. If there is commitment to the concept that this is the best type of care for *most* mothers and their babies, any other necessary adjustments can be made. Alternatives do need to be available for mothers with special problems.

The disinterested mother. Occasionally there is a mother who seems disinterested or even hostile toward her baby yet does not choose to give him up. There is little that we can do for this family on a short-term basis. The brief counseling that the medical or nursing staff can give the mother during the period that the baby is a newborn may afford a beginning and is certainly worth the effort, but it is not a solution. If she has no private physician she must be referred to the public health nurse who may be able to guide her to an agency or individual in the community who can help her and her baby. It is often hard to work with these mothers and easy to lose track of them; unusually a whole complex of factors has affected their attitude. But the attempt to help them must be made and continued to be made.

Bibliography

Armstrong, R. W.: Pentachlorophenol Poisoning in a Nursery for Newborn Infants. II. Epidemiologic and Toxicologic Studies. *Journal of Pediatrics, 75*:317, 1969.

Baker, G. L.: Management of Neonatal Bacterial Infections. *Clinical Pediatrics, 8*:575, 1969.

Bowlby, J.: *Attachment and Loss.* Volume I. New York, Basic Books Inc., 1969.

Craig, W. S.: *Care of the Newly Born Infant.* Baltimore, Williams and Wilkins Company, 1969.

Fantz, R. L., and Neirs, S.: Pattern Preferences and Perceptual Cognitive Development in Early Infancy. *Merrill-Palmer Quarterly of Behavior and Development, 13*:88, 1967.

Gezon, H. M.: Diagnosis and Treatment: Adult Staphylococcal Nasal Carriers in the Newborn Nursery. *Pediatrics, 42*:353, 1968.

Gluck, L., and Wood, H. F.: Staphylococcal Colonization in Newborn Infants with and without Antiseptic Skin Care. *New England Journal of Medicine, 268*:1265, 1963.

Gotaff, S. P., and Behrman, R. E.: Neonatal Septicemia. *Journal of Pediatrics, 76*:142, 1970.

Harlow, H. F., and Zimmermann, R.: Affectional Responses in the Infant Monkey. *In* Mussen, P., Conger, J., and Kagan, J. (eds.): *Readings in Child Development and Personality.* New York, Harper and Row, 1965.

Hervada, A. R.: Nursery Evaluation of the Newborn. *American Journal of Nursing, 67*:1669 (August), 1967.

Hurlock, E.: *Developmental Psychology.* New York, McGraw-Hill, 1968.

Illingworth, R. S.: *The Development of the Infant and Young Child.* Baltimore, Williams and Wilkins Company, 1966.

Klaus, M. H., and Kennell, J. H.: Mothers Separated from their Newborn Infants. *Pediatric Clinics of North America, 17*:1015, 1970.

Klaus, M., Kennell, J. H., Plumb, W., and Zuehlke, S.: Human Maternal Behavior at the First Contact with her Young. *Pediatrics, 46*:187, 1970.

Lutz, L., and Perlstein, P. H.: Temperature Control in Newborn Babies. *Nursing Clinics of North America, 6*:15, 1971.

McBryde, A.: Compulsory Rooming-in in the Ward and Private Newborn Service at Duke University Hospital. *Journal of the American Medical Association, 145*:625, 1951.

McKay, J.: The Fetus and Newborn Infant. *In* Nelson, W. E., Vaughan, V. C., and McKay, R. J. (eds.): *Textbook of Pediatrics.* 9th Edition. Philadelphia, W. B. Saunders, 1969.

Mussen, P. H.: *The Psychological Development of the Child.* Englewood Cliffs, New Jersey, Prentice-Hall, 1963.

Nyhan, W. L.: Newly Recognized Hazard in the Newborn Nursery. *Journal of Pediatrics, 75*:348, 1969.

Richmond, J. B.: The Mother's Tie to Her Child. *Pediatrics, 45*:189, 1970.

Riley, H. D.: Hospital Associated Infections. *Pediatric Clinics of North America, 16*:701, 1969.

Robson, A. M., Kissane, J. M., Elvick, N. H., and Pundavela, L.: Pentachlorophenol Poisoning in a Nursery for Newborn Infants. I. Clinical Features and Treatment. *Journal of Pediatrics, 75*:309, 1969.

Salk, L., and Kramer, R.: *How to Raise a Human Being.* New York, Random House, 1969.

Schaffer, A. J., and Avery, M. E.: *Diseases of the Newborn.* 3rd Edition. Philadelphia, W. B. Saunders, 1971.

Schaffer, H. R., and Emerson, P. E.: Patterns of Response to Physical Contact in Early Human Development. *Journal of Child Psychology and Psychiatry, 5*:1, 1964.

Smith, C. A.: *The Physiology of the Newborn Infant.* 3rd Edition. Springfield, Illinois; Charles C Thomas, 1959.

Smith, N., Schwartz, J. R., Mandell, W., Silberstein, R. M., Dalack, J. D., and Sacks, S.: Mothers' Psychological Reactions to Premature and Full Size and Newborns. *Archives of General Psychiatry, 21*:177, 1969.

Smith, R. M.: Temperature Monitoring and Regulation. *Pediatric Clinics of North America, 16*:643, 1969.

Vulliamy, D. G.: *The Newborn Child.* Boston, Little, Brown and Company, 1967.

Weiss, C.: Does Circumcision of the Newborn Require an Anesthetic? *Clinical Pediatrics, 7*:128, 1968.

CHAPTER 4

The Newborn with
Special Problems

For many reasons, both genetic and environmental, newborns may have special kinds of problems. From 7 to 14 per cent of infants born in the United States weigh less than 2500 gm. and are considered at high risk even if they have no other congenital anomalies. Malformations, birth injuries, infection, asphyxia, and atelectasis are other major sources of difficulty for both term and premature babies.

Regardless of what differentiates an "abnormal" newborn from his normal counterpart, he is affected by the difference in two ways— physically and psychologically. The most obvious effect is the immediate physiological one, but some babies will have long-term physical disabilities as well. These are direct effects.

Equally important are the indirect consequences of abnormality —the way in which the baby's physical appearance and problems affect the attitude of his parents toward him. Prematurity, severe early illness, or deformity can easily, and understandably, arouse many feelings in both mother and father. Since these feelings are shared to a certain degree by many parents, regardless of the specific problem their baby faces, it seems worthwhile to consider them first.

General Family Attitudes

What happens to a man and woman when they find themselves the parents of a baby less perfect than the ideal for which they had imagined and hoped? A big question for them is *why?*; their answer will be a product of both their cultural heritage and their own individual personality. Many parents feel there is something biologically wrong, either with themselves or with their mate. A mother can see herself as a less than adequate woman because she was unable to carry a baby to term or because the baby was defective. The defective baby may be interpreted as God's punishment for past sins or for not desiring the pregnancy (Waechter, 1970).

If the baby has a malformation which makes him appear distinctly different—a harelip, for example—or which carries the probability of prolonged physical or mental abnormality, such as a meningomyelocele or Down's syndrome, parents have to cope with the feelings they have accumulated throughout their own lives toward handicapped persons. They may feel pity, repugnance, contempt, or often ambivalence. A father may remember being with a gang of boys many years before when they teased a "crippled" child. Now he projects his own child into a similar situation. If there are other children in the family, both mother and father are likely to be concerned about their reaction to a less than normal baby and how this new infant will affect them.

The not-so-simple economics of a premature or sick baby can be overwhelming. By the time the infant is ready for discharge, many parents owe the hospital a bill they cannot hope to pay for years.

The kind of relationship mother and father have with one another can also be a factor in their attitude toward the baby. If the baby was unplanned, perhaps coming at a less than propitious time for economic or other reasons, the mother may have already had doubts about what the infant would mean in her relationship with her husband. The added burden of prematurity or illness can shake an already unstable marriage.

We can help parents deal with many of these feelings to a degree. But before considering some of the ways in which this might be done, we need to examine the role of the hospital, particularly the physicians and nurses connected with the nursery, in affecting the attitudes of parents toward their infants. Of special concern in this consideration is the manner in which the hospital makes it more difficult for mothers to become attached to their high risk babies, i.e., the long period of enforced separation that is the most common practice in premature and intensive care nurseries in the United States today.

We need to do some serious thinking about the necessity and even the advisability of separating parents and their babies for the first two to three months of life. Not so very many years ago parents were kept out of all pediatric units, those in which older children were cared for as well as newborns. Fear that infection would be introduced into the unit and that parents would interfere with medical and nursing care were among the popular reasons cited for this exclusion. But as knowledge of emotional needs increased, parents came to be regarded as an indispensable part of good nursing care, even in isolation units, for children over six months of age.

The Problem of Separating Mothers from the Seriously Ill Newborn

In the preceding chapter the meaning of separation for mothers of normal newborns is mentioned. The extent of this separation seems almost inconsequential (although only relatively so) in comparison with the 30-, 60-, even 90-day separations that the parents of premature or sick babies face. This separation of mother and premature infant has not always been the established practice. Pierre Budin, the most famous of the early neonatologists (late nineteenth and early twentieth century) welcomed mother's participation in premature care and encouraged mothers to breast feed their premature infants. (Wet nurses were employed when mothers were unable to do so.) He noted that when a mother did not have to meet her baby's needs, she might lose interest in the baby and abandon it.

The exclusion of the mother began partially as a result of the more rigid measures which were instituted to prevent infection in all areas of the hospital and in part from the example set by the exhibits of Dr. Martin Cooney. Dr. Cooney exhibited premature babies in incubators at fairs in the United States (Fig. 4–1) and England following

Figure 4–1. Dr. Martin Cooney's exhibit of premature infants at the Chicago World's Fair, 1933. (From Klaus and Kennell. *Pediatric Clinics of N. America,* 17:1017, 1970.)

an initial demonstration of his *Kinderbrutanstalt* (child hatchery) at the Berlin exposition of 1896. After this period of early traveling, Cooney settled down on Coney Island where he raised more than 5000 premature infants during a 39-year period. Mothers did not participate in caring for the babies that were exhibited. (They did get free passes so they could come and see them.) It is interesting that sometimes Cooney had difficulty in persuading the mothers to take their infants back.

Thus the precedent was established. When the first hospital premature unit was established in Chicago in 1923, mothers were excluded.

SEPARATION AND MATERNAL ATTITUDES

Is there any evidence that mothers who are separated from their premature or sick babies react to them differently than those mothers who are allowed to have contact with their babies and participate in their care? This kind of study has been limited in human infants, although it has been known for some years that separation of animal young from their mothers shortly after birth results in abnormal behavior. Richmond (1970) showed that even the brief separation of newborn goats for just one hour resulted in an interference with the mother's affection for her baby. Fifty per cent of the separated mothers would nurse any of the kids of the herd—abnormal behavior for goats. The fact that the remaining 50 per cent continued to behave normally seemed to demonstrate considerable individual variation in maternal capacity.

In one London hospital, mothers are now allowed to touch any baby who is in an incubator no matter how sick the infant might be. As soon as the mother is able, she is brought to the nursery; after she washes her hands the incubator port is opened and she reaches in for a "brief fondle." "The joy and delight with which the mothers respond to this contact is truly wonderful to watch. Those mothers whose previous babies have been in incubators have stressed their amazement at the huge difference in their feeling of attachment this time compared with looking through glass" (Gans, 1969).

Liefer and his associates compared the behavior of a group of mothers who had early contact with their infants with a second group who did not. Observations were made of skill in caretaking and of behavior considered to represent attachment (looking at the baby, smiling at him, caressing him, and holding him close). These observations were made at three different times:
1. on the mother's fifth visit to her infant in the discharge nursery
2. in the home a week after discharge
3. in the pediatric clinic a month after discharge.

Differences in caretaking skill were only evident during the visit in the discharge nursery; those mothers with early contact were the more skillful. On the other hand, differences in attachment behavior were greater at the third period of observation, a month after discharge, with the greater degree of attachment being demonstrated by the nonseparated mothers (Klaus, 1970).

Feeding behavior was studied in another group of mothers; comparisons were made between 15 mothers, who had been separated from their premature infants for a period of 20 days, and eight mothers who had physical contact with their premature infants, within the first five days after birth. The technique used was time-lapse photography during the first ten minutes of the feeding period, the photographs being examined for 25 different aspects of cuddling and feeding behavior. Both the amount of time spent "en face" and in cuddling (Fig. 4–2) was markedly increased in mothers with early contact (Fig. 4–3). Follow-up films made a month and nearly 200 feedings after discharge showed that the late contact mothers were continuing to hold their babies differently and were less skillful in feeding in comparison with early contact mothers (Klaus and Kennell).

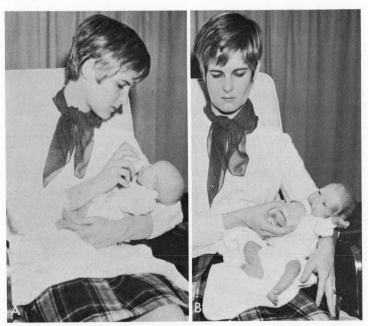

Figure 4–2. A posed mother showing two different caretaking positions. *A*, Infant is held in close contact (cuddling), mother is looking at the infant "en face," and milk is in the tip of the nipple. *B*, Infant's trunk is held away from mother, mother is looking at infant but not en face, and there is no milk in the tip of the nipple. (From Klaus and Kennell: *Pediatric Clinics of N. America, 17*:1024, 1970.)

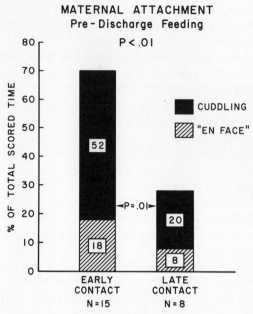

Figure 4–3. Percentage of en face and cuddling times in early and late contact mothers of premature infants. (From Klaus and Kennell: *Pediatric Clinics of N. America,* 17:1025, 1970.)

Klaus and Kennell point out that if, as has been suggested by some studies, early maternal attentiveness is related to later tendencies of the baby to explore, then cuddling and "en face" contact which the baby receives during this early period can affect his later development.

NURSES, MOTHERS, AND MOTHERING

Can the nurse who cares for the high risk baby help a mother feel closer to her baby and facilitate mothering? Since most institutions at the present time still do not allow mothers into nurseries but do let them observe through a window, we need first to consider ways in which we can help mothers within the framework of these existing regulations.

Earlier it was mentioned that the mother of a premature baby, and even more the mother of a baby with an obvious birth defect, may feel that her baby is unacceptable—to her husband, her family, perhaps even to society. We can show her that the baby is acceptable to us by the way we hold him, the way we talk to him, the way in which we talk about him. A baby with a defect must not be concealed in a corner of the nursery so that he is kept from view, nor should his defect be hidden.

Maintaining communication with parents over a long period of time is a nursery responsibility that can assist the mothering process. Keeping these channels of communication open is not always easy. It is not unusual for parents to try to withdraw from the experience of a sick or deformed baby. This is, in part, a kind of anticipatory grief, a preparation for the possible loss of the baby. They are afraid that if they allow themselves to become attached to this baby, and he dies, then the hurt will be even greater. Other parents will be angry, and often the nurses, being readily available targets, will feel the force of that anger. But the resentment and harsh words, if they come, should not be taken personally.

Some mothers will say they feel no love for this baby, particularly if they have had no opportunity to touch him. They need reassurance that feelings of affection often develop gradually rather than spontaneously; that once she begins to care for her baby she will find her love growing.

If the mother is to be allowed in the nursery, she must not only be made to feel welcome but should also be given assurance that it is important to her baby that she be there. Remembering the mother's name and that of her baby, anticipating her questions about the baby's weight and behavior and being ready to answer any other questions she may have, explaining the equipment being used, showing her ways in which she can care for her baby—all are essential parts of nursing care for each mother-infant pair. Fathers, too, when they are able to be at the hospital, should have the opportunity to be with their babies in the nursery.

Once the mother goes home, or if the baby has been transferred from a community hospital to a specialized unit in a medical center, the mother should be encouraged to telephone as often as she wishes —certainly every day if she wants—to ask about her baby. The baby's first name can be put on his isolette (along with the family name, of course) so the nurse can refer to him by name when she talks with the mother. Klaus suggests that the nursery keep a record of all phone calls and visits; where there are fewer than two visits or calls per week there is a subsequent high incidence of severe mothering disorders.

At this time more studies are probably necessary before premature and intensive care nurseries can be open to mothers on a broad scale—studies which not only show positive benefits but also the absence of negative side effects, such as an increased level of infection. Nurses who work with high risk babies each day are in an ideal position to carry out this kind of research.

The Problem of Overprotection

It has become an accepted practice that nurses help mothers feed their babies for a period of several days before discharge and discuss with them other aspects of physical care. If the baby is doing well the mother needs to realize that this care is not different from that of any other baby. Overprotection is a common problem with mothers of babies who have been premature or are ill. And overprotection can, in turn, lead to behavioral changes as the baby grows older. He may become shy and overly attached to his mother; he may be petulant and negativistic. Drillien (1958) found that two-thirds of very low birth weight babies had either major or minor emotional disorders. Overprotection is probably only one reason for such disorders. In studies where socioeconomic level is not controlled, the correlation may be between socioeconomic status and emotional disorder rather than between prematurity and emotional disorders, since increased incidence of emotional problems has been found among the same economic groups which also have an increased incidence of prematurity. Since anoxia is also common in babies of very low birth weight, emotional disturbance, in some instances at least, is probably related to physiologic change.

When the baby is overprotected through his early years, this protection is sometimes supplanted later by a pressure to catch up with his peers, which can again be a source of emotional difficulty. It might help the mother to realize that when her 28-week gestation baby has his first birthday, he is actually only 9 months old (if his age is figured from the time of conception), and he is thus more likely to function on a 9 month level. It may be several years before he "catches up" with his peers, but this is perfectly normal.

The Transportation of a High Risk Infant from a Community Hospital to a Medical Center

When a baby with a special problem—a premature infant, a term baby in obvious distress, a baby who will need major surgery—is born at a small community hospital, current trends indicate that he may very likely be transferred to a medical center specially equipped to care for him. The ever rising costs of both equipment and specifically trained personnel make it likely that this practice will continue to grow. Ideally, high risk mothers would be identified early and assigned to such a center for delivery, but this is obviously not always possible.

The problem, then, is to transport the sick infant both quickly and safely. A transport incubator is almost a necessity. It must keep the baby warm, supply oxygen if it is needed, allow full observation of the baby, and offer easy access for emergency treatment. A nurse, a physician's assistant, or a physician should accompany the baby in order to care for him en route. Certain necessary information should also be sent along with the baby, including the mother's pre- and postnatal history, a record of the delivery, the baby's hospital record (all can be xeroxed copies), and a signed "permission for treatment" sheet, as well as a sample of maternal blood.

Babies of Low Birth Weight and Low Gestational Age

Babies with low birth weight may be premature, with a gestational age of less than 37 weeks, or "small-for-dates" with a gestational age equal to that of a term baby but with a low birth weight, usually because of intrauterine malnutrition. In some ways babies in each category resemble one another. For example, both have limited sub-

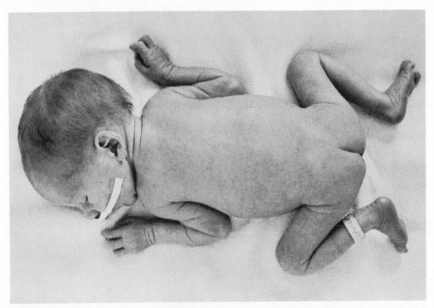

Figure 4–4. In prone position the premature lies with pelvis flat and legs splayed out sideways like a frog. Compare this illustration with that of the term newborn on page 97. (Courtesy of Mead, Johnson, and Company.)

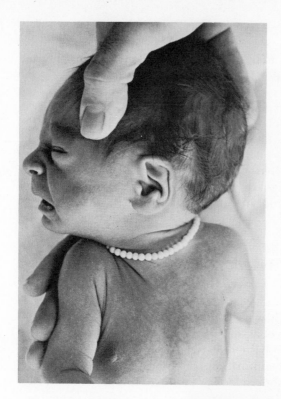

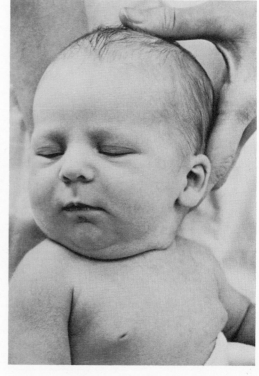

Figure 4-5. In an infant of 28 weeks gestation the chin can be passively rotated well past the acromial tip. As the developmental age advances there is a gradual decrease in the range of motion. (Courtesy of Mead, Johnson, and Company.)

Figure 4-6. When a term infant's head is rotated, the chin stops at the acromial tip. (Courtesy of Mead, Johnson, and Company.)

140

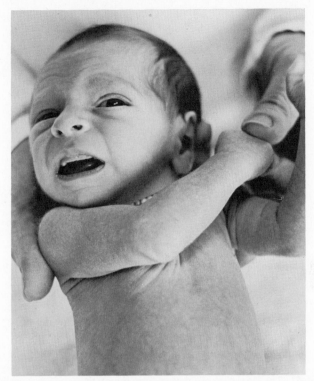

Figure 4-7. The scarf sign is an estimation of muscle tone. In the premature infant, the hand goes well past the acromion. (Courtesy of Mead, Johnson, and Company.)

cutaneous fat, which affects temperature regulation, and a large surface area in proportion to body mass, which influences both heat and water loss. Organ function, on the other hand, will not be as immature in the small-for-dates baby because of his age.

The decision as to whether a baby is truly premature or small for his gestational age is based on a number of criteria, such as the completeness of the Moro response, the descent of the testicles, the pattern of creases on the sole of the foot, and the quality of the muscle tone. Muscle tone is judged on the basis of such factors as posture, consistency of muscles, and range of joint movement (Fig. 4–4).

The range of passive rotation of the head in the premature infant is considerably greater than that of the term baby. At 28 weeks gestation, the chin goes well past the acromial tip (Fig. 4–5). With increased age the range of motion becomes more limited (Fig. 4–6). Another estimate of muscle tone, the scarf sign, also gauges the degree of prematurity (Figs. 4–7 and 4–8).

Figure 4–8.   The scarf sign in a normal term infant; the hand reaches the acromion but goes no farther. (Courtesy of Mead, Johnson, and Company.)

APPEARANCE AND CHARACTERISTICS OF THE PREMATURE BABY

In comparison with most parents' ideal image of what a new baby should be (often based on magazine pictures of six-month-old babies) the "premie" falls far short of expectation. His head is too large, and his body is scrawny. He may also be badly bruised because of the extreme fragility of his capillaries. Such an appearance can be a disappointment to some parents in the first days after birth—a feeling which they may voice or keep to themselves depending on their own personality and on how comfortable they feel with the nurses and doctors who care for mother and baby.

In addition to the obvious differences in weight and proportion, what is this born-too-early baby like? Observe him. He moves far less than the full-term baby and rarely cries. His muscles are poorly developed, a circumstance which affects his respirations and which also means he is unable to shiver in oder to raise his body temperature. And because he cannot perspire either, he is also unable to lower his body temperature in an overly warm environment.

His breathing is largely diaphragmatic, and the rhythm is irregular. During the first few days, a quite early premature baby is likely to have frequent periods of apnea—one minute he is breathing, a moment later he is not.

If he is able to suck or swallow he probably does so poorly. Once food is ingested, regurgitation is not unusual, and in the fairly common absence of a cough reflex, aspiration is a real problem. Because the musculature of his bowel wall is weak, he is easily distended and frequently constipated.

There are also differences which cannot be as readily observed. Resistance to infection is low. The immunoglobulin G (Ig-G) is poorly synthesized, and the immunoglobin M (Ig-M) is at a slower rate than in term infants. Moreover, the mother of a "premie" is more likely to have problems which put the baby at a risk of infection (see page 90).

Kidney tubules continue to be formed until term, so that the premature baby's ability to excrete sodium and chloride is reduced, making him susceptible to electrolyte imbalance and also affecting the excretion of any medication he may receive.

The thinner walls of his blood vessels predispose him not only to bruising, but also to intracranial hemorrhage. Since malpresentation is common in babies born before term, the risk of intracranial hemorrhage is further heightened. Hypoxia, not at all unusual in prematures, also raises the risk of bleeding into the brain.

Enzymes in the premature baby function at reduced levels; one dramatic effect of this is the hyperbilirubinemia of prematurity (see page 153).

APPEARANCE AND CHARACTERISTICS OF
THE SMALL-FOR-DATES BABY

The most common reason for the low birth weight of the small-for-dates baby is placental dysfunction. Degenerative changes in the placenta bring about a reduction in both oxygen and nourishment for the fetus. Maternal malnutrition, smoking, and developmental defects in the fetus which hamper growth can also be factors. In some families in which both parents and other relatives are small, a genetic predisposition may also lead to small babies.

Small-for-dates babies have a limited amount of vernix. Their skin tends to be pale and dry and often cracked or scaling. Frequently both skin and cord are meconium stained. Because the small size of

the baby is frequently related to intrauterine malnutrition, the baby
has a tendency to hypoglycemia.

LARGE BABIES WHO ARE PREMATURE BY AGE

A third group of babies weighs more than 2500 gm. but are
nevertheless premature in terms of gestational age and thus also in
terms of organ maturity. In general these babies have the same needs
and are subject to the same hazards as other premature-by-age babies.
The exception is they do not need an unusually warm environment as
do other premature infants. Because they do have comparatively large
amounts of subcutaneous fat they can easily be overheated and thus
are jeopardized at the temperatures required by smaller infants. The
most frequent reason for a premature baby to be large is maternal
diabetes.

THE NEEDS OF SMALL OR PREMATURE BABIES

The immediate need of all these babies is warmth, nutrition, and
a generous measure of tender loving care along with protection from
infection.

Warmth. The amount of environmental warmth the baby will
need depends upon his size and age. The goal is to maintain the baby
at a neutral temperature, i.e., that temperature at which oxygen consumption will be kept at a minimum. If the environmental temperature drops below the level of neutral temperature, the baby will increase his metabolic rate in order to raise his body temperature. The
term critical temperature is used by some authors to describe that
temperature at which oxygen consumption will begin to rise. If
environmental temperature is higher than the neutral temperature
level, the baby will become restless and his metabolic rate will rise
and consequently so will his oxygen consumption.

Traggis (1969) suggests that it will take an additional two degrees
of environmental temperature during the first two days of life to
keep the premature baby's temperature stable. He proposes the
following isolette temperatures as guides:

	Weight:		
Age	Less than 1500 gm.	1500–2500 gm.	2500 gm.+
First two days	93–95	91–93	89.6–91.4
Three or more days	91–93	89–91	88.0–89.6

Obviously if the baby's body temperature remains low in spite of these temperatures, they will have to be adjusted to meet the needs of the individual infant. A servomechanism, which adjusts incubator temperature to desired body temperature is helpful during these first days while the baby is rather unstable.

Once the infant's temperature is stabilized, incubator temperature should not be routinely altered or it will be difficult (if not impossible) to interpret changes in body temperature. Both increases and decreases in infant body temperature can signal problems such as infection.

Humidity needs to be close to 85 per cent for the first two days and in the range of 60 to 85 per cent afterwards. Humidity is too high if there is mist on the walls of the isolette; the baby's skin can become macerated and his liability to infection is consequently increased. For the same reasons vapojet attachments are no longer used on isolettes. Water used for humidification must be sterile, and water reservoirs kept scrupulously clean.

Nutritional needs. The special nutritional needs of premature infants are discussed on page 210.

Tender loving care. The third need, tender loving care, may be slightly more difficult to document than the first two, but it is no less important. A very tiny, immature baby should probably be handled as little as possible and certainly in the most gentle way. His skin is so tender that it can be broken easily. Because of capillary fragility he bruises from what seems to be a minimum of pressure, even from the electrodes of a monitor or an EKG machine.

The concept of minimal handling for somewhat larger, though still premature, infants has been questioned by Hasselmeyer (Falkner, 1969). In a study conducted in four New York hospitals in 1962 Hasselmeyer found that increased amounts of handling were not detrimental and could possibly be beneficial. Sixty premature infants were studied for 14 days each. "Half of the babies got 'high handling;' half got 'low handling.' The low handling babies averaged 95 minutes of direct contact with another human being in 24 hours. The high handling babies were handled about three times as much as the low handling babies; they got almost five hours of handling in the 24-hour period. To increase sensory inputs, the babies were rocked and cuddled, their hair was combed, and their faces and arms stroked. Nurses and physicians in contact with the babies punched time clocks to verify the amount of handling each baby received.

"There was no difference in the number of infections among the high and low handled babies, and no baby had to be discontinued from the study because of a major infection. The low handling babies, however, were found to have more problems with the eyes, conjunctivitis, stuffy or runny nose and reddened umbilicus.

"At the beginning of the study, the high handling babies had a lower mean weight. The weight gains were not of a statistically significant level, but at the end of the two weeks the high handling babies had overtaken the weight curve of the low handling babies" (Falkner, 1969).

As premature babies grow and begin to gain weight, as they can tolerate oral feedings and brief periods out of the isolette, the tender loving care they require means patience in feeding them at the slow pace they may choose, always taking time to use good isolation technique, and talking and singing to them as their mothers would if they could be with them. As the baby becomes a little older, a mobile or toy suspended above the isolette can add to his pleasure and furnish still more important stimulation.

Protection from infection. The reasons for the "premie's" low resistance to infection have already been mentioned (page 143). The means of protecting him are merely extensions of the protection all newborns need (page 90)—thorough handwashing, exclusion of ill personnel from the nursery, and care that equipment is very clean or sterile. The isolette or incubator offers some protection if good technique is used. Masks are no longer considered necessary or even advisable; unless they are changed with great frequency they act as a harbor for pathogens.

The Baby With Respiratory Distress Syndrome (Hyaline Membrane Disease)

Respiratory distress is one of the major problems of immature babies. A number of theories have been proposed to explain the reason the syndrome exists, and volumes have been written concerning etiology and treatment. One brief review lists 275 articles in the bibliography.

One factor which has been implicated is surfactant. Before birth the alveoli are partially expanded because the lung is filled with fluid. At birth much of the fluid is expelled through the nose and mouth of the baby during a vertex delivery; the remainder is picked up by the lymphatics and blood vessels surrounding the lung. With the fluid gone, the alveoli would tend to collapse on expiration were it not for the presence of a fatty substance, surfactant, which keeps them expanded.

Surfactant is manufactured by enzymes in some of the cells which line the alveoli. When an immature infant is born, the production of surfactant is threatened and may stop altogether. It is theorized that the baby has a supply of surfactant sufficient for approximately 24 hours. Thus he may appear to do well for a period and then begin to have difficulty. If his enzyme system is able to begin functioning he will survive and improve. If his system cannot produce surfactant there is no known way to help him; he will die. However, there is no way to tell which babies will begin to produce surfactant and which will not.

Nelson (1970) views respiratory distress syndrome as an infantile form of shock, which progresses through many stages and affects the function of a great many organ systems. He postulates that following an early decrease in the ability of the heart to contract with consequent hypotension, decreased pulmonary circulation, and atelectasis, other organ systems such as skin, muscle, kidney and gut, to which circulation has been sacrificed in order to preserve heart and brain circulation, begin to produce toxins which further affect the baby.

The physical signs of respiratory distress are:
1. abnormal thoracic and sternal retractions
2. cyanosis except when the baby is in high concentrations of oxygen
3. a respiratory rate of more than 60 per minute
4. an expiratory grunt

CARING FOR THE BABY WITH RESPIRATORY DISTRESS SYNDROME

Warmth. Physiologically the baby is hypoxic and acidotic; he is neither oxygenating his blood nor is he able to rid himself of excess carbon dioxide. He must not be chilled or he will increase his oxygen consumption in an attempt to raise his body temperature, thereby compounding both hypoxia and acidosis. In the hustle of treating a baby—drawing blood, starting fluids, perhaps intubating him—it is easy to forget how absolutely essential it is just to keep him warm. An overbed warmer that allows access to the baby yet keeps his environment warm is one way in which this can be accomplished. Lacking this, a heated mattress or hot water bottle and blankets can be used if the baby must be out of his incubator. His extremities can be wrapped to conserve heat during a procedure in which the abdomen must be exposed, such as umbilical artery catheterization.

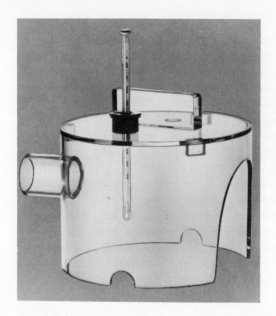

Figure 4-9. With the use of an oxygen hood, oxygen concentrations can be raised to 80–90%, which may be necessary to maintain adequate arterial oxygen levels. (Courtesy of Olympic Surgical Co., Inc.).

Oxygen. In addition to warmth, the baby with respiratory distress syndrome needs oxygen, often at a very high concentration. The level of oxygen concentration is determined by arterial oxygen concentration. The goal of treatment is to keep the pO_2 level between 50 and 100. At pO_2 levels below 50, pulmonary blood vessels constrict and blood cannot get to the lungs so that gases can be exchanged. It is generally believed, although not universally, that there is no danger from retrolental fibroplasia (see page 150) at pO_2 levels below 150. It may take 100 per cent oxygen concentrations to maintain arterial oxygen at the desired level. The average concentration of oxygen in an isolette is 35 to 40 per cent. With the use of an oxygen hood (Fig. 4–9) concentrations can be raised to levels of 80 to 90 per cent. The hood is also useful during examinations and treatments. For all babies receiving oxygen, the concentrations should be checked frequently with an oxygen analyzer and recorded on the baby's chart. When an oxygen hood is used, concentrations should be checked every 30 minutes. Temperature in the hood should also be monitored every 30 minutes; it is possible for temperature to rise considerably over a period of time. The hood in Figure 4–10 comes equipped with a thermometer.

When facilities for monitoring blood oxygen levels are not available, oxygen concentration is kept just at the level at which cyanosis disappears. This means constantly observing the baby and continually lowering the oxygen level while keeping the baby "pink" with no signs of respiratory distress.

Acid-base balance. A third factor in therapy is the correction of acidosis. All babies, healthy term infants as well as immature and sick ones, are born slightly acidotic with elevated levels of carbon dioxide. Normally, the baby will rid himself of this excess CO_2 within the first hour, thereby bringing his pH to within normal limits (7.35 to 7.40). A stressed baby, whatever the source of the stress, is unable to do this. The body's second mechanism for restoring acid-base equilibrium is for the kidney to compensate by conserving bicarbonate. The immature kidneys of newborns and, particularly, of premature babies are very slow to compensate in this manner. So when pCO_2 is high and $pHCO_3$ is low, the baby is given bicarbonate in order to restore pH to the proper limits. With pH levels below 7.32 there is pulmonary vascular constriction just as there is when pO_2 levels fall below 50.

Apnea. In spite of therapy, babies with respiratory distress syndrome are prone to frequent periods of apnea. An apnea monitor is very helpful in detecting these spells. Several varieties are available, some using disc or needle electrodes and others using a small air mattress to signal each breath. For this latter type to function properly, the mattress should be covered with a single layer of material. No monitor, of course, is a substitute for careful observation of the baby.

Frequently, apnea can be resolved by flicking the sole of the baby's foot. Should this fail to restore breathing, bag-and-mask resuscitation is the next alternative, usually with oxygen connected to the bag. "Bagging" an infant requires a very light touch; to squeeze the bag as one would for an adult can cause permanent lung damage. Before a baby is "bagged" he must be suctioned or else any mucus that is in the respiratory tract will be pushed into the lungs. Following suctioning, the baby's neck is hyperextended. The mask is held over the infant's nose and mouth with the thumb and forefinger of one hand, the other hand is then free to squeeze the bag with gentle rhythm.

If in spite of bicarbonate and oxygen therapy the baby continues to have acute respiratory failure, a respirator may be used to maintain life until the alveolar enzymes are able to begin producing surfactant. Symptoms of respiratory failure include:

1. recurrent, prolonged apnea of 20 seconds or more which does not respond to stimulation or bag-and-mask ventilation with oxygen
2. pO_2 of less than 50 in very high concentrations of oxygen
3. pCO_2 of more than 75 after oxygen and bicarbonate therapy.

Should blood gases not be available, the decision may be made to use a respirator on the basis of physical evidence of severe distress.

Since most respirators have detachable equipment, the nurse must be familiar with each attachment so that the respirator can be assembled and made available on very short notice. When a respirator is being used, the infant must be carefully observed. In addition the nursing care of an infant on a respirator includes suctioning through the endotracheal tube, at 15-minute intervals.

Rest. In addition to all of the aforementioned needs, each of which is important, the baby with respiratory distress syndrome should be disturbed as little as possible. He is seriously ill and likely to become apneic even with gentle handling. By using monitors for heart rate and an umbilical artery catheter for fluid therapy and blood sampling and by placing him in an incubator where he can be kept warm yet viewed continuously, we give him the best chance of survival.

Effects of respiratory distress syndrome. What happens to those babies who survive respiratory distress syndrome? Several studies support the theory that they have an increased incidence of subsequent neurological abnormalities in all birth-weight categories. Since deaths from respiratory distress syndrome continue to decrease as ability to regulate acid-base balance and body temperature improves, the problem of abnormalities and their possible prevention is becoming increasingly important.

OXYGEN AND RETROLENTAL FIBROPLASIA

The relationship between high concentrations of oxygen and retrolental fibroplasia has already been briefly mentioned (page 148). Before 1940, the condition was almost unknown. By 1950, it had become the largest single cause of blindness in children in the United States, greater than all other causes combined. The fact that the better equipped, major medical centers had nearly all the cases, while hospitals in small towns and rural areas had virtually none seemed a mystery until 1953 when it was shown that high oxygen concentrations were to blame. The large centers with the newest equipment were able to deliver oxygen ever so much more efficiently.

The incidence dropped as oxygen concentration began to be monitored more closely. But in recent years, evidence that very high oxygen concentrations may be life-saving for babies with many respiratory and cardiovascular abnormalities has led to concern that there will be a resurgence of retrolental fibroplasia. In the United States approximately 40,000 immature infants have respiratory distress syndrome alone; nearly 100 per cent of these babies will require oxygen.

GESTATIONAL AGE OF FETUS

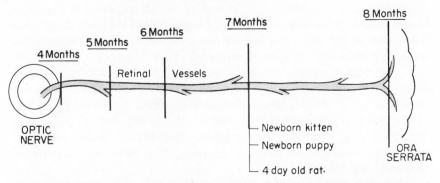

Figure 4-10. Schematic drawing showing the chronology of the development of the blood supply of the retina in the human fetus. (From Patz: *Pediatrics, 19*:508, 1957.)

The basis of retrolental fibroplasia lies in the way in which the retina's blood supply develops. No retinal vessels are present until the fourth month of embryonic life; vascularization of the retina is not complete until after the eighth month. A baby born at seven months gestation has no vessels in much of his retina; they must develop after birth (Fig. 4-10). It is the incompletely vascularized retina that is susceptible to oxygen damage. Once vascularization is complete, added oxygen does not damage the retinal vessels. Unfortunately, the more immature the baby, the more likely he is to have need of oxygen.

Since newborn puppies and kittens also have incomplete retinal vascularization it is relatively easy to demonstrate the sequence of events when oxygen is given. The initial effect is the immediate and almost total constriction of the retinal vessels. This can happen within five minutes after oxygen is given at concentrations of 70 to 80 per cent. It has been suggested that a careful examination of the fundus is one means of determining the level of oxygen concentration to be used, the finding of vasoconstriction indicating an immediate need to lower oxygen concentration. Prompt treatment at this early stage may prevent permanent vasoconstriction (Fig. 4-11) (Patz, 1968).

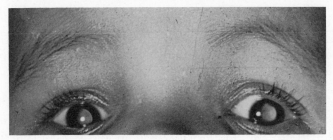

Figure 4-11. Terminal stage of retrolental fibroplasia. The child is totally blind. (From Patz: *Pediatrics, 19*:508, 1957.)

After about ten minutes of sustained oxygen, arterioles and capillaries reopen and remain dilated for the next several hours. New blood vessels appear in the retina. Leakage of fluid and blood from these newly formed vessels and invasion by fibroblasts eventually leads to retinal detachment in the weeks that follow.

A second or cicatricial stage, during which the retrolental membrane is formed, occurs several weeks later. The extent of the damage done in the cicatricial phase depends on the severity of the acute phase and is related to (1) the concentration of oxygen, (2) the length of time during which oxygen is administered, and (3) the degree of immaturity of the eye. There is no cure for a fully developed case of retrolental fibroplasia.

It is felt that by keeping pO_2 levels within the supposedly safe limits of 50 to 100 mm Hg, the danger of retrolental fibroplasia will be minimal. (There is apparently some degree of danger at any concentration above that of room air for some babies.) There is, however, no data which establishes the tolerance of the retina to various pO_2 levels in relation to the length of time the oxygen is administered or the age of the baby. Moreover, arterial oxygen levels can suddenly change without a change in oxygen concentration if the baby's ability to ventilate improves.

The American Academy of Pediatrics has drawn up new recommendations on oxygen therapy for newborns:

1. Oxygen tension of arterial blood should not exceed 100 mm Hg and should be maintained between 60 to 80 mm Hg.

2. Inspired oxygen may be needed in relatively high concentrations to maintain the arterial oxygen tension in the normal range.

3. If blood gas measurements are not available, a mature infant who is not apneic but has generalized cyanosis may be given oxygen in a concentration just high enough to abolish the cyanosis. However, if supplemental oxygen is necessary for an immature infant, he should be taken to a center at which inspired oxygen concentration can be regulated by blood gas measurements.

4. The ideal sampling sites for arterial oxygen tension studies are the radial or temporal arteries. In most circumstances, however, a sample from the descending aorta through an indwelling umbilical arterial catheter is satisfactory.

5. Equipment for the regulation of oxygen concentration (as provided by some incubators and respirators) and devices for mixing oxygen and room air may not function properly; therefore, it is essential that, when an infant is placed in an oxygen enriched environment, the concentration of oxygen be measured with an oxygen analyzer at least every two hours. The performance of an oxygen analyzer must be check daily by calibration with room air and 100 per cent oxygen.

6. Mixtures of oxygen and room air may be delivered to an infant by endotracheal tubes, masks, funnels, hoods, or incubators. Regardless of the method used, the mixture should be warmed and humidified.

7. The condition of infants requiring oxygen may improve rapidly. Under these circumstances, the inspired oxygen concentrations should be promptly lowered. If the infant's recovery is gradual, the oxygen concentrations should be lowered by 10 per cent decrements.

8. It should be appreciated that oxygen is toxic to other organs (e.g., lungs) which may be damaged even if these criteria are adhered to.

9. A person experienced in recognizing retrolental fibroplasia . . . should examine the eyes of all infants born at less than 36 weeks gestation or weighing less than 2000 gm. (4.2 pounds) who have received oxygen therapy. This examination should be made at discharge from the nursery and at three to six months of age.

The Baby Who Is Jaundiced

There are three major causes of jaundice in newborn infants: immature liver function, hemolytic anemia, and sepsis.

The physiologic jaundice due to the lack of the hepatic enzyme glucuronyl transferase is rarely a problem in term infants (see page 107). In immature babies hyperbilirubinemia (indirect bilirubin levels of 15 mg. per cent or higher) and consequently jaundice is more frequent (occurring in 10 to 25 per cent of all premature infants), more severe and prolonged, and somewhat less easy to recognize. Mean peak levels of serum bilirubin in immature babies have been found to range from 3 to 5 mg. per cent higher than the mean peak level of term infants. The lower the gestational age of the infant, the higher the bilirubin levels are likely to be because of the greater immaturity of liver function. While term infants rarely develop kernicterus in the absence of hemolytic disease, babies with low birth weight or low gestational age may do so. Yet these babies may not appear as jaundiced as term infants with lower levels of indirect bilirubin, because in the absence of subcutaneous fat the capillary bed lies close to the skin, reflecting the red of hemoglobin in skin color. Jaundice can be seen if the skin is blanched by pressure of the thumb. Currently phototherapy is being used with increasing frequency for the hyperbilirubinemia of prematurity.

PHOTOTHERAPY AND HYPERBILIRUBINEMIA

None of us can doubt that the careful observations of nurses contribute to the care of individual patients every day. What we do fail to
recognize is that the careful observations of nurses can lead to new
and important developments in patient care which will have far-
reaching effects. It was such an observation that led to the use of
phototherapy as one tool in the treatment of hyperbilirubinemia.

The incident occurred at the General Hospital in Rochford, Essex,
England. The sister (nurse) in charge of the premature nursery, whose
name unfortunately is not recorded in the published report, noted
that jaundice faded after babies had been in direct sunlight for a
short time. Cremer and his associates (1958) then began to place
naked babies in direct sunlight for 15 to 20 minutes, withdrawing
them for a similar period before exposing them again. During exposure the babies' eyes were protected with a plastic shield. It was
discovered that while jaundice quickly disappeared from the exposed
areas, it remained in the shaded areas. The initial test group included 13 infants, weighing from 3 pounds 3 ounces to 5 pounds 14
ounces, whose levels of indirect bilirubin ranged from 10 to 25 mg.
per cent. After two to four hours of exposure the bilirubin levels
dropped from 2 to 12 mg. per cent in 11 of the babies; there was no
change in one infant and in one infant indirect bilirubin rose 2 mg.
per cent. In general the higher the initial serum bilirubin level and
the longer the exposure time, the greater the fall. Cremer next devised a source of artificial light which was tested with nine jaundiced
premature infants and was also found to be effective in reducing
serum bilirubin levels (Cremer, 1958). Subsequent studies have
supported his findings.

There have been some suggestions that light might be used
prophylactically in premature and possibly term nurseries by increasing the level of illumination in the entire nursery. The fact, obvious
for some time, that hyperbilirubinemia varies considerably from one
nursery to another and that the intensity of illumination is one possible variable responsible is considered supportive evidence for this
proposal. (Other factors which are possibly responsible include variations in the laboratory procedures used in determining bilirubin
level, differences in feeding policies, and the use of drugs such as
novobiocin, sulfonamides, and vitamin K.) Five well-controlled
alternate case studies have demonstrated that phototherapy at the
level of 200 to 400 foot candles can significantly reduce the development of the hyperbilirubinemia of prematurity and is effective in its
treatment (Lucey, 1969; Giunta, 1969). Direct sunlight measures
5000 to 10,000 foot candles, while daylight in the shade measures
from 100 to 1000 foot candles. Giunta sees an additional advantage of

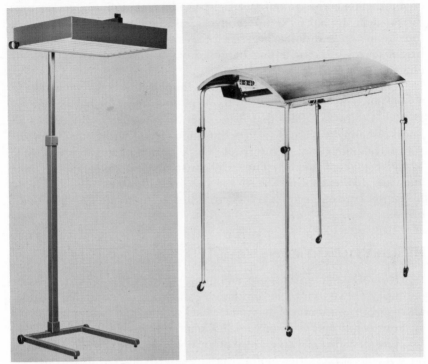

Figure 4-12. Two types of lamps used in phototherapy. They can be rolled into position over the bassinets or isolettes. (Courtesy of Olympic Surgical Co., Inc.)

increased levels of illumination in the greater comfort and ease it affords in performing close visual procedures and the better observation of all babies.

At the time of this writing there have been no reports of any major side effects in human infants from the use of phototherapy. On the other hand, not only is there no clear understanding of the way in which light affects bilirubin metabolism, but there is also no information on the way in which light may affect other metabolic processes, either immediately or on a long range basis. It will be five to ten years before some of these questions can be answered. Because of this consensus seems to support the idea that phototherapy should be used in the treatment of specific babies with hyperbilirubinemia where known dangers exist from the condition, but not routinely as a preventive measure.

When a baby is to receive phototherapy he is undressed completely before being put under the lights. (For examples of the types of lamps available see Fig. 4-12.) The baby may be in either isolette or open bed, depending on his other needs. His eyes are covered to prevent corneal ulceration; they should be closed before they are

covered. Since the amount of light used in phototherapy also produces heat, the baby's temperature should be checked at least every
four hours to minimize the risk of overheating. Stools tend to be
bright green in color. Some babies develop loose stools, rashes, or
changes in activity patterns.

On the average indirect bilirubin levels show a decrease of 3 to
4 mg. per cent after 8 to 12 hours of phototherapy. It has been suggested (Behrman, 1969) that if there is no response within 24 to 36
hours, treatment should be discontinued. Even with a drop in bilirubin, treatment may be interrupted for a period of 6 to 12 hours after
12 to 24 hours of therapy. The baby is usually removed from the light
and has his eyes uncovered for feeding. Rebound elevations of
bilirubin concentration may occur after light treatment has been
discontinued.

HEMOLYTIC ANEMIAS

Hemolytic anemias, most commonly due to Rh_d or ABO incompatibility between mother and baby, constitute a second major cause
of hyperbilirubinemia. The genetic background and pathophysiology
of these conditions is discussed in Chapter 1 (page 44).

The first Rh_d positive baby of an Rh_d negative mother will have
no difficulty unless the mother has previously had a miscarriage or
has been transfused at some time with D positive blood. Her level of
antibodies will not be sufficiently high to harm the fetus. With each
subsequent pregnancy in which the baby is D positive, the risk of the
baby being stillborn increases by 8 per cent. Thus a fourth D positive
baby of a D negative mother would have a 24 per cent chance of
being born dead.

As soon as the baby is delivered, blood is Rh typed and a Coombs
test for the presence of antibodies is done. The reason the Coombs
test is given in addition to the type test, is that a baby with negative
type blood who has a great many antibodies may type positive. If the
Coombs test is negative, there are no antibodies present and the baby
should have no difficulty from Rh_d incompatibility. If the Coombs
test is positive, indicating that the infant's erythrocytes are coated
with antibodies, further blood studies are done (hemoglobin, hema-
tocrit, indirect bilirubin level, reticulocyte count). Even with a positive Coombs test, about 45 per cent of D positive babies born of
D negative mothers do not require exchange transfusions. Phototherapy may be used when babies seem to be only mildly affected
with frequent checks of indirect bilirubin level and other blood
studies.

In contrast to those babies who do not appear to be in serious
danger, other D positive babies are obviously in distress at the time

of birth. They are pale and edematous and have enlarged livers and spleens; blood studies show marked anemia which can lead to heart failure and metabolic acidosis. These babies will nearly always have their blood exchanged shortly after birth. A third group of infants may not appear in such immediate danger but because of subsequent anemia and hyperbilirubinemia will also need exchange transfusion.

Blood for exchange may be O negative which has been cross-mated against maternal serum. If it is suspected before delivery that an immediate exchange will be necessary, this blood should be ready. If there is time following delivery to type the baby's blood before exchange, negative blood of the baby's type which has been cross-matched against maternal serum is used. A sample of maternal serum should be saved for future exchanges. Obtaining additional maternal blood is not a serious problem when the mother is in the same hospital with the baby. But as the transfer of very sick infants from smaller community hospitals to the intensive care units of major medical centers becomes increasingly more frequent, the nurses at both hospitals must make sure that maternal blood accompanies any baby with hemolytic anemia.

Why are D positive babies given negative blood? If D positive blood is used, the antibodies already present in the infant circulatory system will destroy the new erythrocytes just as they are destroying his own cells; nothing will have been accomplished by exchanging one set of positive cells for another.

In addition to proper type, blood for exchange must be the freshest available, never more than three to four days old. Older blood is more likely to hemolyze, exactly the process that exchange transfusion is attempting to prevent. Heparinized blood is always fresh since it must be discarded if it is not used within a 24-hour period. Babies who receive heparinized blood must be watched for bleeding following transfusion; 10 mg. of protamine sulfate may be given intravenously following an exchange with heparinized blood. Blood which has had acid-citrate-dextrose (ACD) added as an anticoagulant can lower blood calcium levels. Because of this, calcium gluconate is given through the exchange catheter after each 100 ml. of blood is exchanged.

The danger that the baby will be chilled during any procedure has already been discussed (see page 76). In addition to the measures normally used to keep the infant warm, the blood for exchange should be warmed. An easy and safe way to do this is to place the blood in a basin of water warmed to, but not exceeding, 98.6° F. (37° C). Overheating the blood can damage erythrocytes and also increase the level of free serum potassium.

The amount of blood that will be used is figured at 85 ml × the weight of the baby in kilograms × 2, 85 ml. per kilogram being the assumed blood volume of the newborn infant. An amount equal to twice the blood volume is used because research indicates that this quantity will assure 85 to 90 per cent effective replacement of circulating erythrocytes.

During the exchange itself there must be one person — doctor or nurse — who can devote full attention to the baby by monitoring pulse and respiration, observing the infant's color and general condition, and suctioning him if necessary. The amount of blood injected and withdrawn and the baby's venous pressure must also be accurately recorded.

After the exchange is completed, the baby is observed closely both for his general condition and for signs of hemorrhage from the exchange site.

About 10 to 20 per cent of babies with ABO incompatibility have hyperbilirubinemia to the extent that they require exchange transfusion. Group O blood, cross-matched against maternal serum, is used.

In less than 5 per cent of all infants with hemolytic anemia, a blood factor other than Rh_d, A, or B is involved. E, C, and the Kell (K) factors may be responsible for severe hemolytic disease and even for hydrops fetalis. The Coombs test is positive. Very careful crossmatching with maternal serum is necessary so that the blood used for transfusion will not contain the antigen responsible for maternal sensitization.

OTHER REASONS FOR JAUNDICE

A third cause of jaundice, much less common than the first two, is sepsis. Some organisms or their toxins may directly damage the red blood cells. Other infectious agents destroy liver tissue, reducing liver function in the conjugation of bilirubin. Included in this group of organisms are the coliform bacteria, cytomegalic virus, and those causing toxoplasmosis, syphilis, serum hepatitis, herpes simplex, and rubella.

KERNICTERUS

The deposition of bilirubin in brain tissue occurs when plasma albumin can no longer bind circulating bilirubin. This usually occurs when there is an excess of bilirubin, but it can also be due to substances which limit the number of albumin-binding sites or to conditions which dissociate bilirubin from albumin. Substances which compete with bilirubin for the albumin-binding sites and thus limit the number of sites include hematin, sulfonamide and salicylate drugs, and fatty acids. Anoxia, a drop in plasma pH, and some drugs, including novobiocin and high doses of vitamin K may dissociate bilirubin from albumin and favor the development of kernicterus (Britten, 1968).

The appearance of any signs of kernicterus calls for an immediate exchange transfusion, regardless of the level of serum bilirubin. The symptoms are lethargy, poor feeding, and loss of the Moro reflex. The baby may be opisthotonic and has the sharp, high-pitched cry of a brain-damaged infant. Seventy-five per cent or more of the babies who have symptoms of kernicterus die; the remainder are usually mentally retarded or deaf and often have spastic quadriplegia. There is, in other words, little to offer these babies in terms of treatment; the brain damage is irreversible. Prevention is the necessity in caring for babies with hyperbilirubinemia.

The Baby With a Congenital Heart Defect

Although the compilation of truly accurate statistics is difficult, it is suspected that one out of every 130 liveborn babies will have a significant congenital heart defect. In a medium sized hospital where 30 to 35 babies are delivered each week, this means that on the average one baby each month will have a cardiac malformation. Approximately 10 per cent of all congenital defects involve the heart.

Many of the symptoms of these defects are vague in the first days of life because certain structures of fetal circulation, such as the patent foramen ovale or ductus arteriosus, may help the baby to compensate. Since hospital stays of apparently normal mothers and babies are often limited to four or five days, clear cut symptoms may not appear until after discharge. Of course, it is better if the defect can be found before this, thus stressing the importance of nursing observations.

Congenital heart defects are usually divided, for obvious reasons, into two groups based on the presence or absence of cyanosis. Here we will consider some of the most frequent defects in three categories based on the anatomical changes involved: the shunts, the blocks, and complex defects.

SHUNTS

Shunts are "leaks" in the septa dividing the heart chambers, openings where no openings should be. There are three types of shunts:

1. Atrial septal defects
2. Ventricular septal defects
3. Patent ductus arteriosus

Atrial septal defects are virtually never discovered in newborns and are seldom a problem in children of preschool age.

Large ventricular septal defects, on the other hand, are one of the chief causes of congestive heart failure in the newborn baby. Fortunately, although ventricular septal defect is probably the most common of all congenital cardiac anomalies, most ventricular defects are small and at least part of them appear to close spontaneously. In these instances the baby need only be examined at frequent intervals until his heart murmur disappears.

When the defect is large, each time the left ventricle contracts to send blood into the aorta, the higher pressure in the left ventricle also sends blood through the defect into the right ventricle. The lungs can then easily become flooded with blood as the right ventricle contracts, hence, congestive heart failure. In addition to the medical treatment for congestive failure (see page 165), surgical treatment, which consists of placing a band around the pulmonary artery, is designed to prevent the flooding of the lungs. Then, when the baby is older—often around two years of age—open-heart surgery is performed to correct the defect in the septum.

The third type of shunt, *patent ductus arteriosus,* is a result of an opening between the aorta and the pulmonary artery which is normal in fetal life but fails to close at birth (Fig. 4–13). Usually the defect

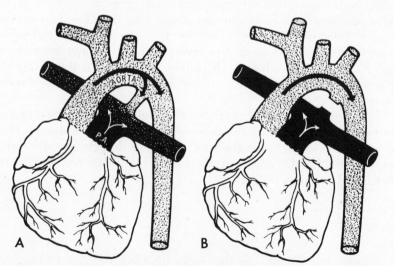

Figure 4–13. Patent ductus arteriosis. *A,* Before surgery. *B,* After surgery. (From *Diagnosis of Congenital Cardiac Defects in General Practice.* Heart Association of Southeastern Pennsylvania and American Heart Association.)

is small and there are no symptoms during infancy and early child-hood. If the shunt is large the baby may develop congestive failure toward the end of the first week. In babies who are hypoxic—a baby with respiratory distress syndrome for example—the patent ductus may remain open.

Only rarely will infants with patent ductus require surgery during the newborn period, the exception being babies who do not respond to treatment for congestive failure. In other infants, the ductus may either close spontaneously or surgery will be performed when the baby is older. The prognosis is usually excellent when surgery can be delayed.

HEART BLOCKS

There are also three varieties of congenital heart blockages:
1. Aortic valvular stenosis
2. Pulmonary valvular stenosis
3. Coarctation of the aorta

Aortic valvular stenosis is relatively rare, and unless it is severe it will usually not be detected in newborns but rather found at some later time during routine physical examination. The prognosis is good for children with mild to moderate stenosis but rather poor for those babies who develop respiratory distress, tachycardia, and pallor in the first few weeks of life. While these babies are initially treated with digitalis and oxygen, prompt surgery (aortic valvulotomy) is necessary to save their lives. The surgery itself also carries a high risk at the present time.

Complete obstruction of the aortic valve (aortic atresia) is always fatal, generally by the time the baby is four to five days old. These babies also have an underdeveloped left heart and ascending aorta, the combination being known as hypoplastic left heart syndrome.

Pulmonary valvular stenosis is also rare in newborns, occurring most often in the infants of mothers who have had rubella in early pregnancy. Rowe and Mehrizi (1968) state that they do not know of a single instance of death in the newborn period from isolated pul-monary stenosis. In combination with other defects, pulmonary stenosis may be an asset in that it reduces excess blood flow to the lungs, just as banding of the pulmonary artery does artificially, and thus protects the baby from congestive failure.

Atresia of the pulmonary artery carries a very high risk; untreated patients die within two weeks to two months after birth and mortality is also very high following transarterial valvulotomy.

Coarctation of the aorta usually occurs in combination with other defects, thus the term coarctation syndrome (Rowe and Mehrizi, 1968).

This syndrome is the most common malformation causing cardiac failure during the newborn period. Often the baby shows no symptoms during the few days he is in the hospital. But the absence of femoral pulses, which should be routinely checked, gives the clue. If the defect is not discovered before the baby goes home, the classic triad of rapid breathing, feeding difficulty (due to rapid breathing), and tachycardia may follow. On the other hand, many children will have no symptoms and the coarctation will only be discovered on a routine examination. As with patent ductus, treatment during infancy is aimed at eliminating congestive failure, with surgery ideally postponed until the baby is at least five years old. Surgery is performed in the newborn period only when heart failure has not responded to medical treatment. To a large extent the success of surgery depends on the nature of the related cardiac anomalies in the coarctation syndrome.

COMPLEX MALFORMATIONS

The most common of the complex heart anomalies are transposition of the great vessels and tetralogy of Fallot.

Cyanosis is the outstanding sign of *transposition of the great vessels* although even with this defect the cyanosis may not be severe in the first days until the ductus arteriosus closes and eliminates the mixing of blood from the two sides of the heart. After it closes, the baby has two separate circulatory systems. The aorta arises from the right ventricle rather than from the left; blood is circulated through the body and returned to the right atrium. This blood never gets to the lungs to be oxygenated. The pulmonary artery carries blood from the left ventricle to the lungs where it is oxygenated and returned to the left atrium. Intercommunication must be established between the two circuits or the baby will die in a very few days. Treatment is the creation of an atrial septal defect which allows the blood to mix. This is commonly done through the use of a balloon cardiac catheter; an inflated balloon is drawn through the foramen ovale to enlarge the opening (Fig. 4–14). Further corrective surgery may be done when the child is older, but not in the newborn period.

The four defects which comprise *tetralogy of Fallot* are:
1. Pulmonary stenosis (occasionally pulmonary atresia)
2. Right ventricular hypertrophy
3. Ventricular septal defect
4. Over-riding aorta which receives blood directly from both right and left ventricles

The embryological basis of the tetralogy is discussed in Chapter 1 (page 8).

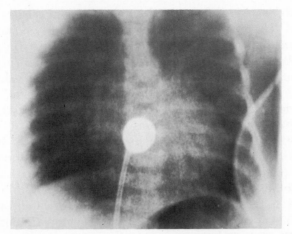

Figure 4–14. Medical creation of an atrial septal defect by balloon for treatment of transposition of the great arteries in the newborn period. Further surgery is postponed until the child is older. (From Rowe and Mehrizi: *The Neonate with Congenital Heart Disease.* W. B. Saunders, 1968.)

Although tetralogy is considered a cyanotic heart disease, even here cyanosis is relatively rare during the time the baby spends in the newborn nursery, even when the pulmonary stenosis is severe. Only half of the newborns with tetralogy will have a murmur, the murmur being due to the ejection of blood through the narrowed pulmonary valve. Lack of this murmur is considered a serious sign, death from anoxia occurring in a few weeks unless high risk surgery can increase pulmonary blood flow. If the baby is having cyanotic attacks during the newborn period an anastomosis between the aorta and the pulmonary artery (an artificial patent ductus) may be palliative until the child is older and better able to withstand open heart surgery. The mortality rate for total correction at the age of six or seven years is now less than 10 per cent.

Obviously every cardiac malformation has not been mentioned here; for descriptions of rarer anomalies the reader is referred to Rowe and Mehrizi (1968).

DIAGNOSIS OF HEART DEFECTS

Once a heart defect is suspected diagnosis is made on the basis of:

1. Clinical signs which have been observed and recorded
2. X-ray
3. EKG
4. Cardiac catheterization

The clinical signs associated with individual defects have been mentioned. The role *of x-ray* in evaluating heart size and some outstanding anatomical changes seems obvious. It is very important that the baby be comfortably at rest and not crying when chest films are taken if they are to be detailed enough to be of any real value. Portable chest films can be taken through isolette walls. If the baby is to go to the x-ray department for films he needs to be transported in a heated bed and to spend as little time as possible outside of it. A nurse should both go with him and remain with him throughout the entire procedure, wearing a protective apron to shield her from radiation while the pictures are being taken. A bottle of water or a pacifier will help to soothe the baby and keep him from crying. A bulb syringe for suctioning and a hand-operated bag resuscitator should go with the baby; infants at times become apneic in x-ray departments and other areas of the hospital away from the nursery, and equipment for resuscitation is not always immediately available. Mouth to mouth resuscitation can be used in acute emergency, of course, but there is always a risk of introducing pathogens into the respiratory tract of an already sick baby. How much easier it is to be prepared.

Electrocardiograms in newborns differ from those of children from age two through adulthood, and those of premature infants often vary from the EKG's of term babies. The problems involved in the interpretation of newborn EKG's are beyond the scope of this book (see Rowe and Mehrizi, 1968, Chapter 4). As with babies who are to be x-rayed, the infant should be warm and comfortable with a full stomach so that he will lie quietly during the procedure.

Cardiac catheterization presents a somewhat different problem in the newborn period than those encountered in other periods. Yet catheterization is highly essential; those conditions which can be treated must be distinguished from those which cannot. Although the mortality rate in newborns is in the neighborhood of 5 per cent, a large proportion of the babies who die have inoperable defects and would have died under any circumstances. Nevertheless, it is a hazardous procedure in the newborn period for several reasons:

1. The hazards of chilling the baby during the procedure are greatest in newborns.

2. The baby is often in very serious condition before the catheterization—he may be cyanotic or acidotic, or in congestive failure.

3. Needle punctures and even traction on small vessels can cause thrombosis and impair circulation.

4. Catheterization in newborns is often combined with angiography so that an accurate anatomical diagnosis can be made, thereby necessarily increasing the risk.

5. Full exploration of the heart, rather than just right-heart catheterization is felt to be necessary in a great many instances.

Measures which minimize the risk include:

1. Early detection of the possibility of a heart defect before the baby is critically ill.

2. Avoidance of premedication and anesthesia; local anesthesia and a cut-down are used. The umbilical artery is sometimes used in the first days of life.

3. Treatment of acidosis with bicarbonate.

4. Treatment of serious arrhythmias by electrical conversion.

5. The use of a minimum of contrast material.

Once the baby returns from catheterization there must be careful monitoring of temperature, which often drops during the procedure, of apical pulse and respiration, and of acid-base balance and fluid intake. The cut-down site needs to be checked for bleeding and the color and pulsation in the limb in which the cut-down was done observed. Thrombosis is a particular danger in tiny newborn vessels. If there is no pulse four hours after the study has been completed, arterial thrombosis has usually occurred. Fortunately collateral blood supply usually prevents gangrene, but occasionally surgery will be necessary.

CONGESTIVE HEART FAILURE

It takes very little time for a baby to progress from the very first sign of heart failure to complete vascular collapse. It becomes a major nursing responsibility, then, to spot that very first sign—not an easy thing to do because the symptoms are so often vague. The instinctive feeling that "something is not quite right about this baby" may be the first indication.

Tachypnea is often the initial symptom. Respiratory rates, after the first two hours, of more than 45 per minute in a term baby or 60 per minute in a premature baby are usually abnormal if the baby is at rest when the observation is made. In term babies respirations are often not counted as a routine measure; perhaps they should be. But because they rarely are, failure of the baby to feed well may be the first sign noticed by the nurse. The baby is breathing so rapidly he cannot suck; he forsakes eating in order to continue breathing, or he may attempt to do both and choke or vomit, possibly aspirating his feeding and further compounding the problem. There are many other possible reasons for tachypnea in the newborn and not all of them are of serious consequence (see Transient Tachypnea of the Newborn, p. 118). Yet any baby who breathes rapidly needs extra watching.

A second sign of possible congestive failure is *tachycardia*. A heart rate of more than 150 beats per minute is unusual in a healthy baby who is not crying.

Edema, if it is present (and often it is not) is more likely to be found about the face; the baby looks "puffy." The ankle edema seen in adults with congestive failure is not present in a recumbent baby.

Older babies, past the newborn period, perspire excessively in congestive failure. While it is rare for a newborn to perspire for any reason, the occasional occurrence of *perspiration* can be a valuable clue in helping to diagnose possible heart failure.

An *enlarged liver and heart* are two additional important symptoms of congestive failure.

Once congestive failure is suspected, treatment is begun as early as possible. The principle agent in treatment is digoxin. Digitalizing doses for newborns are:

For term infants   .06 to .08 mg. per kg. of body weight, orally;
                             .04 to .06 mg. per kg. of body weight, I.M.
For premature infants .045 mg. per kg. of body weight, orally

Two-thirds of the total dose is administered immediately, the remaining one-third being divided into two doses to be administered in the next 12 to 18 hours. The average maintenance dose for newborns is .01 mg. per kg. Toxicity to digitalis is revealed by rate and rhythm changes on EKG. Both full-term and premature infants have an intolerance for digitalis preparations.

Diuretics, commonly used in adults with congestive failure, are not favored for newborns by some physicians because of potential danger to renal tissue. When a diuretic is used it is likely to be a single dose of a mercurial diuretic such as mercaptomerin.

Oxygen is used to relieve dyspnea and cyanosis.

The Newborn Who Needs Surgery

There are some anomalies of the newborn which require surgery shortly after they are detected if the baby is to do well. Ideally, this surgery will be performed within the first 48 hours after birth. During this two-day period, blood volume in relation to body weight is higher than at any other time of life, making normal fluid requirements minimal. Moreover, the baby has the advantage if surgery can be completed before the physiological breakdown of red blood cells begins. Delay not only eliminates these benefits but often allows the baby's physical condition to deteriorate because of vomiting, aspiration, respiratory distress, infection, and similar causes. All of this emphasizes, again, the extreme importance of careful observation which is necessary in early recognition of the infant's problem.

Some of the more common conditions which require or benefit from immediate surgical correction are:

1. Anomalies of the gastrointestinal tract: tracheo-esophageal fistula, diaphragmatic hernia, intestinal obstruction, imperforate anus, and omphalocele.
2. Skull fracture
3. Bilateral choanal atresia
4. Meningocele and encephalocele
5. Certain congenital heart defects
6. Certain disorders of the genitourinary tract: patent urachus; obstructions.

PREOPERATIVE CARE OF NEWBORNS

Preoperative care for newborns is minimal. The baby needs to be kept warm and given oxygen if he is cyanotic. Preoperative medication, with the exception of atropine, is never given. Gastric aspiration helps empty the stomach, and blood and urine studies are completed. A cut-down may be done.

Perhaps the most difficult task is explaining to parents that their new baby has a defect which needs emergency surgery. Although the doctor will undoubtedly make the initial explanation, it is not very long before the father and perhaps a grandmother appear at the nursery door to see the baby and ask many of the same questions again, because they need to hear the answers again. And they need to see for themselves, so they can try to understand what is happening.

SOME SPECIAL PROBLEMS RELATED TO
SURGERY IN NEWBORNS

Three major areas of difficulty for newborns who need surgery are anesthesia, hyperbilirubinemia, and maintenance of adequate warmth during surgery.

Anesthesia is complicated by the limited pulmonary reserve of the baby, by the fact that his rapid respiratory rate must be maintained even during deep anesthesia, and because of his sensitivity to relaxant drugs (Martin, 1969).

Physiologic jaundice may be intensified by the stress of surgery or by conditions related to the surgery, such as sepsis, the initial condition for which the baby is being treated, dehydration, or the anesthesia. On the other hand, adequate hydration, antibiotics, and good general supportive care may bring about a significant fall in bilirubin level without other treatment (Martin).

KEEPING THE BABY WARM DURING SURGERY

One of the biggest hazards to a newborn in a modern, air-conditioned operating room is chilling. Even a healthy, full-term newborn lying on the table for an hour or more, without undergoing a surgical procedure, could experience difficulties because of chilling which might be fatal or at the least, damaging. For an infant who is sick enough to require an emergency operation and, who, in addition, is often of low birth weight, this chilling is a significant danger. Smith (1969) feels that if all covers are thrown off for five minutes during a resuscitative procedure, the child may become so cold that his chances for survival are considerably diminished. Exposure of internal organs, such as the bowel, during surgery, hastens the fall of the baby's temperature.

How can heat be conserved in the operating room?

1. From the standpoint of the baby, an operating room temperature of 85° F. with a relative humidity of approximately 50 per cent is ideal, yet this degree of warmth will probably be unacceptable to many surgeons. An overbed warmer which uses radiant heat keeps the operative area warm, but this too may make the surgical team uncomfortable. If such a warmer is used the distance between the baby and the warmer in relation to the temperature of the warmer is important; hyperthermia is no more desirable than hypothermia (see page 77).

2. The baby should be transported to the operating room (as well as to the x-ray room or any other area of the hospital) in a heated, covered incubator. The bed should be plugged in once he reaches the operating room and he should stay in it until the surgeons are scrubbed.

3. Wrapping the baby's arms and legs in a protective covering, such as the sheet wadding used to line plaster casts, not only reduces heat loss but helps protect his extremities against injury during surgery and also partially immobilizes him. His head should also be covered since babies lose heat through their bare scalp. All of this can be done while the baby is in his own warm bed.

4. During the surgical procedure itself, the baby must be kept warm without being burned or overheated, and his temperature, both rectal and skin, must be monitored and recorded. Of the many methods tried in keeping the baby warm, each has advantages and disadvantages. The problems connected with an overbed source of radiant heat have already been mentioned.

Hot water bottles lose their heat quickly. If water above 105° F. is used in order to retain heat for a longer period, the danger of body burns is great. Smith suggests that an instrument tray be inverted over two hot water bags and then covered with a blanket so that the baby can be warmed without coming in direct contact with the source of heat.

The McQuiston mattress, originally used for cooling in cardiac surgery, can also be used for warming, but here again there is great danger of burning the baby because hot water is continually being added. Water temperature should never exceed 105° F., and the mattress must be covered by at least one thickness of blanket.

A third type of device warms or cools fluid to a designated temperature and then pumps the fluid through coils of tubing which have been incorporated into blankets. If a servomechanism is attached to the unit it will register the baby's temperature and adjust the warming mechanism until the baby's body temperature reaches the temperature for which the machine has been programmed.

5. Nonvolatile liquids should be used for skin preparation since evaporation leads to cooling.

6. Only the area required for operation should be uncovered.

7. Blood for transfusion should be warmed to body temperature (98.6° F.).

8. A warmed incubator should be ready to receive the baby immediately following surgery and should be used to transport him to the nursery.

The Baby With a Tracheo-esophageal Fistula

The signs indicating that a baby has a tracheo-esophageal fistula vary somewhat with the type of anatomical anomaly involved (Fig. 4–15). In the most common type of anomaly (type A), the esophagus ends in a blind pouch (a catheter cannot be passed through it), accounting for the almost immediate vomiting of any fluid taken orally.

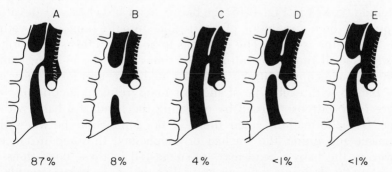

Figure 4–15. The most common forms of esophageal atresia and tracheo-esophageal fistula, in order of frequency. (From Nelson, Vaughan, and McKay (eds.): *Textbook of Pediatrics.* 9th Edition, W. B. Saunders, 1969.)

The trachea is connected to the stomach by a short fistula and thus becomes quickly distended as air enters with each breath. Gastric secretions can enter the tracheobronchial tree through the fistula. When the baby is not being fed there is drooling and frequent bubbly mucus — the classic symptom. Spotting this excess mucus before the baby is fed for the first time is a real contribution to the successful care of these babies.

In type B (Fig. 4–15), air does not enter the stomach nor can gastric juice reach the trachea and lungs, but milk and saliva do overflow the esophagus into the respiratory tract.

Type C is often not suspected in the newborn period because the esophagus does lead to the stomach and the baby can take his feedings. However, there is a fistula, although it may be as small as a pinpoint, and its presence is suspected as the baby grows older and has repeated pneumonitis.

Fortunately types D and E are rare. Because the upper esophagus is connected to the trachea any feeding taken orally will be carried directly to the lungs; the baby will cough and become cyanotic, "drowning" in the fluid.

Maternal polyhydramnios is a diagnostic clue available even before the baby is examined. Polyhydramnios often means that obstruction exists somewhere along the gastrointestinal tract. Under normal circumstances the fetus swallows amniotic fluid, but in this instance, the obstruction prevents him from doing so.

CARING FOR THE BABY WITH A
TRACHEO-ESOPHAGEAL FISTULA

As could be expected, the geatest preoperative problem is aspiration pneumonia. Preoperative nursing care, aside from general support, is largely aimed at preventing this difficulty. In the most common type (A in Fig. 4–15) the baby's head and chest are elevated, to prevent the regurgitation of gastric juice into the lung, by elevating the floor of the isolette. The baby has to be kept in this semi-upright position at all times, including those times when he is being transported from a community hospital to a medical center for surgery.

Babies with each type of anomaly need frequent suctioning, but there is no purpose served by elevating the head of a baby with a type B malformation, since there is no connection between the stomach and either the trachea or esophagus. In some instances, lowering the baby's head may be suggested in these conditions to facilitate the draining of mucus and saliva which the baby is unable to swallow. A Trendelenburg position may cause respiratory distress in a newborn, and some physicians oppose using it for these tiny babies under any circumstance.

Surgery involves ligation of the fistula and anastomosis of the esophageal segments. When the segments are far apart, tissue from another area, such as the colon, must be used to bridge the gap. More than one operation may be required.

The baby returns from surgery with a chest tube and a gastrostomy tube for feeding and for relieving abdominal distention. During the first postoperative hours he needs the individual attention of one nurse. Mucus may plug the respiratory tract, so frequent suctioning is necessary. He must be turned and stimulated to cry so that his lungs will fully expand. Normally there will be a minimal amount of drainage through the chest tube, and the lungs will be expanded within a few hours.

The following standard precautions for any patient, child or adult, with a chest tube have to be observed:

1. If a bottle is used for drainage it is taped to the floor. Some newer types of set-ups use a heavy plastic bag which can be attached to the lower part of the isolette; the advantage here is the bag moves automatically with the isolette when it is moved, so that there is no danger of forgetting to move the bag and causing tension on the chest tube. The bag, like the bottle, must never be raised.

2. No part of the tubing should ever be disconnected, nor should it be compressed or kinked. When the isolette hood is lifted and lowered, caution should be taken to see that the tubing is not caught between the hood and the metal framework.

3. If there are clots of blood in the tube, the tube should be milked away from the baby.

4. Two hemostats, their ends covered with rubber tubing, must always be taped to the top of the isolette so that if for some reason there is a break in the system (a broken bottle, for example, or a hole in the tubing), the tube can be immediately clamped to prevent a pneumothorax as air rushes into the chest.

5. Fluid level in the bottle should be marked on a tape and checked frequently, depending upon the amount of bleeding and drainage.

In the first days following repair of a tracheo-esophageal fistula, feedings are given through a gastrostomy tube, (see page 216), oral feedings beginning in from five to ten days in a baby who is doing well, but delayed much longer in some infants. If total repair was not possible during the initial surgery, gastrostomy feedings will continue for many months, which means that the mother will need to learn to feed her baby and care for him with the tube in place after he goes home.

Postoperatively the biggest problem facing these babies is the healing of the esophagus. Because it has a segmental blood supply, inadequate circulation in one portion of the esophagus is not well compensated. Nor does the esophagus hold sutures well. In spite of these difficulties, surgery is generally successful when (1) the baby is full term, (2) he has no other anomalies, and (3) the esophageal segments are close together. Unfortunately one or all of these requirements may not be fulfilled, and in some studies mortality rates are as high as 45 per cent. If death comes, it is usually from sepsis or pneumonia, or from general debilitation.

The Baby With a Diaphragmatic Hernia

When the diaphragm fails to develop properly, part of the abdominal organs may herniate through the defect into the chest. If the displacement is extensive, the baby will be in acute respiratory distress from the time of birth and is likely to die without early surgery. In addition to cyanosis and retractions, infants with diaphragmatic hernia have small, scaphoid abdomens. There are no breath sounds on the affected side, which is most often the left side, and the heart beat is heard further to the right (in left-sided displacement).

Both pre- and postoperatively, the baby must have his head elevated in order to minimize the pressure of the abdominal organs on the lungs and to allow the diaphragm to move as freely as possible. Postoperatively, the baby will have a chest tube connected to water-seal drainage and either a gastrostomy or nasogastric tube to keep the stomach from becoming distended. First feedings, which will begin the second 24 hours after surgery if the baby is doing well, will be given through the tube.

Since it often takes several days for the lung on the affected side to expand fully, respiratory distress is not unusual postoperatively. Positioning the baby so the affected side is down helps the unaffected lung to expand to its fullest potential in the immediate postoperative period when it is the only one functioning.

Even with superior care, not all of these babies survive. Mortality rates range from 25 per cent in hospitals where surgeons and nurses are specialists in infant care to higher than 50 per cent in studies which include all types of hospitals. At least part of this high mortality is due to associated anomalies of heart, lungs, or intestines.

The Baby With an Omphalocele

The failure of the viscera to return to the abdomen after the tenth week of embryonic life (see page 10) results in an omphalocele—a defect immediately obvious at birth which carries a high mortality rate if the omphalocele is large. Death is likely to come either from postoperative respiratory distress which results from pressure on the diaphragm, when a large amount of bowel is replaced in the abdominal cavity at one time, or from infection of the abdominal viscera.

Before surgery, every effort is made to keep the contents of the sac sterile by covering them with sterile sponges and sterile plastic. The viscera are only partially replaced during surgery and an envelope is created over the remainder, a little more bowel being returned to the abdomen each day, in order to keep respiratory distress at a minimum. An alternative procedure involves suturing the skin over the abdominal contents and deferring return to the abdomen until both baby and abdomen have grown larger.

The Baby With an Intestinal Obstruction

Obstruction, whether it is due to atresia, to stenosis, or to malrotation, may occur in the small or large intestine. Meconium ileus, an early symptom of cystic fibrosis, can also cause obstruction in the newborn. Careful nursing observations of vomitus and stools are most important in recognizing an obstruction and in pinpointing its location (see page 123). Green vomitus, i.e., vomitus containing bile, is the classic symptom. Absence of stool, abdominal distention, and occasionally peristaltic waves from right to left are also significant observations. The lower in the gastro-intestinal tract the obstruction is located, the more likely it is that symptoms will be delayed.

As was true of babies with a tracheo-esophageal fistula, and for the same reason, the mothers of babies with intestinal obstructions often have an excessive amount of amniotic fluid (see page 170).

Surgery is the only treatment. Since an obstruction is not likely to be recognized as early as most other anomalies of the gastro-intestinal tract, the baby may have vomited several times and lost electrolytes as well as fluid, a situation that must be treated before he goes to the operating room.

Postoperatively, as well as preoperatively, vomiting and aspiration are the chief dangers for these babies. Because of this, they should be positioned on their abdomens or sides. A nasogastric tube is inserted before surgery and either a gastrostomy tube or a nasogastric tube will be in place afterward to prevent air and intestinal secretions from accumulating in the stomach until bowel peristalsis is restored. The return of peristalsis is indicated by normal stools and minimal gastric drainage.

The Baby With an Imperforate Anus

The simple expedient of taking an initial rectal temperature on every newborn baby will detect the absence of a patent anus. If the anus is imperforate, urine is tested for the presence of meconium to determine whether or not there is a fistula to the urinary system. Rectovaginal or rectourinary fistulas are common. Nearly half of all infants with an imperforate anus have urinary tract infections as well.

Surgical repair is relatively simple in those instances in which the rectum ends close to the perineum (more commonly in girls) and more complicated when the end of the rectum is high and there is a fistula to the bladder or urethra. In the latter instance a temporary colostomy is created, more extensive surgery being delayed until the baby is several months old.

Following perineal repair, specific nursing care is directed toward keeping the suture line free of feces. A diaper is not used, so that any stool will be observed immediately and washed away. Newborns, when they lie on their abdomens, have a tendency to pull their legs up under them, creating tension in the perineal area. Because of this, following perineal surgery, the baby should be positioned on either side and his position changed frequently.

Colostomy care for infants does not differ from that given to older persons. The mother needs a chance to become accustomed to the colostomy before she takes her baby home. The biggest problem is probably the mother's psychological reaction, i.e., the acceptance of her baby with his colostomy. Knowing that it is only temporary (for about three to six months) and discovering, through practice in the nursery, that care is not really difficult, should help to relieve her anxiety so that she can love her baby and treat him normally.

The Baby With a Meningocele, Meningomyelocele, or Encephalocele

While these obvious defects pose no immediate threat to the baby's life, most neurosurgeons prefer to eliminate them as soon after birth as possible. Not only does early surgery reduce the risk of infection with subsequent meningitis and make baby care far less difficult, it also seems to make it easier for the mother to accept her baby. There is some evidence that rapidly progressing damage may occur to the malformed and partially exposed spinal cord of a meningomyelocele.

Before surgery the sac has to be protected. If it is relatively small, the baby can be kept in a prone position, but when the sac is large, it is difficult to place him in this position; in this case the baby may be more easily positioned on his side.

The ultimate success of surgery depends to a very large extent on the kind of defect that is involved. There are no nerves in the dura mater sac of a *meningocele;* hence there is no loss of either sensory or motor function. The baby should be perfectly normal following surgery.

In a *meningomyelocele,* however, the sac does contain a portion of the spinal cord and terminal nerves. In addition, nearly three-fourths of these babies have, or will have, hydrocephalus. There will be varying degrees of paralysis, due to motor nerve involvement, and loss of sensation, related to sensory involvement. One of the first questions the neurosurgeon is likely to ask is, "Does he move his legs?" Should meconium continually ooze from the anus and urine appear to dribble, it is likely that the baby lacks sphincter control, another significant observation.

Encephaloceles are far less common than meningoceles. The sac may contain fluid, nervous tissue, or a portion of the brain.

If the baby is born in a hospital where there is no neurosurgeon, the sac must be protected during transportation to a medical center. The area is covered with a sterile dressing and sterile plastic and protected by a "doughnut" of foam rubber which has been wrapped in sterile gauze and secured with a binder.

Surgery for a meningomyelocele involves the excision of the sac and the replacement of nerve tissue into the spinal canal. Wound healing takes from a week to ten days. During this time the area has to be kept scrupulously free of urine and stool, which is often more difficult to achieve than with normal newborns because of the frequent lack of sphincter control. To facilitate this aspect of care, the babies are kept in an isolette unclothed and prone; frequently sterile plastic is used to cover the area of the incision.

Because postoperative hydrocephalus is not unusual, daily head and chest measurements must be recorded. By plotting these measurements graphically, the nurse or doctor can detect rapid increases in head, and a shunting procedure can be performed early before there is opportunity for brain damage. The most common shunts are ventriculoatrial, ventriculojugular, and ventriculoperitoneal. Pudenz and Holter valves allow spinal fluid to be drained from the ventricles but prevent a backflow from the blood stream. They can become blocked by blood clots, particularly those which go to the right atrium of the heart. Blockage is sometimes overcome by a pump in the valve which can be pressed through the skin surface. Thus it is important for both nurse and parents to know what kind of apparatus has been inserted. Parents also have to learn to recognize the signs of increased intracranial pressure which is a possibility at any time in a baby who has had a shunt. These symptoms are: (1) failure to feed well, (2) vomiting, (3) irritability, (4) lethargy, and (5) a bulging fontanelle.

Other important observations in a baby who has had surgery to correct a meningomyelocele are:

1. The amount of movement in feet and legs. (Passive exercise is in order when no such movement exists.)

2. Presence of clubbed feet.

3. Urinary retention which, if unrecognized and untreated, can eventually lead to impairment of renal function.

4. Skin breakdown when urine and feces continually dribble.

The Infant of a Diabetic Mother

The babies of diabetic mothers or of mothers who will later become diabetic tend to show the same characteristics. They are plump, sleek and plethoric. Not only the baby, but usually the cord and placenta are oversized. These babies lie quietly, move very little, and cry infrequently. Fifty per cent of these babies will become hypoglycemic, most of them in the first six hours after birth. Of this 50 per cent, most will have transient hypoglycemia, lasting from one to four hours, after which blood sugar level will begin to rise. In a few infants, the hypoglycemia will be prolonged and severe. A small group will have low blood sugar from 12 to 24 hours after birth rather than in the first six hours.

Why are these babies hypoglycemia? The following sequence has been postulated: diabetic mothers who are not well controlled are hyperglycemic. The excess sugar, like other nutrients in maternal blood, crosses the placental barrier causing hyperglycemia in the infant as well. To metabolize this excess sugar, the islets of Langerhans in the fetal pancreas hypertrophy in order to secrete increased amounts of insulin. The sugar is converted to glycogen and stored as excess fat, hence the large size of the baby (which is not due to excess fluid as was once believed). Once the baby is born he is removed from the source of his sugar, but his pancreas continues to work over-time; hence, he becomes hypoglycemic.

The more nearly the mother's blood sugar can be kept within normal limits during pregnancy, the less likely her baby is to develop hypoglycemia following delivery. The higher the maternal blood sugar, the greater the fall for the infant.

A second explanation relates both the large size of the baby and the hypertrophy of the islet cells to the pituitary growth hormone.

Oral hypoglycemic agents seem to be particularly dangerous to the fetus; pregnant diabetic women are maintained on insulin. Pregnancy is usually interrupted in the thirty-fifth to thirty-seventh week, the baby being delivered by cesarean-section or, occasionally, by induced labor.

The resulting danger of hypoglycemia is brain damage; if the hypoglycemia is unchecked, the possibility of mental retardation is considerable. With new microtechniques for blood sugar analysis, the level of sugar can be checked at birth and each hour during the first six hours. A drop of blood from a heel stick is all that is necessary; results are available within minutes. Blood sugar levels below 30 in a term baby or below 20 in an infant premature by gestational age indicate hypoglycemia; the treatment is usually 10 per cent glucose given via umbilical artery catheter.

Not every hospital is equipped to monitor blood sugar so quickly and easily. When there is a choice of institutions it would seem ideal for these high risk mothers to be delivered in large medical centers where the baby can receive special attention, since the chance of complications is one out of two. But often no such choice is available.

In every hospital, the baby can be watched carefully for symptoms of hypoglycemia: apnea, cyanosis, limpness, failure to feed well, tremors, and convulsions. Oral feedings are begun early, within an hour following birth, or shortly thereafter, as a preventive measure.

In caring for the babies of diabetic mothers, it is important to remember that in spite of birth weights of 7 to 9 pounds, in most instances these babies are premature by gestational age, and their organ systems will function accordingly. Thus the incidence of jaundice may be high; these babies are liable to respiratory distress syndrome and to transient tachypnea if they are delivered by cesarean section (see page 118). They may become hypocalcemic or have renal vein thrombosis. There is a difference of opinion as to whether they have a higher incidence of congenital anomalies. Because they have a layer of fat that is usually absent in premature-by-age babies it will take less heat to keep them warm. If the baby is in an incubator his temperature must be monitored closely so that he does not become overheated.

The Baby With an Infection

Like all babies, infants with infections need warmth and humidity and an adequate supply of calories. They may also need oxygen and treatment for the correction of acidosis. For the specific treatment of infection, parenteral antibiotics are used. If the baby is receiving intravenous fluids, adding antibiotics to his fluids will save him the pain of an extra injection. Otherwise, intramuscular injection is the route of choice because of the erratic level of absorption in newborns when oral preparations are used.

Because newborns maintain adequate blood levels of antibacterial agents longer than older children do, 12-hour schedules are usually satisfactory.

Dosage for infants is calculated on the basis of weight or body surface area. The long-standing formulas for calculating infant dosage from adult dosage are not applicable here; they result in some instances in inadequate underdoses and, at other times, in toxic overdoses. Table 4–1 describes infections common in the newborn and the antibiotics commonly used in the neonatal period along with special considerations for their use.

Four antibiotics have been found to be highly toxic to newborns: the sulfa drugs, tetracycline, chloramphenicol, and potassium penicillin. The sulfas compete with bilirubin for albumin-binding sites and can thus cause kernicterus and death at levels of serum bilirubin that would generally be considered safe. Tetracycline inhibits the linear growth of infants because it is deposited in the growing epiphyses and also causes permanent yellow-green staining of the enamel of the baby teeth (as does the ingestion of tetracycline by the mother during late pregnancy). Chloramphenicol, because it is poorly excreted by newborns, can lead to sudden collapse and death known as the "gray baby" syndrome. Potassium penicillin can cause heart block in infants.

The Baby of a Mother Addicted to Narcotics

As drug use among young women increases, as it has during recent years, the incidence of infants being born to mothers addicted to narcotics has increased. In some urban medical centers relatively large numbers of newborns addicted to morphine, heroin, and methadone are currently being seen. The problem for the nurse is to recognize these babies.

The most prominent sign is central nervous system irritability: the baby is frantic and inconsolable; he may have tremors; and the

TABLE 4–1. *Common Infections in Newborn Infants*

ORGANISM	COMMONLY CAUSES	PREVENTION	TREATMENT
E. coli	Pneumonia Septicemia Meningitis Diarrhea		Kanamycin, 15 mg/Kg./ day in two equal doses Ampicillin sometimes used in combination with Kanamycin
Staphylococcus aureus	Pneumonia Septicemia Enteritis	Exclusion of persons with skin infection from nursery Hexachlorophene handwashing Care of umbilical cord stump Avoidance of over-crowding in nursery	Aqueous penicillin 50,000 U./Kg. q 12 hours for first 5 days; q 6 hours after 6 days old Ampicillin, 50 mg/kg. q 12 hours first 5 days, then q 6 hours thereafter Kanamycin, 7.5 mg./kg. q 12 hours Bacitracin ointment to skin lesions
Pseudomonas	Bacteremia Pneumonia Meningitis	Careful and frequent cleaning and sterilization of respiratory equipment Avoidance of equipment or procedures which promote stasis of respiratory secretions Use of silver nitrate or vinegar in the humidification pans of incubators	Treatment unsatisfactory; organism is rarely sensitive to bacterial agents Polymyxin B, 1.5–2.5 mg./Kg. q 12 hours I.M. Colistin (polymyxin E) 2–4 mg./Kg. q 12 hours I.M.

Moro response may be incomplete. His shrill cry is not unlike that of babies with central nervous system damage. In addition, there may be a large amount of mucus or such generalized symptoms as diarrhea and vomiting. Either excessive weight loss, due to fluid loss from vomiting or diarrhea, or failure to gain weight, because of a very high expenditure of energy, prevents these babies from growing normally in the nursery.

Since all these symptoms are common to many other kinds of newborn problems, it is important that the nurse be alert to signs of addiction in mothers, such as scarred veins and withdrawal symptoms, in order to evaluate the symptoms in babies. Addiction can be suspected and the possibility should be evaluated in mothers with venereal disease, hepatitis, cellulitis, and thrombophlebitis.

The diagnosis in the baby is confirmed by the discovery of narcotic breakdown products in the blood and urine. Specimens need to be collected shortly after birth because these narcotic metabolites disappear quickly.

The care of addicted babies includes minimal handling, because of their hyperirritability, adequate hydration, and correction of any electrolyte imbalance. Phenobarbital and Thorazine are the medications most commonly used for treatment; paregoric may be given for diarrhea. Methadone has been used experimentally for newborn withdrawal symptoms but is not, at the present time, commonly employed in treatment.

Bibliography

Barnett, C.: Leiderman, P. H., Grobstein, R., and Klaus, M.: 1970, Neonatal Separation: The Maternal Side of Interactional Deprivation. *Pediatrics, 45*:197, 1970.

Behrman, R. E.: Phototherapy and Hyperbilirubinemia. *Journal of Pediatrics, 74*:989, 1969.

Behrman, R. E., and Hsia, D. Y.: Summary of a Symposium on Phototherapy for Hyperbilirubinemia. *Journal of Pediatrics, 75*:718, 1969.

Braine, M. D. S., Heimer, C. B., Wortis, H., and Freedman, A. M.: Factors Associated with Impairment of the Early Development of Prematures. *In* Mussen, P., Conger, J., and Kagan, J. (eds.): *Readings in Child Development and Personality.* Harper and Row, 1966.

Britten, A. F. H.: A Neonatal exchange Transfusion: Present Status. *Clinical Pediatrics, 7*:125, 1968.

Callon, H. F.: The Premature Infant's Nurse. *American Journal of Nursing, 63,2*: 103(February), 1963.

Cavanagh, D., and Talisman, M. R.: *Prematurity and the Obstetrician.* New York; Appleton-Century-Crofts, 1969.

Craig, W. S.: *Care of the Newly Born Infant.* Baltimore, Williams and Wilkins, 1969.

Cremer, R. J., Perryman, P. W., and Richards, D. H.: Influence of Light on the Hyperbilirubinemia of Infants. *The Lancet,* 1, 1094, 1958.

Cross, V. M.: *The Premature Baby.* Boston, Little, Brown and Company, 1966.

Darnell, B.: We Give our Premies Family-centered Care. *RN,* March: 57, 1966.

DeLeon, A., Elliott, J. H., and Jones, D. B.: The Resurgence of Retrolental Fibroplasia. *Pediatric Clinics of North America, 17*:309, 1970.

DeMarco, J. P., and Reed, R.: Care of the High Risk Infant in the Intensive Care Unit. *Nursing Clinics of North America, 5*:375, 1970.

Drillien, C. M. Growth and Development in a Group of Children of Very Low Birth Weight. *Archives of Disease in Childhood, 33*:10, 1968.

Drillien, C. M.: School Disposal and Performance for Children of Different Birthweight Born 1953–1960. *Archives of Disease in Childhood, 44*:562, 1969.

Falkner, F.: *Key Issues in Infant Mortality.* Bethesda, Maryland, National Institute of Child Health and Human Development, 1909.

Fisch, R. O., Froven, H., and Engel, R. R.: Neurological Status of Survivors of Neonatal Respiratory Distress Syndrome. *Journal of Pediatrics, 73*:395, 1968.

Fleming, J. W.: Recognizing the Newborn Addict. *American Journal of Nursing, 65*:83, 1965.

Fosson, A. R., and Fine, R. N.: Neonatal Meningitis. *Clinical Pediatrics, 7*:404, 1968.

Fyler, D. C.: Diagnosis and Treatment: The Salvage of Critically Ill Newborn Infants with Congenital Heart Disease. *Pediatrics, 42*:198, 1968.

Gans, B., Kooner, H., Orebiji, E., and Macleod, J.: Mother-Baby Contact in Special Care Baby Units. *The Lancet, 2*:692, 1969.

Giunta, F. and Roth, J.: Effect of Environmental Illumination in Prevention of Hyperbilirubinemia of Prematurity. *Pediatrics, 44*:162, 1969.

Gotaff, S. P., and Behrman, R. E.: Neonatal Septicemia. *Journal of Pediatrics, 76*:142, 1970.

Goulding, E. I., and Koop, C. E.: The Newborn: His Response to Surgery. *American Journal of Nursing, 65*:84 (October), 1965.

Klaus, M., Kennell, J. H., Plumb, W., and Zuehlke, S.: Human Maternal Behavior at the First Contact with Her Young. *Pediatrics, 46*:187, 1970.

Klaus, M. H., and Kennell, J. H.: Mothers Separated from Their Newborn Infants. *Pediatric Clinics of North America, 17*:1015, 1970.

Leifer, A., Leiderman, P., and Barnett, C.: Mother-Infant Separation: Effects on Later Maternal Behavior. *Child Development:* to be published.

Lewis, C.: Nursing Care of the Neonate Requiring Surgery for Congenital Defects. *Nursing Clinics of North America, 5*:387, 1970.

Lucey, J.: Nursery Illumination as a Factor in Neonatal Hyperbilirubinemia. *Pediatrics, 44*:155, 1969.

Martin, L. W., Gilmore, A., Peckham, J., and Baumer, J.: Nursing Care of Infants with Esophageal Anomalies. *American Journal of Nursing, 66*:2463 (November), 1966.

Martin, L. W., Altemeier, W. A., and Reyes, P. M.: Infections in Pediatric Surgery. *Pediatric Clinics of North America, 16*:735, 1969.

Medovy, H.: Outlook for the Infant of a Diabetic Mother. *Journal of Pediatrics, 76*:988, 1970.

Milby, T. H., Mitchell, J., and Freeman, T.: Seasonal Neonatal Hyperbilirubinemia. *Pediatrics, 43*:601, 1969.

Miller, H. C.: Prematurity. *In* Cooke, R. E. (ed.): *The Biologic Basis of Pediatric Practice.* New York, McGraw-Hill, 1968.

Moore, M. L.: Recognizing Illness in the Newborn. *RN*, December: 40, 1965.

Morse, T. S.: Transportation of Critically Ill or Injured Children. *Pediatric Clinics of North America, 16*:565, 1969.

Nelson, N. M.: On the Etiology of Hyaline Membrane Disease. *Pediatric Clinics of North America, 17*:943, 1970.

Owens, C.: Parents Reactions to Defective Babies. *American Journal of Nursing, 64*:83 (November), 1964.

Patz, A.: Retrolental Fibroplasia. *In* Cooke, R. E. (ed.): *The Biologic Basis of Pediatric Practice.* New York, McGraw-Hill, 1968.

Raffensperger, J. C., and Primrose, R. B.: *Pediatric Surgery for Nurses.* Boston, Little, Brown, and Company, 1968.

Richmond, J. B.: The Mother's Tie to Her Child. *Pediatrics, 45*:189, 1970.

Rowe, R. D., and Mehrizi, A.: *The Neonate with Congenital Heart Disease.* Philadelphia, W. B. Saunders, 1968.

Rubin, A.: *Handbook of Congenital Malformations.* Philadelphia, W. B. Saunders, 1967.

Schaffer, A. J., and Avery, M. E.: *Diseases of the Newborn.* 3rd Edition. Philadelphia, W. B. Saunders, 1971.

Slobody, L. B., and Cobrinik, R.: Neonatal Narcotic Addiction. *Quarterly Review of Pediatrics, 14*:169, 1959.

Smith, R. M.: Temperature Monitoring and Regulation. *Pediatric Clinics of North America, 16*:643, 1969.

St. Geme, J. W.: Preoperative Evaluation. *Pediatric Clinics of North America, 16*:573, 1969.

Traggis, D. G.: The Care of the Premature Newborn. *In* Cavenagh, D., and Talisman, M. R. (eds.): *Prematurity and the Obstetrician.* New York, Appleton-Century-Crofts, 1969.

Vulliamy, D. G.: *The Newborn Child.* Boston, Little, Brown and Company, 1967.

Waechter, E.: The Birth of an Exceptional Child. *Nursing Forum, IX*:202, 1970.

Wortis, H., Heimer, C. B., Braine, M., Redlo, M., and Rue, R.: Growing Up in Brooklyn: The Early History of a Premature Child. *American Journal of Orthopsychiatry, 33*:535, 1963.

CHAPTER 5

The Nutritional Needs
of Newborns

Nutrition for newborns, whether they are full-term or premature babies, whether they are apparently normal or obviously ill, involves providing water, electrolytes, and nutrients in adequate but not excessive amounts.

Water and Fluid Balance

For several reasons fluid balance in newborns is much more precarious than in older children and adults:

1. Metabolic rates in the newborn are higher. A newborn produces 45 to 50 calories per kilogram of body weight every 24 hours. The basal metabolic level for adults in the same period is from 25 to 30 calories per kilogram. Since metabolism utilizes water, a higher rate of metabolism utilizes a proportionately higher quantity of water.

2. The larger surface area of the newborn in relation to his body mass means a higher ratio of water loss through evaporation, the rate of loss per kilogram being twice that of an adult. This means that his fluid balance is much more susceptible to environmental temperature and humidity. His water loss can be very high in a high temperature, low humidity environment such as an incubator which has been heated but has not had the water chamber filled.

3. The proportion of water in relation to total body mass is greater than at any other period of life—a total of 70 to 75 per cent. About 30

to 35 per cent of total body weight in the newborn is extracellular water, compared with 25 per cent in the older infant and an average of 20 per cent in adults. Because of this, the infant has proportionately less reserve; any fluid loss or lack of intake will deplete his extracellular fluid very rapidly. In a 24-hour period an infant puts out about 50 per cent of his extracellular water; in the same period an adult excretes only about 14 per cent of his extracellular water. A large part of the difference between the newborn and older infant disappears by the time the baby is ten days old, for it is the loss of this large proportion of extracellular water that accounts for much of the weight loss that occurs in the first three days of life.

4. The kidneys of both premature and term infants have about half the concentrating capacity of the normal adult. They function satisfactorily under usual conditions, but they are less able to conserve fluid when the baby is stressed. In an older individual, scanty urine is a fairly reliable sign of dehydration, but because of the newborn's limited ability to conserve water by concentrating urine, his urinary output may not decrease. His normally higher blood levels of phosphate and potassium are also related to renal immaturity.

WATER REQUIREMENTS OF NEWBORNS

The amount of water a newborn needs is related to his weight— about 80 to 100 ml./kg. of body weight in his first week to ten days, increasing to 125 to 150 ml./kg. after ten days. For a baby weighing 6½ pounds (3 kg.), this would mean an intake of 250 to 300 cc. during the first week or approximately 45 cc. at each of six feedings. Slightly higher intakes of formula at usual strengths are given by the end of the first week in order to meet caloric needs, with 2- to 2½-ounce feedings six times a day meeting both requirements. At this level of fluid intake there is no need for extra water unless the baby is in a very hot environment where his water loss from evaporation will be extraordinarily high.

Since intake is based on body weight, larger babies will have an increased water and caloric need.

Rarely do babies take the same amount of formula at each feeding, but this is unimportant as long as the day's total is adequate.

ELECTROLYTES

As might be expected, because of the rapid exchange of water during infancy and the ease with which water balance is upset, electrolytes are also exchanged rapidly so that electrolyte balance is also relatively unstable. Changes in sodium and potassium balance especially are likely to be affected. Any loss of fluids and secretions, caused by vomiting, diarrhea, and gastric suction, also results in the loss of sodium, chloride, and potassium. The amounts needed for replacement are determined from laboratory reports of electrolyte blood levels.

Babies with the salt-losing form of congenital adrenal hyperplasia (comprising about 30 per cent of all infants with this condition) must receive sodium chloride (usually 4 to 8 gm. as an initial 24-hour dose followed by 2 to 6 gm. per day maintenance) as well as desoxycorticosterone acetate (DOCA) and hydrocortisone throughout their lives. Since the condition is an autosomal recessive trait it may be suspected from family history, but there is just as likely to be no such clue. Girls with adrenal hyperplasia often have hermaphroditic external genitalia, but there is no similar indication in affected newly born boys. Symptoms which may occur in the newborn nursery or in the first month include anorexia, vomiting, and diarrhea which leads to extreme dehydration and weight loss.

PARENTERAL FLUID THERAPY

Once fluid or electrolyte balance is upset, parenteral fluid therapy is often necessary. In most cases fluids are given intravenously, but hypodermocylsis is also occasionally used to treat newborns. In a nursery caring for full-term healthy infants, parenteral fluid therapy would be a rare exception. But in low birth weight and intensive care nurseries the administration of intravenous fluids is very much in evidence—for the tiny infant who is unable to take sufficient food and calories orally, for the baby who is being prepared for surgery or is a recent "post-op," and for the baby with persistent vomiting or diarrhea whose fluid and electrolyte losses are substantial.

The type of solution and the total amount to be given as well as the amount of solution to be given each hour should be a part of the physician's order. Once the fluids are started, their maintenance at the proper rate becomes a nursing responsibility that involves the monitoring of both baby and intravenous equipment at the minimum of once every hour. If too small an amount of fluid is given, the baby will become increasingly dehydrated and circulating fluid volume will be decreased; if the proper fluid level is not restored, he will die in a relatively short period of time. On the other hand, too much fluid in too brief a period of time will lead to pulmonary edema and water intoxication, and again, if uncorrected, to death. The margin for error is narrow in a newborn baby.

A first requirement for assuring accurate intake is an intravenous set designed specifically for pediatric patients (Fig. 5–1). A small amount of fluid can be transferred from the main fluid bottle to the burette — not more than the baby is to receive in a three-hour period. In this way, even if by some accident the fluid should begin to run at a faster rate than ordered, the baby will be protected against an overwhelming fluid intake. From 5 to 10 cc. of fluid should remain in the burette at all times as a buffer so that if an emergency does arise and fluid intake cannot be checked exactly on the hour all of the fluid will not be gone and the needle clogged with blood.

The amount of fluid the baby receives should be checked and charted each hour. Readings are made at the fluid level at the bottom of the meniscus. The chart should be a type which can be kept at the baby's bedside and quickly checked to see the kind of fluid he is receiving, the amount he has received, and the rate of flow.

The pediatric intravenous set is commonly calibrated so that if the baby is to receive 3 cc. per hour, for example, then a rate of 3 drops per minute should be used. The correct rate of flow can be maintained with a small pump, such as the Holter pump, which is attached to the tubing between the fluid bottle and the burette and which adjust the rate to keep it constant. When the Holter pump is used, the burette must be lowered 4 to 6 inches above the pump; fluid in a bottle too high above pump level will exert too much force on the pump and cause it to work improperly. The Holter pump is not calibrated directly in drops per minute and is unable to regulate fluids at rates of one to two drops per minute.

Equipment of this sort varies from one institution to another. The special requirements of the Holter pump are mentioned to illustrate how important it is for each nurse to be thoroughly familiar with the use and special requirements of the available equipment so that it may be used to maximum benefit. Since these pumps are monitoring devices they usually may be used by nurses without a specific physician's order. Using a monitor for any reason, however, does not eliminate the need to check the baby himself and to keep complete and accurate records of fluid intake.

The fluid site is one area to be observed on the baby. A scalp vein, an umbilical artery, and veins in the hands and feet are frequent sites for the administration of intravenous fluids in newborns. If it is suspected that the baby will receive fluids for a number of days, a "cutdown" to deeper vessels may be done. The site needs to be checked for swelling at least every hour. Occasionally, in adults, the continued position of a needle in a vein is ascertained by lowering the fluid bottle to see if blood returns in the tubing. This should not be done in newborns because of the small gauge of the needle; the back-up blood may easily clog the needle and the fluids will have to

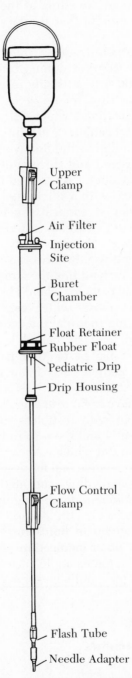

Upper
Clamp

Air Filter

Injection
Site

Buret
Chamber

Float Retainer
Rubber Float

Pediatric Drip

Drip Housing

Flow Control
Clamp

Flash Tube

Needle Adapter

Figure 5-1. Special equipment is necessary in order to safely administer intravenous fluids to infants.

be restarted at another site. Swelling at the fluid site may indicate infiltration of fluids or merely that the tape holding the needle in place is too tight.

Umbilical artery catheterization, which allows frequent blood sampling as well as the administration of fluids, is a procedure developed in the early 1960's. It is usually reserved for very small premature babies who have tiny, fragile veins and respiratory distress syndrome or other serious illness which will require fluid therapy for several days. An umbilical catheter can minimize the number of times a sick baby must be handled in the first week which is decidedly to his advantage. After the cord and surrounding area are washed with an antiseptic solution, a catheter is inserted into one of the umbilical arteries and fixed in place with a silk thread. The tip of the catheter should be in the abdominal aorta at the level of the diaphragm. The position of the catheter is usually confirmed by x-ray.

Because there is always the possibility of infection through the cord stump, even in healthy newborns, an antibiotic ointment may be ordered for the area surrounding the stump.

Babies with umbilical catheters should be checked for leg blanching, due to arterial thrombosis which can occur shortly after the catheter is inserted, during the time the catheter is in place, or after the removal of the catheter. The baby's leg may appear cold and white with no pulse or it may be mottled, pale, and dusky.

After an umbilical catheter has been removed there may be bleeding from the cord stump.

Even small babies have to be restrained while they are receiving fluids. Like older people with restraints they need to have their position changed frequently and the restraints checked often, as well as the skin under the restraint which is so very delicate and can easily be injured. If a baby is to receive oral fluids while he is restrained, his head should be lifted for feeding, and after feeding he should be turned on his side or abdomen, depending upon the fluid site. Each time the baby is turned or moved, the site and flow must be rechecked.

If medications are added to fluids this must also be included in the record, just as any other medications would be. Some medications, calcium gluconate, for example, may have a sclerotic effect on surrounding tissues if the needle becomes dislodged from the vein.

Other Necessary Nutrients

In addition to fluids and electrolytes, newborn infants, like all of us, need protein, carbohydrate, fats, vitamins, and minerals in amounts suited to their needs.

PROTEIN

A dietary intake of approximately 9 gm. of protein per day is necessary to provide for growth (3.5 gm.) and to cover losses in urine and from the skin (5 gm.). Advisable intakes are generally calculated at the slightly higher level of 14 gm. per day during the first month, 15 gm. for the second month, and 16 gm. from the fourth month throughout the remainder of the first year. (While infants in the later months of the first year need increased protein for maintenance, their rate of growth decreases and thus their overall protein need remains stable.)

There are several conditions, like PKU and other disorders of amino acid metabolism, in which the advisable level of protein intake is reduced to a lower level than that generally required. In nations where dietary sources of protein are limited, achieving minimum levels becomes the goal, with even this level being out of reach at times. This can have a deleterious effect, because protein malnutrition in the early months has serious consequences (see page 222).

CARBOHYDRATES

In human milk, 37 per cent of the calories come from carbohydrates. Since cow milk derives only 29 per cent of its calories from carbohydrate, cow milk formulas are sometimes supplemented with some form of sugar. Research indicates that infants can grow normally on formulas consisting only of evaporated milk and water (Fomon, 1967).

Commercially prepared formulas vary in their percentage of carbohydrate calories from 32 to 51 per cent, with the majority ranging from 40 to 45 per cent. When the proportion of calories from carbohydrate is too low, i.e., below 20 per cent, babies are not able to tolerate the high percentage of protein and fat that would then comprise their formula. On the other hand, carbohydrate in excess of 50 per cent of the total caloric content can lead to loose stools due to the baby's inability to hydrolize disaccharides, resulting in impaired growth and development.

FAT

Just as neither too much nor too little carbohydrate is well tolerated, so too the proportion of caloric intake from fats needs to fall within certain margins. From the standpoint of fats alone, a formula providing 1 per cent of the caloric intake from the essential fatty acids, linoleic and arachidonic, is evidently sufficient for healthy development. But such a formula would necessarily be so high in protein that the renal solute load would be excessive (see page 196), or the carbohydrate content would be so high that diarrhea would result. Too high a fat content is also poorly tolerated. Those formulas which derive 30 to 35 per cent of their calories from fat are generally the most acceptable.

VITAMINS

In the United States a great many babies receive vitamin supplements during their early months, in addition to the vitamins and minerals with which many formulas are supplemented. As a result, vitamin deficiencies are rare, although rickets (due to insufficient Vitamin D) and scurvy (due to too little Vitamin C) still occur occasionally. A mild Vitamin K deficiency is not unusual in newborns, but appears more frequently in premature babies. Chemical substances with Vitamin K activity are synthesized by normal intestinal flora, which are established after birth. In many hospitals a single dose of Vitamin K is given as a prophylactic measure to all babies shortly after birth.

Folic acid deficiency may occur more frequently than is generally thought, because the megaloblastic anemia, which is caused by inadequate folic acid and is due to a failure of the primordial erythrocytes to mature normally, may be masked by iron deficiency anemia which is rather common in infants.

The danger with Vitamin A is not of deficiency but of overdosage. Healthy infants who are receiving human milk, cow milk, and most commercial formulas do not need additional Vitamin A. About 600 I.U. per day is considered an adequate intake; many commercial formulas contain from 1500 to more than 2700 I.U. per liter. Babies receiving skim-milk formulas or milk-free formulas not supplemented with Vitamin A and infants with chronic steatorrhea do need to receive supplementary Vitamin A in a water-miscible preparation.

The possibility of toxicity due to excessive Vitamin D has been suggested but is unproven. The recommended daily intake of Vitamin D is 400 I.U. In the 1950's some British pediatricians recognized that the fortification of milks and cereals and the use of supplementary vitamins was raising Vitamin D intake for many British infants to a level of 3000 to 4000 I.U. per day, nearly ten times the amount recommended. There was a suspicion that these high dosages were related to infantile idiopathic hypercalcemia, and the fortification of food with Vitamin D was subsequently reduced, although no definite link between the vitamin and the condition was established. The reduction brought maximum daily intake of Vitamin D to less than 1500 I.U., without increasing the incidence of rickets, a matter of some concern at the time.

In the United States evaporated milk, most commercial formulas, and most fresh whole milk is fortified at the level of at least 400 I.U. of Vitamin D per quart. Human milk, however, contains less than 100 I.U. of Vitamin D per quart, and some commercial formulas contain less than 400 I.U. Infants receiving these formulas and those who are breast fed will need supplementary vitamin D.

MINERALS

A number of minerals play a role in newborn nutrition, but the need for most of them is apparently met with little difficulty. An exception is iron. Various studies have shown that the incidence of iron deficiency anemia (defined as a hemoglobin concentration of 10 gm. per cent or less) ranges from 25 to 76 per cent in infants over six months from economically deprived areas to 1 to 2 per cent in babies from more affluent families.

Iron requirement during the first year equals the difference between the level of iron at birth and the amount of iron required for growth and hemoglobin production between birth and the first birthday. Premature and low birth weight infants and twins accumulate limited iron stores in utero, as do babies of iron deficient mothers. Bleeding after birth, from cord or circumcision, for example, and too early clamping of the cord before pulsation has stopped deplete iron stores.

Formulas fortified with iron are frequently used for babies with a high risk of iron deficiency anemia. Cereals which have been iron fortified are offered early and parents are encouraged to continue the use of these cereals beyond the age of five or six months when they are normally discontinued in many families.

Breast or Bottle

The decision of a mother to breast or bottle feed her baby is almost always a culturally based decision rather than a medical one. In societies which are just beginning to develop technologically, there is no real choice but breast feeding, either by the infant's own mother or by another lactating female. But even in traditional societies breast feeding is on the decline as mothers become aware of Western practices. This is hardly surprising; cultural change in some aspects of life does not take place in isolation from the rest of life. But it is unfortunate that the switch from breast to bottle feeding has taken place in many instances before water has become safe and before adequate sanitary conditions and practices are established. Thus gastrointestinal disease remains the major cause of infant mortality in many developing nations.

There was also little choice in the manner of feeding infants in our own country until late in the nineteenth century when technology made bottle feeding a reasonable alternative to breast feeding. As recently as 1946 approximately 65 per cent of American infants were breast fed during the newborn period. By 1965 the figure had dropped to 26 per cent. In the early twentieth century breast feeding was more common among women from the lower socioeconomic classes. Today, however, the reverse is true; the incidence is higher among upper- and middle-class women. In one study, wives of students were found to be the most likely to breast feed. In the process of cultural change, innovations are usually accepted first by the best educated people of the community and later by the economically poorer peoples who have limited access to new ideas. The trend toward bottle feeding followed this pattern; it may be that the current increased incidence of breast feeding among better educated women will, in time, affect the practices of the rest of the community.

Schmitt (1970) emphasizes that the cultural values of nurses, as articulated by the nursing literature, are strongly in favor of breast feeding. In her review of the literature on breast feeding, from both the social as well as the biological sciences, she sees this bias as resting on no firm scientific evidence, a premise that cannot be entirely supported. She also feels that such strong predispositions can interfere with good nursing care, and in this she is entirely correct. If a mother feels that nurses expect her to breast feed, she may do so while she is in the hospital, but switch very quickly to bottle feeding when she returns to her own home.

There are several disadvantages to this. Having changed her baby to the bottle, the mother may subsequently feel uncomfortable in the presence of nurses who favor breast feeding. She may equate the attitudes of hospital nurses with those in the clinic of doctor's office or with the public health nurse who comes to her home. It is not too difficult to imagine the mother fearing the nurse's disapproval in other aspects of child care. Thus a barrier arises between mother and nurse, and the infant receives less than the best of medical care. Anthropologists have noted just this sort of barrier between Western medical personnel and the tradition-oriented peoples of developing nations. Such barriers are just as real in our society.

Moreover, too strong an insistence on breast feeding may create some nagging measure of guilt or feeling of inadequacy in mothers who really prefer bottle feeding, particularly in the mother whose feelings are ambivalent to begin with. Since the mother who has really decided to bottle feed will probably do so shortly after she returns home regardless of what she has done in hospital, it would be much wiser to spend the time that is available in the hospital for instructing her about bottle feeding rather than teaching her a technique she plans to discard.

Recognizing the validity of these arguments, it is also important to face some other realities. It is easy to say that breast feeding from the standpoint of infant health is important today only in developing nations where environmental standards in terms of water and sanitation are low. This argument fails to recognize that for a significant proportion of our own population, both sanitary and economic resources are limited. There are homes, both rural and urban (and I have visited in them), where mothers feed their babies from "coke" and whiskey bottles topped with nipples because these are the only kinds of bottles available; where a hungry, runny-nosed toddler drinks from the baby's bottle which has dropped from the crib to the floor and then puts the bottle back in the baby's mouth; and where refrigeration is inadequate and a pan for sterilization of equipment just doesn't exist even if the mother had the time, energy, and knowledge to carry out daily formula preparation. That some middle- and upper-class mothers can purchase presterilized, individually packaged formula is virtually as remote for these mothers as it is for a southeast Asia tribeswoman or an Australian aborgine mother. The babies of these mothers suffer a high rate of neonatal and postneonatal mortality and could certainly benefit from breast feeding during their early months, but as we have already pointed out, they are the least likely to be breast fed.

It would be tremendously worthwhile if we could find some effective way to encourage poor mothers to breast feed their babies, not only because poor techniques in bottle feeding increase the likelihood of introducing infection into milk but also because the lactobacillus flora in the gastrointestinal tract of breast-fed babies produces an environment unfavorable to E. coli, the organism most commonly associated with infection in infants. Low pH produced by the lactobacillus is thought to be the primary inhibiting factor. Cow milk, on the other hand, produces an environment favorable to the growth of enteric bacteria.

Perhaps the kind of techniques used by cultural-change agents (public health nurses, agriculturalists, sanitary engineers, anthropologists, and others), who work in developing nations, can offer some ideas. One or two key members of a neighborhood group are won to the new idea, and it is they, rather than the change agent, who bring about change on a larger scale. Nurses who work with programs which aim to bring about significant change need to know the neighborhoods in which they work; they need to be able to recognize who the leaders in that neighborhood are, and they need to have a large measure of rapport with the people for whom they care.

NUTRITIONAL COMPARISON: BREAST AND COW MILK

A nutritional comparison of breast and cow milk can be made on several counts. In making such a comparison it is necessary to realize that there is wide variation in human milk. This applies not only to the milk from different women but also in the milk from different breasts of the same woman at the same time and in the milk of the same woman at different times of the day. This is true of cow milk as well, but in our urban society where most milk is obtained from the grocery store, rather than from the family cow, a child will be getting milk from many cows and usually many herds of cows, so that this difference becomes insignificant.

The reasons for these differences are not known. They do not seem to be related to changes in the mother's diet. Poor nutrition affects the quantity of milk produced, but it does not appear to affect the relative proportions of carbohydrate, fat, and protein. Only vitamin content seems to be directly related to maternal intake.

Protein. One of the major differences between human and cow milk is in the protein content. Cow milk contains approximately three times the protein in grams per liter that human milk contains. The type of protein also differs. The principal protein in human milk is lactalbumin, while casein is the primary protein of cow milk. The fact that breast-fed infants have historically had a lower incidence of disease and a better growth record, was at one time attributed to the differences in protein. But now it seems that at least part of this difference in infant health was due to the bacterial contamination of bottled milk and the relatively high curd tension of the formulas. The curd tension is related to the amount of casein, and the curd in fresh, unprocessed cow milk is tough and rubbery in comparison to the soft, more easily digested curd of human milk. However, the modern processing of cow milk results in a softer curd and eliminates the major cause of its indigestibility.

Carbohydrate. Carbohydrate accounts for 37 per cent of the calories in human milk and 29 per cent of the calories in cow milk. Many formulas increase the amount of calories from carbohydrate by adding some form of simple sugar.

Fat. The fat content of cow milk is higher than that of human milk and is composed of different proportions of fatty acids. As a result, the fat of human milk is more easily digested in the early weeks of life than the fat of cow milk.

Vitamins. As for vitamins, human milk in adequate quantity satisfies the infant's requirements with the exception of vitamin D, in which cow milk is also deficient. Cow milk contains more thiamine, riboflavin, pyridoxine, vitamin B_{12}, and folic acid than does human milk. Because of the length of time between the time the cow is milked and the time the baby is fed, some of these vitamins are lost. The losses are, as far as we now know, of little nutritional significance where the B vitamins are concerned, but in the case of Vitamin C it has been shown that the levels of Vitamin C 24 hours after the milk is drawn drops from 20 mg. per liter to 5 mg. per liter. The vitamin C content of human milk, provided that the mother's intake of Vitamin C is adequate, is in the range of 40 mg. per liter, a level which satisfies the baby's requirements.

Minerals. The concentration of minerals is greater in cow milk than in human milk, although human milk supplies adequate amounts of all minerals with the exception of iron and flouride. The quantity of these two minerals in cow milk is also too low to assure adequate intake. Full-term infants, whose mothers had adequate iron intake in pregnancy, will have a store of iron sufficient for the first three to four months, at which time iron must be added to the diet, by giving cereal or meat or ferrous sulfate or using a formula which includes iron. Premature babies, having had less time to store iron, will deplete their store at an earlier age.

OTHER COMPARISONS BETWEEN HUMAN AND COW MILK

Antibodies. Antibodies in human milk seem to offer some protection to infants, although many of the antibodies transferred from the mother are probably involved in the digestive process and are more important in terms of local immunity in the gastrointestinal tract than they are in protection against generalized infection. Stools of breast-fed babies have been shown to have significant amounts of antibody to pathogenic strains of E. coli which play such a major role in infant infection. When mothers have a high serum titer of poliomyelitis antibodies, their infants show a resistance to the attenuated live polio vaccine virus, indicating some transfer of immunity. Antibodies for mumps, vaccinia, influenza, and a Japanese B encephalitis have also been found in human milk, but the extent to which these antibodies protect the baby has not been determined.

Renal solute load. Renal solute load refers to the quantity of urea and electrolytes excreted in the urine. The renal solute load of cow milk, even when it is diluted with water and carbohydrate, is considerably greater than that of human milk. In the healthy infant this difference is of little practical concern, but it becomes significant in a number of pathological conditions, such as the inability of the kidney to concentrate properly, and in conditions in which there is a high insensitive water loss, such as high fever or exposure to high environmental temperatures.

COMMERCIALLY PREPARED FORMULAS

In the United States today a great many infants, instead of receiving human milk or cow milk in unmodified form, are given commercially prepared formulas of various types. Some of these formulas are designed for the "average" baby under normal circumstances; others are planned to meet very specific needs, such as those of the baby with PKU or galactosemia or are used for the baby who does not tolerate cow milk. Some formulas, while initially designed for babies with no special problems, are more adaptable than others for babies who do have special needs, such as the baby with a congenital heart defect.

The type of formula the baby will take in the hospital is prescribed by the doctor. It does, however, seem just as important that a nurse understand why a certain formula is chosen for a particular baby as it is for her to know why she is giving a particular medication. When any baby goes home on formula, especially a baby who has been ill or has special dietary needs, the mother needs to know why that particular formula has been chosen for her baby. Without that kind of understanding, mothers may change formulas in line with the advice of a grandmother or sister. Or they may add sugar to a formula already supplied with carbohydrate or omit sugar when it is needed, on the basis of the formula used for a neighbor's baby.

The discussion of formulas here does not cover all of the available preparations. Its purpose is to point to some of the kinds of problems that formula companies have solved or attempted to solve and some of the ways in which babies may react to specific preparations.

A first group of formulas consists of evaporated milk plus carbohydrate (lactose or corn syrup). Since the fat absorption of butterfat is lower than that of vegetable oils, low birth weight infants on these formulas may lose mild to moderate amounts of fat in their stools so that they fail to gain weight even when their caloric intake is adequate. This, however, seems to present no problem to term babies. Carnalac, Lactim, and Purevap are examples of this type of formula.

A second group of formulas is designed to solve the problem of butterfat absorption by combining nonfat cow milk and vegetable oil. Of this group Varamel is the only formula which does not have added carbohydrate, which must be added when it is prepared. Varamel and Olac have a relatively high renal solute load, but another formula in this group, Formil, has a renal solute load low enough to allow it to be fed in a more concentrated form in order to increase the number of calories per ounce for some low birth weight babies or babies with congenital heart disease. A fourth formula in this group, Modilac, has a lower fat content than other prepared formulas and also a low renal solute load.

Two formulas, Similac and SMA, are prepared by combining whey proteins, nonfat cow milk, carbohydrate (lactose), vegetable oils, minerals, and vitamins, so that the end product resembles human milk in terms of the relation of whey proteins to casein and minerals. The renal solute load of Similac and SMA is sufficiently low that they may be fed in concentrations of 100 calories per 100 ml. or greater (30 calories per ounce). By comparison, Modilac and Formil may be fed in concentrations of 80 calories per 100 ml.; the majority of milk formulas can be fed at concentrations of 64 to 74 calories. Because of this, Similac and SMA are often given to infants who need high caloric feedings, such as infants with congenital heart disease. The fact that these two formulas have low, though adequate, amounts of sodium increases their value for babies with heart problems. A low renal solute load at normal concentrations is also helpful for babies who have a problem concentrating urine, as do infants with diabetes insipidus or renal disease.

One further difference between SMA and Similac and other types of cow milk formulas is their relatively low concentration of radionuclides. This is due to a method of processing which removes a part of the minerals naturally present in milk and substitutes minerals which are free of radionuclide contamination (see page 225).

Protein Milk, Hi-Pro, and Probana are three cow-milk based formulas. Because of low-fat and low-lactose content, Probana is sometimes given to infants with persistent diarrhea. However, as in any formula with a high renal solute load, there is a danger in using it with babies who have an increased extrarenal water loss or diarrhea.

In addition to these formulas, all of which utilize some form of cow milk, there are formulas for those babies who cannot tolerate cow milk. Soy is a common source of protein in many of these formulas, as well as the source of fat. Some form of sugar is added to formulas of this type. Sobee, Mull-soy, Soyalac, and Isomil are soy based formulas. Meat Base Formula and Lambase use beef and lamb hearts respectively as the protein source, with fat and carbohydrate added. Nutramigen is a nonmilk formula which is used in the treatment of galactosemia (see page 220); a similar formula, Lofenelac, has amino acid phenylalanine removed and is specific for the treatment of phenylketonuria (see page 220).

Helping the Mother Who Wants to Breast Feed her Baby

To suppose that breast feeding is instinctive and that the mother who wants to nurse her baby will automatically know how to do so is pure fallacy. Very little human behavior can be considered truly instinctive; most of what we do is dictated by the culture of the society in which we live. In tribal societies and traditional villages where a girl grows up observing her mother, her aunts, and her sisters feeding infants at the breast, she will have learned almost unconsciously a great deal about nursing before she has an infant of her own. But many young mothers in our own society have never seen another infant breast fed. They may live many miles from any female relative, and it is very possible that none of their friends have breast fed their babies. A nurse cannot walk in, hand these mothers their babies, and expect them to know how to begin breast feeding with any degree of success.

Usually (and ideally) the decision to breast feed is made at least several weeks before the baby is born. In the time that remains before delivery the mother can learn something of breast anatomy and physiology and the most effective way to breast feed. Also during these weeks some simple exercises will help to assure that the nipple will be protractile after the baby arrives (Fig. 5–2). The breasts should be bathed only in plain water both before and after delivery. Newton (1967) found that soaps could cause sore, cracked nipples. No creams or toughening agents should be used.

THE ANATOMY AND PHYSIOLOGY OF BREAST FEEDING

Milk is produced by the gland-secreting cells (Fig. 5–3) of the alveolus which surround a central ductule opening. Each

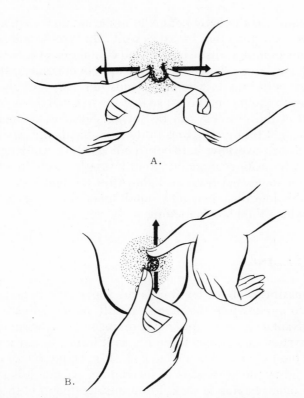

Figure 5-2. Hoffman's exercises to make the nipple more protractile. *A*, The nipple is stimulated by opposing thumbs in a horizontal plane. *B*, The procedure is repeated with thumbs in a vertical plane. The purpose of these exercises is to break adhesions at the base of the nipple and assure maximum protractility. (From Applebaum: *Pediatric Clinics of N. America, 17:207, 1970.*)

alveolus is partially surrounded by a contractile cell (c). As the infant begins to suck, nerve endings in the nipple and areolar margin of the breast are stimulated and impulses are sent to the hypothalamus via the central nervous system and somatic afferent nerves. The hypothalamus first stimulates the anterior pituitary to secrete prolactin, which in turn induces the alveoli to produce milk. Then within two or three minutes, the hypothalamus stimulates the posterior pituitary to secrete oxytocin. Oxytocin causes the contractile cell to contract, squeezing milk through the duct system to the milk reservoir in the areola. This second process is known as the "let-down" reflex.

The presence or absence of the let-down or milk-ejection reflex is related to both physiological and psychological stimuli. The sound of her baby crying can start the flow of milk in a nursing mother. Emotional upsets can interfere with it.

Frequently as the baby begins to nurse at one breast, a let-down of milk occurs in the other breast as well. This excess and sometimes copious flow of milk is disturbing to some mothers. One reported that she felt like an "unwashed milk bottle" most of the time. If the mother will expose both breasts when she feeds her baby and place a hand towel beneath the second breast so that it will catch the overflow, the major part of the problem can be solved. Soft cotton liners can be made or bought for nursing bras (old cotton handkerchiefs make fine ones) to absorb overflow between feedings. Just realizing that this reflex is an indication of adequate milk supply can help a mother to view it in a somewhat positive light. After the first weeks of breast feeding, the let-down becomes conditioned to occur only in the breast at which the baby is feeding.

FIRST FEEDINGS

The maxim in breast feeding is the sooner the better. Allowing the baby to nurse while the mother is still on the delivery table has several advantages. It assures rapid drainage of colostrum that is in the duct system and allows the milk, as it forms, to move down the system to the milk reservoirs (Fig. 5–3). It is believed that colostrum may also aid in the peristalsis of meconium. Lactation is stimulated when the infant begins to suck. From the standpoint of the mother's well being, oxytocin, in addition to causing the contraction of the contractile cells of the breast, also causes uterine smooth muscle to contract and helps to prevent postpartum hemorrhage. (It is this same mechanism that causes the mother to experience the uterine contractions commonly called "afterbirth pains" in the days immediately following delivery.

The practice of putting the baby to breast in the delivery room does not seem to be very common in the United States, although apparently many traditional peoples do so. The use of anesthesia during delivery makes it difficult, not only because the mother is asleep or groggy but also because large amounts of anesthesia make the infant suck poorly, both immediately after delivery and in the first days of his life. Applebaum (1970) recommends minimum analgesia and anesthesia for mothers who plan to breast feed.

If the first feeding is delayed, the baby should not be fed for a few hours after delivery. In some institutions it is the practice to offer the baby a small amount of plain water about an hour before his first breast feeding in order to observe him for signs of excessive mucus.

Before the baby begins to nurse, his mother needs to be in a relaxed, comfortable position. For the first feedings following de-

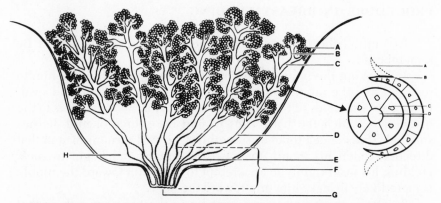

Figure 5-3. *Left,* Diagram of the breast. *A,* Alveolus; *B,* ductule; *C,* duct; *D,* lactiferous duct; *E,* lactiferous sinus; *F,* ampulla; *G,* nipple pore; *H,* areolar margin.

Right, Diagram of an alveolus. *A,* Uncontracted myoepithelial cell; *B,* contracted myoepithelial cell, *C,* gland-secreting cell, *D,* ductule opening. Gland-secreting cells are arranged in a circle about the ductule opening. About the alveolus is a contractile cell. When sucking begins, this cell, under the influence of oxytocin from the pituitary gland, contracts and squeezes milk into the duct system. This is the "let-down" reflex. (From Applebaum: *Pediatric Clinics of N. America, 17*:205, 1970.)

livery, she will usually need and prefer to lie on her side, supported by pillows behind her. This is particularly helpful if the mother has a considerable amount of discomfort from her episiotomy or if there is a contraindication to raising her head.

Later, the mother may prefer to sit with the head of the bed raised and the knee support elevated slightly. After she is able to be out of bed, she may sit in an armchair or a rocker, with a footstool for propping her feet. One advantage to a sitting position, other than personal preference, is the ease it affords in switching the baby from one breast to another if he is to be nursed on both sides. Mothers breast feeding for the first time will need to experiment in order to find the most comfortable position.

The reason some mothers, especially multiparas, experience rather severe uterine contractions while nursing has already been mentioned. Physiologically these contractions are very beneficial to the mother and lead to more rapid involution of the uterus. But occasionally the discomfort is so severe that the mother is found nursing her baby with tears running down her face — she is truly miserable. If medication for pain has been ordered for the mother, and she has been grossly uncomfortable during a previous nursing period, the nurse might suggest that medication be taken in advance of the breast feeding period. If no medication has been ordered, the mother's discomfort should be called to the attention of her obstetrician. The mother should know, too, that these strong contractions will last only a few days and not as long as she is nursing her baby.

PROCEDURE IN BREAST FEEDING

In putting the baby to breast, the following points should be remembered:

1. Stroking the infant's mouth with the nipple will cause him to root and find the nipple with his mouth. Rooting, sucking, and swallowing are examples of true instinctive behavior. Rooting refers to the instinct by which the baby tries to find the source of milk he has smelled. If his cheek touches something, he will turn his face in that direction, open his mouth to grasp the breast, and begin to suck. Holding his head rigidly in an attempt to push him toward the nipple is more likely to make him turn toward the hand.

2. The entire areolar area must be in the baby's mouth so that the milk reservoirs will be compressed as the baby sucks (Fig. 5–3). The baby can be helped to grasp the areolar margin rather than the nipple if it is held between the thumb and forefinger. Not only is this necessary if the baby is to get any milk, but if the baby grasps only the nipple and chews on it, the result may be cracked and fissured nipples.

3. The breast must not press against the infant's nose. Babies can breathe only through their noses; they can't nurse if they can't breathe.

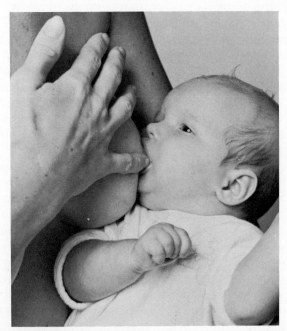

Figure 5–4. Breaking suction by placing a finger at the corner of the baby's mouth before pulling him away will help to prevent sore nipples. (From Applebaum: *Pediatric Clinics of N. America,* 17:211, 1970.)

4. When nursing is completed, the baby may be asleep but still clinging tenaciously to the breast. The suction can be broken by placing the tip of a finger at the corner of the baby's mouth *before* pulling him away, thereby preventing sore nipples (Fig. 5–4).

How long should the baby be nursed at the first feeding? It has been fairly common practice to limit first feeding to two minutes, but the most recent literature suggests nursing each breast for five minutes at each feeding on the first day, increasing the length of time on each following day. These longer periods are believed to lead to more complete drainage of colostrum and consequently better access to milk as it forms and moves down the duct system.

Milk begins to replace colostrum in the second to fourth day after birth. The baby needs to nurse for longer periods now — for as much as 15 minutes on each side at each feeding. He will probably need to nurse about every three hours since breast milk is more readily assimilated than cow milk. Ideally, even in a hospital with fixed feeding hours, breast-fed babies should be fed *on demand.* The baby should not be wakened and taken to his mother when he is not hungry, to be nursed briefly and then returned to the nursery only to be genuinely awake and hungry an hour later. If he is then given a supplemental feeding, the whole mechanism of milk production adequate to meet the baby's needs becomes jeopardized. Moreover, sucking from a rubber nipple requires the use of different muscles than does nursing at the breast (Fig. 5–5).

If breast feeding must be interrupted temporarily for some reason, such as fever in the mother, a tubal ligation, or perhaps a mother who returns home before the baby can be discharged, it can be resumed with a minimum of problems if, first, the mother's breasts are pumped so that she can continue to produce milk and, second, the baby is fed with a rubber-tipped medicine dropper rather than a nipple so that he does not become accustomed to the kind of sucking action nipple feeding requires.

A mother who is nursing her baby should not be given sleeping medications. Not only will such medication make it more difficult to wake her for a middle of the night feeding, but sedatives lower the baby's basal metabolic rate and in so doing also lower the mother's milk production.

Most mothers, and especially those breast feeding for the first time, are concerned about whether the baby is getting enough milk. We have already mentioned that a good let-down reflex is one indication of adequate milk supply. A second indication is the infant's behavior. If he seems satisfied, sleeps well between feedings, and is gaining weight there is little doubt that he is being adequately fed. At one time it was popular to weigh breast-fed babies immediately before and after feedings. Except in rare instances this is not con-

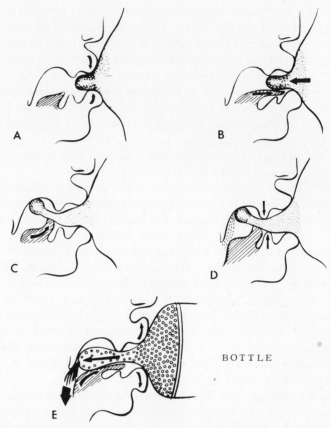

Figure 5–5. The use of muscles in breast and bottle feeding is distinctly different. (From Applebaum: *Pediatric Clinics of N. America, 17:*216, 1970.)

sidered a good idea today. The amount of milk an infant takes varies from feeding to feeding by as much as several ounces. Focusing such close attention on each feeding can add to a mother's anxiety, which may in turn reduce the milk supply.

POSSIBLE BREAST FEEDING PROBLEMS

Difficulties in breast feeding may be physiological or psychological. In both instances nurses can offer some very specific help.

Sore nipples.   Sore nipples at the very beginning of a nursing period are not unusual. Before the let-down occurs, the pressure of the baby's lips on the nipple is stronger than the pressure of the milk in the nipple. Within a couple of minutes, the milk reservoirs fill with milk, the negative pressure is decreased, and the discomfort also disappears. Even this initial discomfort diminishes in the second week or soon afterward.

The nipples of some mothers, especially those with very fair skin, are more tender than those of other mothers. Exposing the nipples to air or to a heat lamp for very brief periods helps to overcome this temporary tenderness. Some physicians prescribe an ointment for nipple soreness; such an ointment is harmless to the baby and does not have to be washed off before feeding. Any drying substance, including soap, should not be used on the nipples.

Breast engorgement. Referring again to Figure 5–3, it is easy to see that when the breast is not emptied milk will accumulate in the duct system. This leads to a rise in pressure not only in the affected duct but in adjacent ducts as well, because of the way in which the ducts are interconnected. There will be "caking" of the breast tissue and a decrease in milk production. If the tension is not relieved, redness, swelling, and eventual mastitis can result. Engorgement creates breathing difficulties for the baby during nursing and can lead to sore nipples for the mother (Fig. 5–6).

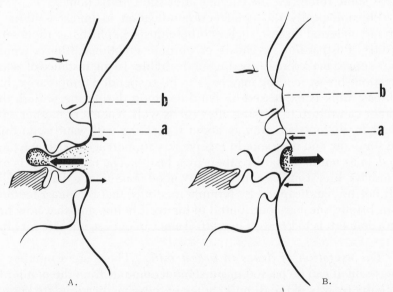

Figure 5-6. The relationship of breast engorgement and sore nipples. *A*, When an infant sucks at a normal breast, his lips compress the areola and fit neatly against the concave nipple-areola junction (a) He also has room to breathe (b). When breasts are engorged, as in *B*, the baby can neither breathe (b) nor grasp the nipple properly (a). Attempts at sucking then damage the nipple. (From Applebaum: *Pediatric Clinics of N. America,* 17:218, 1970.)

The major factor in prevention of engorgement is drainage of at least one breast at each feeding. Breast massage while the baby is nursing helps achieve this, although many babies seem to drain the breasts adequately without massage. Massage is used toward the end of the nursing period when the baby begins to suck intermittently with shallow movements. The mother massages her breast with her fingertips, beginning near the armpits. This helps the milk still in the alveoli to move down the ducts to the milk reservoirs so that the baby will have access to it. As one area of the breast softens, the fingers are moved to an adjacent area until the whole breast is soft. Breast massage is not used in the first minutes of nursing when the baby is making long, continuous sucking movements as it would make the milk flow faster than the baby can handle.

Mothers who are nursing their babies will have many questions after they return home. Some hospitals and physicians provide excellent guide sheets to reinforce what nurses and physicians have told the mothers in the hospital. A comprehensive and very readable book, *The Womanly Art of Breastfeeding,* is available from La Leche League, Franklin Park, Illinois, 60131. La Leche also has a folder, *When You Breastfeed Your Baby,* which briefly summarizes most of the essential information and is available at a minimal cost. No matter how good a job the nursing and medical staffs have done, the mother needs some reference she can use after she returns home.

Physiologically the chief contraindication to breast feeding is chronic maternal disease such as tuberculosis, nephritis, or rheumatic carditis. Postpartum psychosis or chronic emotional illness would also seem to make breast feeding undesirable. In the instance of acute infection, breast feeding may have to be suspended temporarily, but if breast milk is expressed by hand or pump during the period, the mother can return to nursing after she is well. Not every mother who breast feeds feels so strongly about it that she will want to do this. But some do, and they should receive any support and assistance they need so as not to jeopardize their own health. The mother who is too ill to have breast milk expressed may need reassurance that her baby will not be handicapped by formula feedings, that by breast feeding even briefly she has contributed to his well being, and that now her main concern is to get well herself so she can once again care for him.

The excretion of drugs in breast milk. There are a number of drugs which can be passed in substantial amounts from the mother to her baby by way of breast milk. Some of these medications are known to cause difficulty in the baby. For example, thiouracil can cause goitre in the infant; radioactive iodine has a suppressant effect on the development of the thyroid; and reserpine causes nasal stuffiness.

Other drugs such as atropine affect milk production. Smoking also has been shown to decrease the volume of milk excreted, and oral contraceptives may inhibit lactation if given early in the postpartum period.

Following is a list of drugs to be avoided when the mother is breast feeding: diuretics, oral contraceptives, atropine, hallucinogens, morphine, anticoagulants, bromides, antithyroid drugs, antimetabolites, reserpine, and steroids.

In addition, any new or unusual drug and excess amounts of any drug should not be taken by nursing mothers.

Helping the Mother Who Wants to Bottle Feed

Just as we cannot hand a mother her baby and expect her to nurse it without some instruction and assistance, neither can we assume that the mother who plans to bottle feed her baby can do so without guidance, both as to feeding techniques and the method of preparing the formula. The mother should be aware that while the baby is being fed he needs (1) to be warm and dry, (2) to be held in a semi-sitting position, (3) to drink from a nipple that is always filled with milk, and (4) to be given frequent opportunities to burp.

Most mothers seem to be familiar with "over-the-shoulder" burping. There is nothing wrong with this; it is very satisfying to have a warm, well-fed sleepy baby lying with his head on your shoulder. An alternate method is to hold the infant in a sitting position, his chest supported with one hand while his back is gently rubbed or patted with the other hand. After feeding, the baby should be laid on his side or stomach, so that if there should be some regurgitation, the milk will not be aspirated.

Many hospitals now buy formula already prepared and in bottles, a procedure which is apparently more economical than running a hospital formula room and which seems to have the added advantages of greater sterility and safety. Once the bottles and nipples are used they are thrown away. Bottles are kept at room temperature and are not warmed. Occasionally this may disturb a mother because our traditions tell us that baby's milk should be warm, although studies some years ago demonstrated that babies who were fed only formula taken directly from the refrigerator could thrive. A formula too hot poses many more dangers than a cool to cold one.

When do bottle feedings begin? The trend is toward earlier feeding, within the first 12 to 24 hours. Plain water, rather than glucose water, is now considered best for the first two to three feedings because the aspiration of glucose water has been found to be as damaging to lung tissue as the aspiration of milk. First feedings usually measure 5 to 15 cc., depending upon how awake the baby is, with increases of about 15 cc. each day so that by the end of the first week the baby is taking approximately 2½ ounces (75 cc.). The size of the baby has a direct bearing on the amount of formula he needs and often on the amount he seems to want. The ideas that "if a little is good, a lot is wonderful" and "bigger babies are better babies" seem to be a part of our cultural heritage, but there are distinct disadvantages to overfeeding a newborn. An immediate danger is that the infant's stomach may become distended, causing him to vomit and aspirate. As a long-range consideration, the possibility has been advanced that overfeeding in infancy conditions the baby physiologically to eat more food than he actually needs and is one factor responsible for the high level of obesity in the population of the United States. Whether obesity results because the baby overeats in his first weeks or because the same mother who takes pride in the large quantities consumed by her newborn continues to overfeed the child throughout his infancy is a moot question at this time. However, the presence of obesity in our society is in itself reason enough to give mothers some guidance about feeding and about a philosophy of feeding.

After the first week, about 2 to 2½ ounces of formula per pound of body weight is the rough rule for feeding in the first month. The length of time between feedings and the amount of formula taken at each feeding vary; the mother needs to know this so that she will not be overly concerned. Consistent failure to feed well at nearly every feeding, on the other hand, is often the first indication of illness—infection or congenital heart disease, for example—and needs to be reported to a physician.

A baby, who begins gaining weight on the fourth day of life, who has regained his birthweight somewhere between 7 and 12 days, and who gains, on the average, 6 to 8 ounces a week after that, is likely to be well nourished. The fact that he also sleeps well between feedings and is generally content, also confirms that probability. Fluctuations in weight gain are normal, periods of rapid growth being followed by slower gains and vice versa. Baby scales at home can sometimes do more harm than good when they focus undue attention on daily and even weekly changes.

FORMULA PREPARATION

There are several alternatives in formula preparation today. The entire formula may be purchased in a disposable nurser, a system which is easy, aseptic—and somewhat expensive, so that most likely it is the upper-middle-class mother who is able to take advantage of this convenience and who is also able to prepare the formula correctly and with a minimum of difficulty.

Expense can be minimized by using two to three bottles which are washed thoroughly after each feeding with cold and then warm water and then boiled and kept sterile in the same pan. Bottles are prepared individually as the baby requires them, a single can of formula or evaporated milk being opened at a time and kept refrigerated. Powdered formulas have the advantage of not requiring refrigeration, making them ideal where cold storage space is limited or inadequate. They are also very useful for the occasional supplementary feeding of a breast-fed baby, since the unused portion will not spoil. Boiled water is used if the formula requires the addition of water. Such a method eliminates the need for a large sterilizer and extensive refrigerator room for a number of prepared bottles and saves a good deal of time out of each morning.

Perhaps the hardest thing for the mother in financial distress to do is throw away that portion of the formula which the baby leaves in the bottle, particularly if a great deal remains. The temptation is to refrigerate it and then rewarm it and offer it again at the next feeding. Meanwhile bacteria have had several hours in which to multiply. Mother needs not only to understand why this can be harmful to her baby; she needs concrete suggestions as to how the left-over milk can be used, such as in the making of puddings.

Feeding Schedules

Whether the baby is breast or bottle fed, a constant concern of mothers leaving the hospital is how often the baby should be fed. "Feeding by the clock and not by guess or when the baby cries" was the advice in a 1922 nutrition text, *Dietetics for Nurses*. After that we went through a period in which food was offered at every cry, but now we have come to the conclusion that the answer lies somewhere between the two extremes.

It is easy for a mother to get the idea from her hospital experience that there is a specific time for feeding a baby because her baby has been brought to her on a rather rigid schedule. When she gets home and her baby begins to cry at all the wrong times she is likely to be distressed, particularly if this is her first baby. She needs to know that not every cry represents hunger. She also needs to understand that because babies have relatively immature central nervous systems and digestive systems, they are somewhat erratic in their eating habits in the first couple of months.

Feeding on demand, as it is currently understood, does not mean a complete absence of any schedule. It is more nearly a substitution of a schedule suited to the needs of an individual baby rather than an arbitrary schedule based on the assumption that certain hours of the day are the best ones at which to feed every infant. The parents of Baby C, an 8½-pound boy born two weeks before his expected date, kept a record of how often their baby ate during his first weeks home from the hospital. They found he was nursing every three hours except for one two-hour interval which occurred at approximately the same time each day and one four-hour interval, resulting in a total of seven feedings. By the beginning of his fourth week he had lengthened the time between feedings so that he was nursing six times in 24 hours. Still the intervals were not equal; there was a three-hour span in the afternoon followed by a five- to six-hour stretch after supper.

How can an inexperienced mother interpret her baby's cry? Crying that is accompanied by rooting behavior, as if the baby were searching for the nipple, and is not relieved, even when the baby is held, probably means that he is hungry. If he is truly hungry, allowing him to cry for 20 or 30 minutes until he is exhausted will generally mean that he will go to sleep before he has had as much milk as he really needs and will then awaken in a fairly short time to begin the cycle again.

It seems worth considering whether "demand" feeding might not be a possibility in hospital units in which rooming-in is not available. It is particularly important for breast-fed babies, as we have already discussed, but it has something to offer every baby.

Infants with Special Feeding Problems

As the discussion of formulas indicated there are a number of instances—some of them fairly common, others relatively rare—in which special kinds of feedings are necessary. Low birth weight infants, babies with congenital heart disease, babies with cleft lips or palates, and infants with inborn errors in metabolism such as PKU and galactosemia need special attention. Later in the neonatal period, evidence of allergy to cow milk or conditions with associated vomiting and diarrhea may also require special kinds of feedings.

LOW BIRTH WEIGHT INFANTS

Infants with a low birth weight, particularly those born prematurely, have several potential problems with feeding. Even more than term newborns, low birth weight infants can differ greatly from one another, and so their feeding must be planned on a very individualized basis (Fig. 5–7).

Since neither the skeletal muscles nor the smooth muscles of the gastrointestinal tract are as well developed in the premature baby as in term babies, premature babies suck less vigorously and have a greater tendency toward abdominal distention. In addition, sucking, swallowing, and gag reflexes are less well developed and may be entirely absent in a very young infant (in terms of gestational age).

The smaller the baby, the smaller his stomach capacity, hence the necessity for smaller, more frequent feedings. If the baby is overfed the likelihood of regurgitation and the associated danger of aspiration are very real.

There also appears to be a difference in the physiology of digestion in prematurely born infants, in that they are less able to handle fats. Protein and carbohydrate digestion is similar to that of a term baby, but if prematures are fed cow milk with none of the fat removed, a great deal of fat is then excreted in the stool.

There are differences of opinion among competent pediatricians concerning numerous aspects of premature feeding—the best choice of food, the optimum number of calories per pound of body weight, and the time at which feedings should be started. Very rarely would these decisions be made by a nurse at this time, but it seems important to recognize that honest differences of opinion do exist and that future research may change some of our ideas about premature feeding just as it may change many of our other current ideas about nursing care.

What is the best type of feeding for premature babies? In England breast milk is till considered highly desirable. One consideration in breast feeding is the inability of many premature babies to suck with sufficient vigor to nurse. Under these circumstances breast milk is often expressed and fed to the baby by bottle or dropper. Even when the mother leaves the hospital several weeks before her baby is ready for discharge, she may continue to express milk at home and send it to the hospital. For very small infants, breast milk is diluted and carbohydrates are added during the first week (Craig, 1969).

In emphasizing the value of human milk, one British physician points out that while weight gain will be more rapid in babies who are given a higher intake of protein (as is advocated by some pediatricians in the United States), the advantage of the easy digestibility of human milk with reduced abdominal distention and regurgitation is equally important (Vulliamy, 1967).

Nelson sees human milk as being satisfactory for premature babies weighing more than 4 pounds (2000 gm.) but inadequate in phosphorous, protein, and possibly calcium for smaller premature

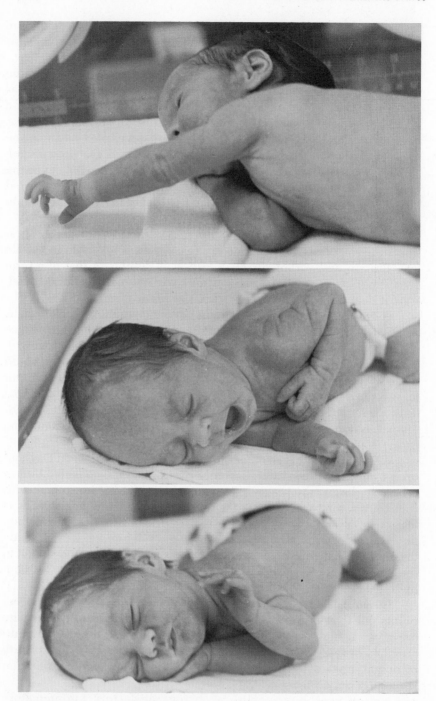

Figure 5–7.   The development of feeding behavior in a premature baby. Top to bottom: prefeeding tension, rooting, and hand-mouth activity. (From O'Grady: *American J. Nursing,* 71:736, 1971.)

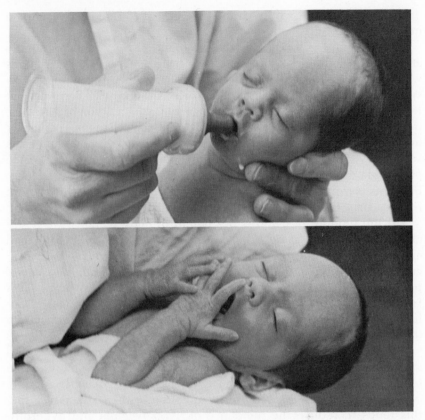

Figure 5-7 (continued). Top, characteristic weak grasp of the nipple but strong suck. Bottom, satiety and relief of tension. (From O'Grady: *American J. Nursing,* 71:736, 1971.)

infants. It is suggested that these smaller infants need 4.0 gm. of protein per kilogram of body weight, nearly twice the estimated need of a term infant. Mineral content is higher in cow milk than in breast milk, an advantage for small babies in one respect, but a cause for concern if water intake is limited or water losses are high so that the minerals cannot be properly excreted.

The number of calories per pound of body weight needed by the small baby is also subject to discussion. Some feel that the total calories per pound should be approximately the same for premature and term, full-sized infants. They argue that the increased requirements brought about by increased basal need, more rapid growth, and increased fecal loss if unskimmed milk is used are counterbalanced by the relative inactivity of the small baby. Others suggest that the premature infant needs 60 to 80 calories per pound or more because of his accelerated growth in contrast to the 40 to 50 calories per pound needed by the full-sized newborn.

The amount of formula a small premature baby is able to tolerate at a single feeding is quite small — as little as 3 to 5 cc. for babies weighing in the neighborhood of 2 pounds. It is the physician's responsibility to order the amount as well as the kind of formula, but just as a nurse must be able to recognize when the amount of a medication ordered is excessive, so too should a nurse realize when an order for formula is likely to exceed the baby's capacity. For example, to a surgeon who cares primarily for adults and older children, an ounce of formula every three hours may seem a very small quantity indeed, but if his patient is a newborn weighing 2½ pounds, even this amount is more than the baby can handle.

If the number of calories per pound of body weight is to be increased and at the same time the infant is able to take only small amounts of formula, the caloric content of the formula can be increased above the approximately 67 calories per 100 ml. (20 calories per ounce) that is commonly offered to average sized newborns. This is done either by supplementing the formula with additional carbohydrate or by increasing the concentration of the formula preparation (liquid or powder).

Just as there are differences of opinion as to what should be fed to premature infants, there are also differing ideas about when feedings should be started. The chief argument for early feeding (within the first 12 hours after birth and often by the sixth hour) is that this tends to reduce the incidence of hypoglycemia and hyperbilirubinemia. The risk of vomiting and aspiration is considered minimal if the feedings are small and given by an experienced nurse.

The rationale for postponing feeding until the premature infant is 36 to 72 hours old or even older is that the comparative inactivity of very small babies and their lowered heat production (if body heat is conserved in a warm incubator) reduce the immediate need for calories, water, and electrolytes.

Methods of feeding low birth weight infants. Careful observation of each infant can help determine the best method of feeding. There are several alternatives for feeding the premature infant. Direct breast feeding or bottle feeding is only possible for a few relatively large and vigorous premature babies whose sucking and swallowing reflexes are well developed. If the baby is able to swallow well but seems too weak to suck, he can sometimes be fed with a medicine dropper.

When the baby has neither sucking nor swallowing reflexes, or when sucking and swallowing seem to exhaust him, gavage feeding is necessary, either through the nose or mouth. The technique of gavage feeding is as follows:

1. For very small infants of 2 to 3 pounds a #8 gavage tube is used; in larger babies a #10 tube may be satisfactory.

2. The tube is measured from the bridge of the nose to the xiphoid process, if it is to be inserted through the mouth, and from the bridge of the nose to the lobe of the ear to the xiphoid process, if it is to be passed through the nose. The catheter may be premarked, but since there are all sizes of even tiny infants, the tube should still be measured at each feeding.

3. A small quantity of sterile water run through the tube before it is inserted assures its patency.

4. Nasal catheters may be lubricated with sterile water; oral catheters do not need to be lubricated.

5. After the catheter is passed, the baby should be observed for a moment for signs of dyspnea, an indication that the tube may be in the trachea rather than the esophagus.

6. If the catheter is not already attached to a syringe, the syringe is attached and the formula poured into it and allowed to flow by gravity.

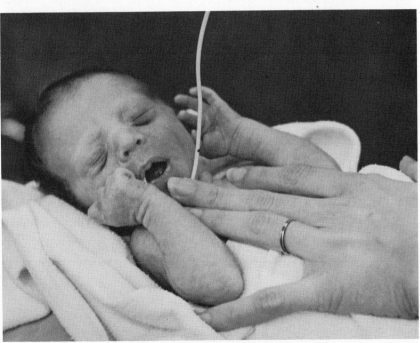

Figure 5–8. Hand-mouth gestures and a capacity to "mouth" the feeding tube are indications that this 3½-pound premature baby will soon take feedings from a nipple instead of a tube. (From O'Grady: *American J. Nursing,* 71:737, 1971.)

7. If the tube is not to be left in place it is pinched and removed when every drop of formula has passed through the tube.

8. A baby should be "burped" following gavage feeding just as he is after a bottle or breast feeding. If he must remain in the incubator he can be held in a sitting position and have his back gently stroked toward the neck.

9. After feeding the baby is placed on his abdomen or right side.

If a baby begins to suck on his gavage tube during feedings, he may be ready to graduate to a medicine dropper (Fig. 5–8). Bottle feedings should begin gradually, initially at only one feeding during the 24-hour period, and gradually increased when the baby shows that he is not overly tired from sucking on the nipple.

THE BABY WITH A CLEFT PALATE

Since the hard palate is essential to sucking, the baby with a cleft palate may have to be fed by some means other than breast or bottle. Some babies with cleft palates can be successfully bottle fed; others seem to feed more easily with a Breck feeder. Only the tip of the nipple should be in the baby's mouth. Then, with a little practice, the baby will gently suck the tip. Nipple holes need to be small enough to keep the baby from being flooded with milk which will then flow into his respiratory tract, depositing curds in the nasal passages and making the danger of infection of both the nasopharynx and the ears a very real possibility. Holding the baby upright to feed him also helps to prevent this regurgitation.

If the cleft is large the baby may push the nipple up into the open area with his tongue. This can be avoided both by keeping most of the nipple outside of his mouth and by positioning it at an angle to the cleft.

Once the baby has begun to feed well his mother should begin to feed him under nursing supervision. I am continually amazed at how well and how quickly many mothers are able to feed their babies with a Breck feeder. The baby is ready for discharge (barring other complications) when the mother feels comfortable about caring for him and feeding him.

THE INFANT WHO IS TO BE FED THROUGH
A GASTROSTOMY TUBE

The most common reason for gastrostomy feedings in newborns is the repair of a tracheo-esophageal fistula. The tube is inserted during surgery and sutured in place. Initial feedings of glucose and water (5 to 10 cc.) begin on the second to third day after surgery. If they are well tolerated they are followed by small amounts of milk which are gradually increased as the baby shows his ability to handle it. Vomiting or abdominal distention are signs that feedings need to be decreased for a period.

The gastrostomy tube is connected through the hole in the top of the isolette to an asepto-syringe without the bulb. It is never clamped until the baby is taking oral feedings and then only during the feedings themselves. This allows any gas and the contents of the baby's stomach to reflux up the tube and into the syringe when the baby cries or strains. Because of this reflux there is no advantage to rinsing the tube with water after each feeding. If the baby is able to tolerate the extra amount of fluid that would be used to rinse the tube, his milk intake should be increased, giving him needed calories and nutrients as well as liquid.

HYPERALIMENTATION AS A MEANS OF INFANT FEEDING

Infants with congenital malformations of the gastrointestinal tract may survive surgery and then, because they cannot be adequately nourished, die of starvation. Traditional intravenous fluids containing electrolytes and sugars reduce body wasting, but they do not contain the protein that is essential for the maintenance of body tissue.

Hyperalimentation is an attempt to remedy this situation by giving the infant intravenously a solution which contains glucose, protein in the form of fibrinhydrolysate (Aminosol), vitamins, and electrolytes. In addition plasma transfusions are given to provide the baby with essential fatty acids and trace minerals. Calcium and phosphorus are given when laboratory studies show that they are needed. Electrolytes are checked twice weekly and they too are added to the solution as necessary.

The catheter through which the solution is delivered is inserted under local anesthesia into the right external jugular vein and guided into the superior vena cava, this location being chosen because the high blood flow of the superior vena cava helps to avoid inflammation and thrombosis in the vein. The proximal end of the catheter (i.e., the end which is not in the vena cava) is passed from the neck subcutaneously to a stab wound in the parietal area of the scalp (Fig. 5–9). This procedure serves three purposes:

1. By displacing the point of the catheter entrance from the skin exit site, additional protection against infection is provided.

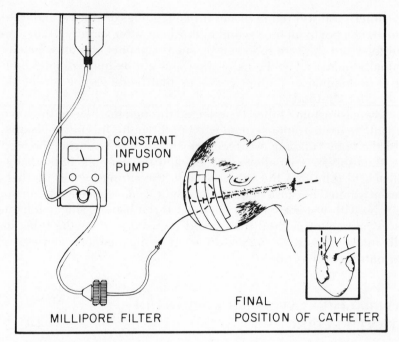

CONSTANT
INFUSION
PUMP

MILLIPORE FILTER

FINAL
POSITION OF CATHETER

Figure 5-9. Technique of catheter insertion and delivery of fluids for total intra-venous alimentation.

2. Contamination by the baby's oral and nasal secretions becomes less likely.

3. The catheter is out of reach of the baby's ever-searching hands. After the catheter has been inserted an x-ray is taken to insure proper placement.

The intravenous system includes a millipore filter, which serves to remove particles or micro-organisms which may have contaminated the solution from the system before they can reach the baby, and a peristaltic constant-infusion pump (such as a Harvard or Holter pump) to insure that the solution is delivered at a constant rate throughout the 24 hours. Both filter and pump are changed at least every three days.

Because there are a number of serious complications possible with hyperalimentation, constant nursing attention is an absolute necessity. Septicemia is a major danger, because the glucose-protein solution is a nearly perfect medium for the growth of bacteria, particularly monilia. The prevention of infection depends upon careful technique not only at the time the catheter is inserted but throughout the period it is in place. Frequent changing of the intravenous set-up has already been mentioned. The catheter should never be used for the administration of medications or for the withdrawal of blood; both procedures heighten the possibility of contamination. A careful record of temperature and frequent blood cultures are important in detecting infection as early as possible. If the catheter is needed for more than 30 days it is usually inserted on the opposite side.

Fever may occur in the baby in the absence of positive blood culture or other signs of infection. It has been suggested that fever of this nature may be an antigenic reaction to peptides in the solution. Such fever begins early, usually within four hours after therapy has been started, and may subside within a week.

The utilization of the amino acid solution by the baby's body is dependent upon the addition of a quantity of glucose sufficient to stimulate insulin production. The insulin, in turn, stimulates both the transport of amino acids into the cell and the synthesis of protein. If relatively large amounts of glucose are not given, the amino acids will be utilized for energy by the body rather than for the synthesis of protein.

However, the high quantity of glucose necessary (as much as twice that normally given to infants) can cause a rapid and severe dehydration. Urines are tested for glucose at least every six hours during the first days of treatment. If two or more consecutive samples reveal a 3+ or 4+ glucose by the Clinitest method, either the rate of the infusion or the glucose content of the solution is decreased. Some physicians add insulin to the solution under these circumstances. Others begin therapy with a 10% solution of glucose during the first 24 hours, followed by a 15% solution during the next 24 hours, and a 20% solution thereafter to prevent this initial glycosuria.

Hypertonic sugar solutions in combination with amino acids may, after several days of administration, lead to a hypoglycemic response within the body, whether insulin has been added or not. If insulin is added it is generally not needed after the first few days. It is important to be watchful for signs of hypoglycemia at this time.

As in all newborns, weight gain is a significant observation. If the baby was not malnourished before the feedings began and has no infection, weight gain may be comparable to that of a normal infant, although it will also be influenced by the infant's original problem. If the baby was nutritionally depleted at the time therapy started, his weight is likely to remain constant for several days even though he shows other signs of improvement.

A number of other side effects are possible including demineralization of bone and cerebral edema. However, in spite of the hazards, which admittedly are great, with very good care hyperalimentation does indeed mean a difference between life and death for some newborns.

INFANTS WITH CONGENITAL HEART DEFECTS

Not every baby with a congenital heart defect will have feeding problems. There are, however, two possible sources of difficulty. The baby may tire so easily that he takes an insufficient amount of formula, or he may choke and become dyspneic, and the mother will discontinue feeding him. Yet because of an increased cardiac work load and an increased expenditure of energy he actually needs more calories than usual. When this happens it is necessary to use a formula which increases the concentration of calories within the limits of a small fluid intake. In addition the formula should have a fairly low concentration of sodium and a low renal solute load.

THE INFANT WITH PHENYLKETONURIA

The inheritance of phenylketonuria, an autosomal recessive trait, is described in Chapter 1 (page 25). Mass screening for the presence of phenylalanine in urine or blood is now required by law in a number of states. This is only the preliminary step in the recognition of PKU, for there are other conditions in which phenylalanine is found in urine and blood. Children with these conditions other than PKU will be harmed by a low phenylalanine diet and the use of Lofenalac, which is essential for children with PKU.

The dietary treatment of PKU must be constantly monitored by regular blood testing (daily during the first week, then weekly until the baby is two months old, twice a month from two months to a year and monthly after that) and urine testing (daily during the first month, twice weekly until the baby is six months old, weekly until his first birthday, and twice a month from that time on). The reason for this constant monitoring—one which parents must understand—is that while a normal dietary level of phenylalanine will cause mental retardation, a diet too low in this essential amino acid will not meet the baby's growth requirements. In the newborn period the restriction of phenylalanine is met by the use of Lofenalac with a small amount of cow milk added to the diet to provide the phenylalanine needed for growth. Later, strained foods low in protein are added to the diet (Fomon, 1967).

THE INFANT WITH GALACTOSEMIA

Like PKU, galactosemia is also inherited as an autosomal recessive trait. An infant with galactosemia lacks a specific enzyme—galactose-1-phosphate uridyl transferase. Because of this he is unable to metabolize lactose and galactose, so that galactose-1-phosphate accumulates in the red cells (hence galactosemia), and reducing sugars, for which specific tests are available, are found in the urine. Glucose, however, is not present in the urine.

The symptoms of galactosemia are not always easy to detect. Common findings are failure to gain weight and jaundice, which persists beyond the first week unlike physiological jaundice. There may also be subcutaneous bleeding, vomiting, diarrhea, and subsequent dehydration. If the disease is not detected the baby usually deteriorates progressively with physical and mental retardation, signs of malnutrition, cirrhosis of the liver, and cataracts.

The treatment is simple in theory. Since lactose occurs naturally only in milk, the newborn infant who shows signs of galactosemia is fed a formula, such as Nutramigen, which does not contain milk. Soy bean formulas have also been found to be satisfactory if the baby does not have diarrhea. Problems in feeding arise as the baby grows older and needs a more varied diet since milk and milk-components such as lactose, casein, and whey are incorporated into so many commercial foods. Lactose, for example, is added to many canned and frozen fruits and vegetables during processing.

The removal of lactose from the diet changes the course of galactosemia markedly, even when the condition has gone unrecognized for several months. Appetite improves, vomiting, diarrhea, and jaundice subside, and liver function improves. In some instances, cataracts disappear (Cornblath and Schwartz, 1967).

THE BABY WITH CYSTIC FIBROSIS

In the newborn nursery the recognition that a baby has an obstruction due to meconium ileus (see page 173) leads to the diagnosis of cystic fibrosis. Only about 10 per cent of cystic fibrosis babies are diagnosed this early, the remaining 90 per cent being recognized in later infancy or early childhood. Obstruction in the bronchi may not appear for weeks or even years after birth. The characteristic bulky foul stools may or may not be evident in the newborn period.

Several dietary changes are necessary for babies with cystic fibrosis. Total caloric intake has to be increased because of the abnormally high loss of calories in stools. Fecal losses are reduced, but not entirely eliminated, by giving the baby pancreatic enzymes before each feeding. A formula is chosen that is high in protein and carbohydrate but has a low to moderate fat content, the fat being one that is readily absorbed. Fomon suggests Olac as the best choice because corn oil is the source of fat; Nutramigen (which also utilizes corn oil) and Probana are also used. Banana flakes may be added to the diet to supplement caloric intake.

Water-miscible preparations of the fat-soluble vitamins A, D, E, and K are given to the baby. The dosage of vitamin D is adjusted to blood levels of calcium, phosphorus, and alkaline phosphatase and to wrist x-rays, while the dosage of vitamin E is correlated with levels of blood alpha-tocopherol. The adequacy of vitamin K intake is determined by checking prothrombin time at intervals of one to two months.

Nutritional Deprivation in the Newborn Period

What happens when nutrition is not adequate in the newborn period? Obvious effects may be inadequate growth in length and failure to gain weight. It is strongly suspected that nutritional deficiency may affect the central nervous system as well. The results of nutritional deficiencies on the central nervous systems of very young animals have been demonstrated in a succession of studies over nearly 50 years. Rats with inadequate caloric intake during the period of most rapid postnatal brain growth exhibited marked retardation (Scrimshaw, 1968). Severe undernutrition has been shown to influence the chemical composition of the brains of infant pigs so that their brains resemble those of considerably younger pigs (Fomon, 1967).

Even more important than a lack of calories is a lack of protein. A number of animal studies have examined protein deficiency in the presence of adequate caloric intake. In a London study, weanling rats, piglets, and puppies born of well-nourished mothers were fed diets adequate in calories but severely deficient in protein. The animals showed signs of degenerative changes in their nerve cells. Electroencephalograms were abnormal; one researcher noted certain resemblances in the EEG's of these pigs and those of children with kwashiorkor, a condition involving severe protein deficiency (Nelson, 1959).

The animal studies showed that the time at which nutritional restriction occurs is significant. Food restriction prior to weaning was associated with permanent changes in the size and chemical composition of the brain in rats. Food restriction for an equal period of time, but imposed at the time of weaning, also led to brain alterations, but these later alterations disappeared during a subsequent period of adequate nutrition (Winick, 1966).

Evidence from another study is corroborative. Abnormalities in myelination of rat nervous systems brought about by undernutrition after weaning (age 3 weeks) until 11 weeks of age was corrected by normal diet between 11 and 19 weeks (Fomon, 1967).

Lack of specific vitamins and minerals also led to deformities in animals studied.

In human infants prodigious development of the brain occurs after birth. Head circumference increases from approximately 34 cm. at birth to 46 cm. at the first birthday and then at a rate of roughly 0.5 cm. each succeeding year until the adult size of 52 cm. is reached. Similarly the weight of the brain, about 400 gm. at birth, more than doubles in the first year to 1000 gm. and continues to grow for many years. Brain mass increases until about 25 years of age.

In addition to these changes in size, a major change in brain structure occurs in the first years of life. At birth, the infant brain contains most of the ten billion neurons that it will have during the individual's lifetime. But neurons are packed very densely in the small infant skull. The neurons enlarge and the connecting links between them increase in number and complexity very rapidly until the age of four and more slowly until the age of 12. Because of this, it is believed that when nutritional deficiencies, particularly protein deficiencies, are severe enough to limit height and weight gains in the first years of life, brain development and the related motor, language, and adaptive behavior is also likely to be affected. The earlier the period of deprivation, the more serious the consequences. In studies of children with kwashiorkor, rates of progress in behavioral development were related to the age at which the children were admitted to the hospital. Relatively little progress was made by children who had kwashiorkor at the age of three to six months; there was better development in children who were 15 to 29 months at the time they were admitted. Children who were 37 to 41 months at the time of admission demonstrated the best rate of behavior development (Fomon, 1967).

MATERNAL DEPRIVATION AND UNDERNUTRITION

Whitten (1969) has proposed that undernutrition may not always be recognized for what it is. Studies in the 1940's (Spitz, 1945; Talbot, 1947; Fried and Mayer, 1948) suggested that emotional deprivation in an infant or young child could be directly responsible for the child's failure to grow and thrive. Whitten points out that none of these psychological studies determined the babies' caloric intakes. His own study involved 13 maternally deprived infants, 11 of whom gained weight at an accelerated rate when they were fed adequately in a hospital environment which deliberately simulated their home situations, i.e., they were confined in windowless rooms and were neither talked to or smiled at nor held for feeding. The two babies who did not gain remained anorectic. Both of them had a history of repeated attempts by the mother to force feed them. It was reported that one father, reacting to his baby's poor intake, had tried to "ram a hamburger down the infant's throat."

In a second group of seven infants, all seven gained rapidly in their own homes when they were fed an adequate diet in the presence of a public health nurse acting as observer. Whitten believes that there was no improvement in home environment which could account for the increase in weight. For example, one infant, who was visited 42 times by the nurse (three times a day for 14 days) was found alone in a crib in a back room on every occasion. Forty-one times the baby was returned to the back room before the nurse left. Yet during the 14-day period the baby gained 26 ounces.

A second infant gained 22 ounces during an eight-day feeding program in spite of the fact that during that period his family was evicted for nonpayment of rent and he had been physically abused by his father.

When the mothers were questioned prior to the period of the observed feedings most of them had claimed that their babies ate adequately. During supervised home feeding, however, some mothers began to realize that their babies actually had been underfed.

The Environmental Contamination of Milk

As mentioned earlier, in Western society we have the knowledge and means to deal with the biological contamination of milk through pasteurization, sterilization, and refrigeration, although these means are still not used by everyone in our society. Environmental contamination, on the other hand, is a potential threat to all infants regardless of socioeconomic factors. Two sources of environmental contamination of the milk given to newborns are DDT and radioactive material.

DDT. In 1969 the DDT residue level in human milk was reported to be 0.1 to 0.2 parts per million, two to four times the level permitted by the Food and Drug Administration in cow milk that is to be shipped in interstate commerce. One reason the level is higher in human milk is that DDT becomes more concentrated at each step in the food chain. Animals, poultry, and fish all store DDT in their tissues and pass it on to humans as meat and milk. Women also secrete a higher percentage of DDT in their milk than do cows. Just what effect these high levels of DDT have, or will have, is not directly known. Animal studies have implicated DDT as a cancer-causing substance, which at least raises the question of a similar possibility in humans. In some animal populations DDT has apparently affected reproduction and has led to a decline in some species (Wurster, 1970).

Is the problem of DDT contamination of such magnitude that mothers should no longer nurse their infants? Wurster feels that this is not the answer. Other foods also contain DDT, and since DDT is also known to pass the placental barrier, even before birth, the baby has already stored DDT in his tissues. Two suggestions for nursing mothers are avoiding household sprays containing DDT or other chlorinated hydrocarbons and minimizing the intake of eggs, fatty meats, and fish.

Radiation. Another source of potential environmental contamination of infant milk is radiation. As in the past, the major source of radiation today is from natural sources, such as cosmic rays and atmospheric and terrestrial radiation. Man-made sources, including diagnostic x-ray (the most important), therapeutic x-ray, and luminous dials account for about seven times as much radiation as fall-out. Even if there should be no further testing of atomic weapons in the atmosphere, the increasing peacetime uses of atomic energy as power sources and the expanding use of radioisotopes in medicine and industry will increase radiation in the environment. The hazard from fall-out, probably the most feared source, is small in comparison with the potential radioactive contamination from sources which we tend to accept as necessary.

Radioactivity relates to infant feeding on several counts. Unlike DDT residuals, the radioactive content of human milk is considerably lower than that of cow milk. The length of time during which milk is stored affected some radioisotopes. For example, since only 0.6 per cent of the original amount of iodine-131 remains in cow milk after the milk has been stored for two months, it cannot be considered a real hazard in evaporated and powdered milk formulas. Barium-140 and Strontium-89 also have short half-lives and are biologically important only for a few months after a bomb has been exploded. Strontium-90, on the other hand, has a half-life of 20 years (half-life being the time required for half of the atoms of a radioactive substance to disintegrate). Increases in the concentration of Strontium-90 occurred in the United States in 1963 and 1964 following the atomic testing of 1961.

As mentioned earlier in this chapter, SMA, Similac, Nutramigen, and soy-based formulas use calcium from uncontaminated sources predominately and are therefore very low in strontium contamination. It is conceivable that this could influence infant feeding in future generations.

Bibliography

Applebaum, R. M.: The Modern Management of Successful Breast Feeding. *Pediatric Clinics of North America, 17*:203, 1970.

Arena, J. M.: Contamination of the Ideal Food. *Nutrition Today, 5,4*:2 (Winter), 1970.

Bain, K.: The Incidence of Breast Feeding in Hospitals in the United States. *Pediatrics, 2*:313, 1948.

Beal, V. A.: Breast and Formula Feeding of Infants. *Journal of the American Dietetic Association, 55*:31, 1969.

Birchfield, M.: A Mother's Views on Breast Feeding. *American Journal of Nursing, 63,3*:88 (March), 1963.

Cornblath, M., and Schwartz, R.: *Disorders of Carbohydrate Metabolism in Infancy.* Philadelphia, W. B. Saunders, 1967.

Craig, W. S.: *Care of the Newly Born Infant.* Baltimore, Williams and Wilkins Co., 1969.

Filler, R. M., Eraklis, A. J., Rubin, V. G., and Das, J. B.: Long-Term Total Parenteral Nutrition in Infants. *New England Journal of Medicine, 281*:589, 1969.

Fomon, S. J.: *Infant Nutrition.* Philadelphia, W. B. Saunders, 1967.

Fried, R. and Mayer, M. F.: Socio-emotional Factors Accounting for Growth Failure in Children Living in an Institution. *Journal of Pediatrics, 33*:444, 1948.

Goldberger, E.: *A Primer of Water, Electrolyte and Acid-Base Syndromes.* 4th Edition. Philadelphia, Lea and Febiger, 1970.

Harley, L. M.: Fussing and Crying in Young Infants. *Clinical Pediatrics, 8*:138, 1969.

How the Nurse Can Help the Breastfeeding Mother. Franklin Park, Illinois, La Leche League International.

How to Avoid Difficulties in Early Breastfeeding. St. Louis, Missouri, St. Mary's Hospital.

Hurley, L. S.: The Consequences of Fetal Impoverishment. *Nutrition Today, 3,4*:3 (December), 1968.

Kerr, G. R., Chamove, A. S., and Harlow, H. F.: Environmental Deprivation: Its Effect on the Growth of Infant Monkeys. *Journal of Pediatrics, 75*:833, 1969.

Meyer, H. F.: Breast Feeding in the United States. *Clinical Pediatrics, 7*:708, 1968.

Meyer, H. F.: Current Feeding Practices in Hospital Maternity Nurseries. *Clinical Pediatrics, 8*:68, 1969.

Michener, W. M., and Lau, D.: Parenteral Nutrition: The Age of the Catheter. *Pediatric Clinics of North America, 17*:373, 1970.

Nelson, G. K., and Dean, R. F. A.: The Electroencephalogram in African Children: Effects of Kwashiorkor and a Note on the Newborn. *Bulletin of the World Health Organization, 21*:779, 1959.

Newton, N., and Newton, M.: Psychologic Aspects of Lactation. *The New England Journal of Medicine, 277*:1179, 1967.

O'Grady, R. S.: Feeding Behavior in Infants. *American Journal of Nursing, 71*:736, 1971.

O'Keefe, M.: Advice From a Nurse-Mother. *American Journal of Nursing, 63,12*:61 (December), 1963.

Proudfit, F. T.: *Dietetics for Nurses.* New York, Macmillan, 1923.

Sarto, Sister Joseph: Breast Feeding: Preparation, Practice, and Professional Help. *American Journal of Nursing, 63,12*:58 (December), 1963.

Schmitt, M. H.: Superiority of Breast-Feeding: Fact or Fancy. *American Journal of Nursing, 70*:1488, 1970.

Scrimshaw, N. S.: Infant Malnutrition and Adult Learning. *Saturday Review, 16*:64, March, 1968.

Sinclair, J. C., Driscoll, J. M., Heird, W. C., and Winters, R. W.: Supportive Management of the Sick Neonate. *Pediatric Clinics of North America, 17*:863, 1970.

Spitz, R. A.: Hospitalism: An Inquiry Into the Genesis of Psychiatric Conditions in Early Childhood. *Psychoanalytic Study of the Child, 1*:53, 1945.

Talbot, N. B. et al.: Dwarfism in Healthy Children: Its Possible Relation to Emotional, Nutritional and Endocrine Disturbances. *New England Journal of Medicine, 236*:783, 1947.

Vulliamy, D. G.: *The Newborn Child.* Boston, Little, Brown and Company, 1967.

When You Breastfeed Your Baby. Franklin Park, Illinois, La Leche League.

Whitten, C., Pettit, M. G., and Fischhoff, J.: Evidence that Growth Failure from Maternal Deprivation is Secondary to Undereating. *Journal of the American Medical Association, 209*:1675, 1969.

Wilmore, D. W., and Dudrick, S. J.: Growth and Development of an Infant Receiving All Nutrients Exclusively by Vein. *Journal of the American Medical Association, 203*:860, 1968.

Winick, M., and Noble, A.: Cellular Response During Malnutrition at Various Ages. *Journal of Nutrition, 89*:300, 1966.

Womanly Art of Breast Feeding. Franklin Park, Illinois, La Leche League.

Wurster, C. F.: DDT In Mother's Milk. *Saturday Review,* May 2, 1970, p. 58.

CHAPTER 6

Culture and the Newborn Infant

Culture, the sum of a society's beliefs, customs, knowledge, and capabilities, is a significant factor in the health and well being of every newborn infant. Culture affects him even before his conception, as it determines the childhood experiences of his mother—her exposure to illness, the organization of her family, the amount and kind of education she has, the kind of food she eats as she grows up, whether she will come to pregnancy strong and healthy or ill and malnourished. Culture determines her beliefs about pregnancy, whether she will seek medical care or the counsel of her relatives or a midwife, or whether she will consider herself sick or well during pregnancy. To a degree, culture will determine the age at which she first becomes pregnant, the number of children she will have, whether or not she will breast feed her infant, how often she will hold him, and so forth.

Of course, within any society, all mothers will not act identically, regardless of similar cultural backgrounds. Individual differences, determined by both heredity and environment, are always important factors in behavior. Yet culture does exert its influence; the middle-class American mother would not be likely to pin a charm on her baby's dress to protect him from the "evil eye," nor would she use a cradle board, rather than a carriage, to transport him.

The United States is a nation of many subsocieties, each with its own distinct cultural heritages. When the beliefs of these groups come in conflict with those of nurses and doctors, misunderstandings can and do arise, creating barriers which in the long run can hurt the infant. For example, many Spanish-American mothers believe in *el mal ojo,* the evil eye, which leads them to care for their babies in certain ways. Because we do not share their belief, we may ridicule their behavior. But consider how odd the Spanish-speaking mother would consider the previously popular American notion that babies must be "fed by the clock." She must surely think that any woman who watches the clock as her baby cries vigorously and sucks his fist is cruel and unloving. Or consider the practice of most American hospitals of separating mother and infant immediately after birth. To most of the world's women this must seem peculiar.

It is important, then, for us to know something of those traditional ideas of infant care which differ from our own. But it is also important that we realize the extent to which our own beliefs—some of which stem from middle-class culture and some of which are taught to us as nursing students and passed on to patients as "scientific" principle—may themselves be products of a particular heritage.

What is the source of our own ideas about infant and child care? Wolfenstein (1953) studied the effects of changing attitudes toward child care in our society and the concomitant changes in child-care practices. Using the United States government publication *Infant Care,* which was first issued in 1914 and has since undergone a number of revisions, she traced changes in the advice given about weaning, masturbation, thumb-sucking, and toilet-training.

Considering how rapidly our society has changed technologically in the 40-year period covered by Wolfenstein's study, it is not surprising that ideas have also changed in the same period of time. Wolfenstein points out, however, that many of the changes in child-care practices are not related so much to new knowledge as to the widespread belief in our society that new ideas are always better than old ones—the latest suggestion becomes *the* way to care for the new infant.

Breast feeding, for example, was recommended from 1914 through 1945, with warnings about the dangers of early weaning beginning in 1921. In 1914 stress was placed on gradual weaning—it might begin as early as five months and not be completed until the baby is a year old. By 1921 early weaning was in growing disrepute. Ideally, weaning was to be postponed until the baby was nine months old, but once begun it "need not take more than two weeks." Both in 1921 and 1929 there was emphasis on being very strict with the baby; "the child will finally yield" was the statement made in 1921, and "soon the baby will give in" was the phrasing used in 1929. Similar attitudes are expressed in 1938.

Not every pediatrician in this era was so severe in his advice. Bartlett (1932) suggests that there is no set time for weaning and that gradual weaning is more pleasant for mother and safer for baby unless serious illness in the mother makes rapid weaning necessary.

By the 1940's *Infant Care* was back to stressing the idea of gradual weaning; at the same time the age at which bottle feeding was to be given up for good became a matter of "little difference." But by 1951, while gradual weaning was still advocated, there was apprehension lest weaning to the cup be delayed too long.

Wolfenstein found similar vacillation in the other areas she examined: thumb-sucking, masturbation, and toilet-training. The change in ideas is not so important as the fact that at any given time the dominant ideas expressed in the culture are accepted and professed by so many of us as *the* correct way to care for an infant, other methods being considered "old-fashioned" and "unscientific," if not completely damaging.

Perhaps the realization that we, as nurses, are influenced by our own cultural biases can make us more tolerant and understanding of some of the biases we encounter in those families whose newborn infants we attend.

What is our reaction to beliefs that we see as based on "superstition" and folk lore rather than on "fact"? Sometimes these beliefs are ignored, at other times ridiculed. Very often an attempt has been made to exorcize such ideas as one might exorcize the devil himself. Saunders (1953) points out that "such an approach is likely to be less harmful to the persistence of folk medical beliefs than it is to the quality of the relationship between the physician and his patient, and is more effective in drawing patients deeper into a dependence on folk medicine than drawing them into the folds of enlightened followers of science."

Even the most rural tenant farmer or the poorest resident of the urban ghetto is aware of the attitudes of many doctors and nurses toward his cultural beliefs, and he knows that he had best keep those beliefs to himself. His faith in them is no less firm; they are discussed freely within family and community, but almost never are they shared with the health team — if there is any contact with the health team at all.

Role of Folk Beliefs

There are three reasons why we cannot overlook the importance of folk beliefs:

1. If a belief is accepted by a mother (or father), whether or not we feel the belief has any scientific validity or not, it will be valid in the mother's eyes and will affect her baby both before and after birth. Many of these beliefs are not usually based on reason but have strong religious overtones. For example, if a mother feels she must eat certain foods or perform certain acts during pregnancy to insure her baby's

well being, telling her that this is not so is not likely to make very much of an impression. "Who are they to question the wisdom of my people?", she thinks.

2. Re-examination of some traditionally held beliefs shows that not all of them are completely valueless. If we can work with some beliefs and see them as being neutral, causing no special good but causing no harm either, we may be in a better position to deal with those beliefs which do have a potential for harming the infant.

3. Often folk beliefs fulfill a very special need of the people who hold them.

THE POSSIBLE VALIDITY OF SOME FOLK BELIEFS

For at least 30 centuries in India, a drug, known today as pegal-ke-sawa the insanity herb, and sold at village fairs, has been used by the people of that land. Holy men have chewed it during meditation; mothers have bought it to give to fretful babies; and people in general have used it for vomiting, fever, certain eye problems, and a variety of other symptoms. The claims made for the drug were so extravagant that Western scientists ignored it for hundreds of years. It was not until 1947 that Western researchers began to consider seriously the properties of this drug, known as, Rauwolfia, although Indian physicians and chemists had begun to take a scientific interest in its properties in the late 1920's and early 1930's (Kreig, 1964).

Rauwolfia has also been known in Africa for a number of centuries. Dr. Raymond Prince, a psychiatrist from McGill University who has spent a considerable amount of time in the western bush country of Nigeria studying the methods of witch doctors in the treatment of mental illness, found that their therapy included, along with "talking things over," the use of a yellow liquid medication. Analysis revealed that it chemically resembled reserpine, widely used by contemporary Western psychiatrists (Kreig, 1964).

Should we tend to overlook the possible merits of these traditional beliefs it seems worth remembering that Western medicine "discovered" the concept of psychosomatic medicine approximately 40 years ago; traditional peoples have known for generations that body and mind are not separate entities and that no treatment can be completely effective if it does not cope with psychological as well as physiological needs.

In an article in *Science News* (1968) Lopez Mar, a Mexican herbalist, reports that in pre-Columbian times Indians ate a paste of moldy corn, a form of penicillin, to cure infections.

Willow bark tea, taken by the Chinese for centuries as a remedy for stiff joints and rheumatic pains, is chemically related to the salicylates which are used for similar purposes today (Kreig, 1964).

Ross and van Warmelo (1965), in reporting on the Bantu approach to skin disease, comment, "It is not generally recognized how advanced the ideas of some native tribes are on the identification, causation, and treatment of skin diseases. At times their knowledge is surprising. . . There is always a theory behind their viewpoint, and a meaning attached to many of the names for the conditions they recognize."

There is no suggestion here that every folk belief, whether about pregnancy, newborn infants, medical treatment, or whatever, is valid. For each jewel hidden in the rubble of folk belief there are thousands of ideas representing beliefs that do neither harm nor good, and some which can actually cause harm. One such practice in this last category is geophagy—the eating of clay (see page 42)— which can cause harm to an unborn baby. While a practice such as this is harmful in itself, other beliefs can have a more subtle effect by keeping the mother away from the medical care which she or her baby needs (although folk traditions are not the only reason mothers fail to seek medical help).

FOLK BELIEFS THAT MAY MEET SPECIAL NEEDS

While it is interesting to consider the possibility that some folk beliefs can prove valid, it is even more important to realize that these beliefs often fulfill some special need for the women who hold them. In this regard we might consider a very widely held traditional belief, even among middle-class Americans, that certain foods are craved during pregnancy. Folklore suggests that if a woman does not get the food she craves, her baby will be marked, often in the shape of the food desired.

Obeyesekere (1963), in dealing with the customs of the Sinhalese of Ceylon, discussed a possible function of such cravings in that country, where the term *dola duka* refers both to food cravings and to certain other "minor complications" of pregnancy, specifically nausea, vomiting, and weakness. While recognizing physiological and individual psychological components in *dola duka*, Obeyesekere sees it chiefly as an opportunity for the pregnant woman to express pressing needs in a socially approved manner:

A Sinhalese girl marries shortly after puberty. In a brief period of time she must make a rapid change from carefree girlhood to the role of wife and mother. In addition she often must leave her own village to live in the village of her husband. The young wife is very likely to have an ambivalent feeling toward pregnancy or toward having a child, for children are associated with the social roles of wife and mother, roles which determine a woman's inferior status in Sinhalese society. Moreover, the continual birth of babies virtually destroys any freedom a woman might have and ties her down to a life of domesticity.

Dola duka is a defense provided by the culture — an opportunity for expressing some important needs in a way that society sees as appropriate. Its most conspicuous aspect is a craving, not equated with hunger, that has to be satisfied. The woman will not be satisfied with a larger quantity of food, but only with the consumption of a specific kind of food. To deny a woman what she craves may seriously damage one's chances of rebirth. More immediately it is believed that the ears of the fetus will rot if the cravings are not satisfied.

And so for the woman who takes on an adult role at an early age *dola duka* offers the opportunity to escape from that role into an emotionally gratifying phase of childhood. For the woman who is ambivalent toward her pregnancy, again there is a certain amount of gratification. From another standpoint *dola duka* might be considered a culturally approved way of expressing male envy. While normally Sinhalese women are expected to obey and serve their husbands, *dola duka* inverts the roles and the husband is compelled by custom to serve his wife.

For another example of the possible function of folk belief, consider the following ways in which the sex of a coming child is supposedly foretold:

"If a woman is larger in front during pregnancy, the child will be male."

"If a father wears his boots while his offspring is being born, the child will be male."

"If your first-born is a girl and you want a boy, turn your bed around."

"A child born on a shrinking moon will be a boy." (White, 1961).

"If a woman carried a baby high, it's a girl; low, its a boy."

"If a baby first moves on its left side, its a boy; and vice-versa." (Clark, 1966).

Could these beliefs not reflect a certain amount of anxiety over the sex of the coming child and thus afford a way to deal with that anxiety through what can seem like a never-ending wait? Once the child is born, that anxiety will disappear. One will rarely look back to validate prior assumptions, particularly if one has been incorrect. And at any rate, any prediction has a 50 per cent chance of being right — far better odds than are necessary to keep traditions in active circulation.

Some Specific Cultural Ideas Affecting Newborns

It is not possible here, nor is it our purpose, to catalogue the wide variety of beliefs that are held about newborn infants. The examples that follow are meant to serve as illustrations. Each nurse, whether she works in a hospital or a clinic or with mothers at home, has to understand the varying life styles, ideas, and beliefs of the people she is serving. The available literature, particularly that of medical sociology and medical anthropology, can be helpful. But it will never substitute for being a sensitive listener.

SOME BELIEFS OF SPANISH-SPEAKING PEOPLES

There are Spanish-Americans in many areas of the United States today—the Southwest, the Northeast, and the Southeast. Some are descendants of families who came to the United States many years ago; others are recent immigrants. Because of language barriers, low social status, poverty, fear of discrimination or insult by Anglos (a fear that for many is based on experience), and a desire to avoid the conflict caused by introducing new ways of doing things, many Spanish-speaking Americans have retained their own cultural heritage rather than accepting the beliefs and practices of twentieth century America.

Among these beliefs and practices are some very specific ideas about the cause, prevention, and cure of illness, about how an individual must act in the face of illness, and about the way in which the curer—whether doctor, nurse, or curandera should behave. Baca (1969) feels that many Spanish-speaking people are unable to seek care from someone who does not understand their beliefs.

As previously mentioned, many Spanish-speaking people behave in *mal ojo*, the evil eye; it describes symptoms of restlessness and unusual crying, which are believed to be caused by the admiration or coveting of the baby. The intention of the admirer need not be malicious; usually he is not accused of wishing the baby ill. But in spite of himself he brings sickness to the infant. As a result "Hispanos" do not admire or praise babies as many American mothers do. Or if they do they follow any praise with a mild slap. Consider the consternation, then, that a nurse could cause in a clinic waiting room filled with Spanish-speaking mothers if she should go from one baby to the next commenting on how pretty or how good each seemed to be.

When a baby falls ill and *mal ojo* is believed to be the cause, the parents can resort to several types of folk cures. It is generally considered useless to consult an Anglo doctor who may deny the existence of the evil eye and thus prove himself either a liar or a fool.

Clark (1959) quotes a resident of Sal si Puedes, California: "How can a doctor cure something he doesn't even know about?"

Another Spanish belief concerns a condition called "fallen fontanel" (*mollera caida*) and illustrates the difference which may exist between traditional ways of thinking and medical beliefs as regards what is cause and what is effect. One common symptom of dehydration in infancy is a depressed fontanel; rugae of the soft palate are also often exaggerated. Since severe diarrhea and vomiting produce dehydration rather quickly in a small baby, a depressed fontanel and elevated rugae are often associated with vomiting and diarrhea. But in Spanish folk belief the symptoms are seen not as the end result of dehydration but as the cause. A *bolita* (elevated rugae) on the hard palate is thought to cause the baby to nurse poorly, with the gastrointestinal symptoms as sequellae. Folk treatment is directed toward elevating the fontanel — by suspending the child upside down over a pan of tepid water, by slapping the soles of his feet while he is held inverted, and so on. In view of the belief about cause, the treatment seems logical to the people who hold that belief.

Since gastrointestinal disorders are the major cause of infant morbidity and mortality in most of the countries from which Spanish-Americans come, depressed fontanels and elevated rugae are hardly uncommon conditions. But the belief concerning this condition is not limited to the poor and uneducated, or even to Spanish areas. A graduate student from British Honduras revealed an identical belief among his people (where the mollera is simply called "the mole") in asking about the size of his own new infant's fontanel.

Air (*aire, mal aire*) is seen as another source of illness. Air and particularly night air is thought to enter the body through any of its cavities. In the newborn, the cord stump is seen as a portal of entry for the air, and a surprised nurse may find a raisin placed over the umbilicus as a preventive measure (Baca).

To people who hold a belief in air as a cause of illness, the fear of surgery takes on an added dimension, for any incision increases the avenues through which air may enter the body. Thus the intestinal distention which frequently accompanies abdominal surgery only serves to support this traditional belief.

Sometimes the reactions of a Spanish-American mother to treatment recommended for her sick infant may confuse the nurse or physician involved. But it should be remembered that culture plays a major role in determining how a mother will act when she learns that she or a member of her family is ill. For example, if a middle-class American mother is told by her doctor that her infant has pyloric stenosis and requires immediate hospitalization and surgery, she would most likely accept the diagnosis and carry out the physician's directions. Undoubtedly either she or her doctor would call her husband to tell him what was taking place, but the diagnosis of the illness lies in the physician's hands and is accepted by the parents.

This is not as likely to be true if the family is Spanish-American. There may be a discussion between family members, relatives, and neighbors as to the proper course of action. All of this talk may seem to be a waste of valuable time to the medical team, and there is no question that the time involved can be a real problem in some instances. The delay, however, is not due to a lack of concern over the baby's welfare; actually it is a sign of truly conscientious parents. The opinions of nurses and doctors are not accepted as final; it is the family group that has the ultimate authority to make the decision. In the eyes of the Spanish community, the role of the curer is to advise, not to dictate. Authoritarianism is likely to drive patients away. The parent will rarely be openly defiant; she will smile and answer, "si." But unless family consensus confirms medical opinion, medical advice may be ignored: medicine is not given, a return appointment is not kept, and we wonder why the mother is so unfeeling and uncaring (from our point of view).

Culture, then, decrees the way in which the doctor or nurse is expected to behave. Clark (1959) describes the behavior of Paula, a curandera in California, who typifies the role.

"Paula's manner is as warm and friendly as her kitchen-dispensary."

"She observes the requisite social amenities and always behaves in a manner which her clients regard as courteous. For example, she is always careful to wait for an invitation to enter the house before she goes in. She knows that she is expected to sit down with the family, drink a cup of coffee, and make small talk before getting down to the business at hand. . . . After a decent interval, the illness can be mentioned and the patient seen."

SOME BELIEFS OF AMERICAN INDIANS

American Indians also have a distinct cultural heritage. In fact, many Indians have never been assimilated into what we call American culture. Most are isolated both geographically and culturally from other Americans; the majority are poor economically; and many are limited in their comprehension of English. Because of poverty and isolation, health care for Indian people has also been limited. Even when care has been available, the lack of understanding of Indian culture on the part of many of the doctors and nurses has complicated Indian acceptance of new health measures.

While ideas and beliefs vary from tribe to tribe, a majority of American Indians, like traditional people in many parts of the world,

Text continued on page 242

Figure 6–1. An Eskimo mother with her infant son checks in at the outpatient clinic of the Public Health Service Hospital in Barrow, Alaska. In many societies, mothers and babies remain in close physical contact after birth. (Courtesy of U.S. Public Health Service: Indian Health Service.)

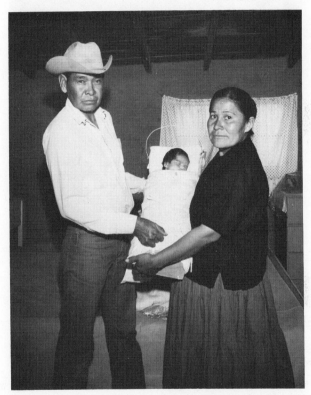

Figure 6-2. A Navajo family living in Arizona. Note the traditional cradle board. (Courtesy of U.S. Public Health Service: Indian Health Service.)

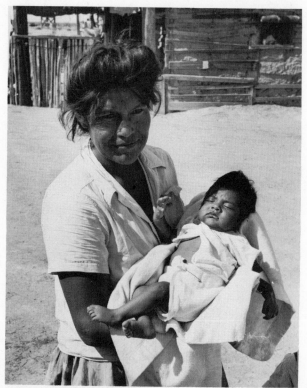

Figure 6-3. A Papago Indian mother and her baby. Because of isolation and poverty, perinatal and infant mortality is high in many Indian societies. (Courtesy of U.S. Public Health Service: Indian Health Service.)

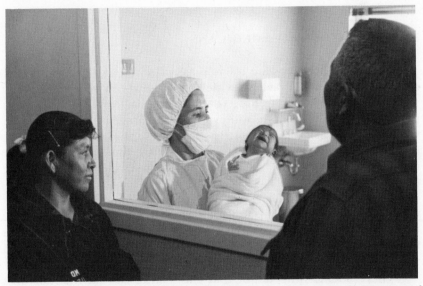

Figure 6-4. Some Navajo babies are now born in modern hospitals. (Courtesy of U.S. Public Health Service: Indian Health Service.)

tend to see health and illness as intimately connected with religious life. Yet changes and innovations can be made. Just as ways of curing have been borrowed by one tribe from another tribe (for example, the Navaho have borrowed hand trembling from the Apache and masks and fetishes from the Pueblo), certain aspects of Western medicine have been integrated into Indian culture when shown to be truly helpful. Today most medicine men, as well as their patients, recognize that there are conditions — appendicitis, for example — which Western medicine can treat far better than Indian medicine. Other conditions, however, are virtually unknown to Western medicine; only the medicine man is able to help people with these illnesses. In still other instances both physician or nurse and medicine man are called upon. The medicine man may begin to care for a baby, feel that the baby needs additional help, send him to a clinic for treatment, and then complete his rites when the baby returns, even if several weeks have passed in the interim.

PICA AMONG SOME AMERICANS

Cultural differences are by no means limited to those who speak a different language. Practices which affect newborn infants can occur right in our own communities. Yet many medical professionals, both physicians and nurses, are either totally ignorant of them or are so vaguely aware of their existence as to consider them insignificant in scope. One such example is pica, including the eating of dirt or clay (geophagy) and the related practices of starch and flour eating (Fig. 6–5).

Clay eating, an ancient practice recorded from the time of Pliny in the first century, A.D., and undoubtedly dating to much earlier times, very much a factor in the United States today. The practice in this country apparently originated in the south, but it exists as well in many northern cities to which Southerners have migrated.

There seems little doubt that clay eating can have an adverse effect on the newborn (see page 42). But is it really prevalent enough to be of major concern? Only a limited number of studies, both as to incidence and specific effects on the fetus and newborn, have been conducted to date, but more extensive investigations are being undertaken. A recent survey (Li and White, 1970) of 49 pregnant teenagers in one southern community revealed that 46 of them, all black, were familiar with clay and starch eating. Forty-five admitted that they had eaten starch at one time or other. Twelve of these women had also eaten clay or dirt, as well as the starch, but expressed a distinct preference for clay, which is the more deleterious from the standpoint of the fetus' health.

Figure 6-5. The eating of clay and starch, particularly during pregnancy, is a cultural practice that affects the newborn. (From Moore, Mary Lou: "The Clay Eaters," in *RN*, August, 1970. Photographed by Ray Solowinski. Courtesy of RN magazine.)

In a smaller sample of 13 women in another community, one-fourth reported eating clay, half favored starch, and the remaining fourth preferred raw flour (Hochstein, 1968).

Various reasons have been offered to explain the phenomenon of pica. They include spasms due to hunger, the relief of menstrual cramps or uterine sensations which occur during pregnancy, and the belief that the clay may contain substances essential to the well being of mother or child. Hochstein points out that just as the physician may recommend soda crackers to the middle-class mother who is nauseated during early pregnancy, neighbors and relatives of the poorer mother may guide her to clay or starch for the same purpose.

Regardless of the historically reported reasons for pica, Li found that the girls in her study ate clay because it was "good," "gummy," "crunchy," or "bitter." Their descriptions of starch included "good," "smooth," "sweet," "bitter," and "thick." In short, they enjoyed eating the clay or starch, just as the woman who smokes or chews gum enjoys that particular habit. In no way did the girls in the study attribute any special food value to either starch or clay. The habit seemed so natural to them that there was no reluctance to discuss it; it was no different than expressing a preference for a candy bar. The findings of other researchers support this matter of fact attitude.

The Culture of Poverty

The practice of eating clay or starch is but one aspect of the culture of poverty, in this particular instance for the black poor. There are many differences between the culture of the very poor and that of the middle-class. Lower-class behavior may be just as difficult for nurses to understand as is the behavior of a Spanish or Indian mother.

There are approximately 39 million families in the United States with incomes of less than $3000 annually for a family of four (Sehan, 1970) — an arbitrary poverty line. These families, whether they live in crumbling tenements or rural shacks, often have inadequate sanitary facilities and suffer all degrees of malnutrition and disease. Many poor mothers have no prenatal care, and even in 1972 many deliver their infants outside of the hospital. In fact, the incidence of prenatal care is actually decreasing in some areas. One reason is economic. A mother must pay in some clinics before she can be examined, even though the charge is a somewhat lower rate than she would pay a private physician. But if she appears at the emergency room in labor it is more difficult to turn her away, even though she has no money. So she just waits until this moment arrives.

Long delays in clinics, poor facilities, seeing a different doctor on each visit, the attitude of many clinic personnel, and a tendency to face today's problems rather than plan for tomorrow's (i.e., to be oriented to the present rather than the future) are other factors limiting prenatal care among the poor.

What is the very poor mother like? She may be very young and black or white. Her education is likely to be limited and, perhaps because school and formal learning may have been an unpleasant experience for her, she may be hostile to people in authority (including nurses). She may have difficulty in making herself understood, and she may have just as much difficulty understanding us.

Barriers to communication can include differences in the pronunciation of words, differences in the meanings attached to the same words, and different words used by nurse and mother to refer to the same object or behavior. In addition many words the nurse may feel are rather commonplace may be totally unfamiliar to the patient.

The limited education of the low-income mother has special significance for nurses interested in mother-baby health, for there is so much to teach the mother about caring for her baby. One test of mothers who came into the pediatric emergency room of Los Angeles County Hospital revealed that 15 per cent read at the fourth grade level or below, 30 per cent at the sixth grade level, and 55 per cent at the eighth grade level or above. (The test consisted of four paragraphs about pediatric health problems which the mother was asked to read, followed by four multiple choice questions which the mother answered on the basis of what she had just read.) Reading level correlated with the number of years of education; those who had the highest levels of education also tended to have the highest scores. But only 60 per cent of those mothers who had attended high school were able to read at the eighth grade level (Wingert, 1969).

It seems likely that most of the printed material we give to mothers from low-income neighborhoods is probably beyond their comprehension and thus of little value. Wingert suggests that reading material should be no higher than a sixth grade level for it to be understood by approximately 85 per cent of all mothers. In addition, printed material of this type should be extensively illustrated so as to catch the attention of the nonreading mother, and it should certainly be discussed thoroughly with all mothers and not just handed to them.

Husband-wife relationships in the lowest socioeconomic class also differ from those in middle class families. Men and women tend to operate in separate spheres for both work and play. This has real significance when a baby is born. In most lower class families the father, if he is present at all, is going to feel uncomfortable about performing tasks such as changing diapers and feeding or even holding the baby; this is "women's work." He is probably uncomfortable about visiting his wife in the hospital and probably would not want to stay with her in the labor or delivery room (nor would she be comfortable having him there). The worlds of men and women are too far apart for this kind of sharing.

It is easy for nurses with a middle-class bias to interpret this behavior as an indication of a lack of affection. All the family pictures in our textbooks and the articles in popular magazines reinforce our beliefs of family togetherness, which is generally accurate for middle-class patients like ourselves. But here again both our attitudes and our teaching must be modified to fit the life-style of the people for whom we care.

Working Within the Framework of a
Mother's Beliefs

Perinatal and infant mortality and morbidity in the United States are, in general, higher in those groups whose cultural heritage differs from that of middle-class America. It does not necessarily follow that these increased rates are merely the results of different beliefs. Both the increased incidence of death and illness and the maintenance of traditional values and ideas are related to the isolation of groups of people—because of poverty, color, differences in language, and a multitude of related factors. To introduce better health measures into these communities, nurses and their fellow health workers must overcome these barriers.

Aichlmayr (1969) has described what can happen when nurses have some understanding of, and appreciation for, cultural beliefs and values different from their own. In this instance the project began when six students in a community nursing class observed a government speaker addressing a group of Indians in a highly condescending manner. The purpose of the meeting had been to explore the health and welfare needs of the Indians, yet it seemed that the speaker ignored both the expressed needs of the Indians and their contributions. He appeared to typify a very common attitude: that the Indians were "lazy, unappreciative and unreachable"—a sentiment resulting from the Indians' failure to cooperate with health programs which the white community had prescribed without first consulting them.

It was only with difficulty that Aichlmayr and her students were able to arrange a meeting with health aides in the Indian community, not because the Indians were reluctant to meet but because the local director of the Office of Economic Opportunity (OEO) felt that as a result of previous bad experiences with whites the Indians would be unwilling to accept the students and their instructor on their reservation. Nevertheless, a meeting was arranged. When the Indian aides were told that the students wanted to get to know the Indian people and that it was up to the Indians to decide what information they wanted to obtain from the students, the aides began to discuss among themselves topics such as their high rate of infant mortality and the paucity of medical facilities for their people.

In a subsequent meeting on the reservation, one Indian woman said, "We are so tired of having people come to the reservation with their prescribed programs and telling us what our needs are and how we should live." One example cited was the manner in which whites from large cities admonished the Indians to bathe daily, without ever considering the availability of bathing facilities or the supply of water, a tremendously scarce item on many reservations.

Aichlmayr and her students came to be accepted by the Indian women as the Indians discovered that the student truly did want to help in the way in which the Indians desired. At the same time the nurses learned things about the Indians; they found that the Indians valued sharing more than saving, co-operation more than competition, anonymity rather than individuality—all in direct contrast to the values of most middle-class whites. They learned that even such a seemingly simple act as asking a woman a direct question about herself violated valued anonymity.

Perhaps most important of all was the fact that they did learn. By going to the reservation with neither fixed ideas nor a set program they were able to win friends and offer specific help in a number of health areas. It may be another generation before all the results of such a program can be evaluated; cultural change is usually a long, slow process that can't be hurried. But it would seem that the right kind of beginning has been made in this instance.

Project in a Negro Ghetto

As we have already mentioned, we don't have to go to an Indian reservation to enter a world with ways that seem foreign to us. But we can learn from the experience of Aichlmayr and her students. The same principles of listening first to the mothers so they can tell us of their needs and then planning with them, rather than for them, are equally applicable in an urban ghetto or a rural southern county.

"The Mom and Tots Neighborhood Center" is an example of an attempt to meet the needs of poor, black, urban mothers in one of the "most deprived and alienated" areas of the city of Detroit (Milio, 1967). Even the name of the center came from the women of the community; Milio had planned to call it the "Maternity Satellite Center" but was told by the women that no one would understand such a title.

The center was envisioned by the Visiting Nurse Association of Detroit, but it actually began only after Milio, the only full-time professional person on the project staff, talked with neighborhood mothers in their block clubs and at their church meetings. The mothers pointed out that they were often unable to go to prenatal and birth control clinics because they had neither transportation nor baby-sitters; that they often had to spend long hours in waiting if they did go; and that no one had time to answer their questions. They were concerned about keeping their children away from the streets and keeping the rats away from their babies. Some mothers wanted the project to be staffed only by local Negroes. Many wanted full-time day-care for the children of working mothers. A great many of the ideas were incorporated, in whole or in part, into the plans for the center. An empty neighborhood store was found, local men and women renovated and decorated it, and operations began.

In Milio's description of the prenatal clinic the planning that went into meeting specific community desires was obvious.

"Cribs, playpens, and a baby-sitter are available for the children while their mothers wait to see the doctor."

"Coffee is served by our clinic aide, Tommie, who lives two blocks away. Tommie brings her own year-old daughter, so that she can work an eight-hour day. While waiting, the women may be shown a pertinent sound filmstrip or color slides made by the center staff. They may discuss with Tommie and the public health nurse the pictures, diets, or sample intra-uterine contraceptive devices displayed on the walls. They may go to the kitchen to observe a bath demonstration using one of the center babies. Group discussion is encouraged and enjoyed. Increasingly, we are filtering more health information through Tommie, who is a most effective intermediary."

Projects in Other Countries

Understanding what a particular group of mothers value and what motivates them can solve specific problems as well as long-range ones. While both of the examples which follow are drawn from experiences outside of the United States, the situations are similar to those many of us have met or will meet.

PRENATAL CARE IN MEXICAN HEALTH CENTERS

In Mexico City's prenatal programs, the major goals were to:
1. Persuade women to come to the health centers at the first sign of pregnancy and to return at regular intervals until delivery, and
2. To promote hospital delivery rather than home delivery.

One hospital in the city, the *Maternidad Isidro Espinosa do los Reyes* is considered the most prestigious of the government hospitals because of its location in an elegant section of the city. If a woman comes to the health center early in pregnancy and keeps all of her appointments, she then receives a card entitling her to delivery at this hospital. Women who delay their prenatal care or who are less regular in attendance are admitted to hospitals which offer competent medical care but are located in less affluent neighborhoods. In a study of the factors influencing mothers to use government maternity services, Garcia found that many mothers carefully followed the rules of the health center for the status they gained by having their infants born at the prestigious hospital (Foster, 1969).

THE DISTRIBUTION OF POWDERED MILK IN A VENEZUELAN HEALTH CLINIC

Powdered milk has been distributed in many areas of the world, as well as in the United States, in an attempt to improve nutrition at relatively low cost. In Venezuela powdered milk was distributed at maternal-child health clinics for nutritional purposes and as an incentive and a reward for faithful attendance. Clinic attendance did indeed improve, but there was little evidence of change in nutritional status. Investigation revealed that rather than drinking the milk, mothers were exchanging it for adult food and liquor. Several factors were found to be responsible:

1. Giving powdered milk implied that the mother's breast milk was inadequate and threatened their role as a mother.

2. The mothers were never shown how to mix the milk or how to incorporate it into other foods.

3. Some mothers felt that by exchanging the milk for other food, the whole family, not just mother and baby, would share in the benefits of a government program.

Clinic nurses then began to spend more time in teaching the mothers how to mix and use the milk powder; they awarded prizes for ingenious ideas from the mothers themselves; and they began to open cans of milk before giving them to the mothers, so that it was more difficult to exchange them. As a result of these steps milk consumption seemed to increase (Foster, 1969).

Summary

Cultural beliefs determine to a large extent the way in which each of us views every aspect of our lives. The term *ethnocentrism* describes how all people believe that the ways of their group are better than those of any other group. As nurses in the United States, we are products of a particular cultural point of view. From this cultural heritage, we have derived certain ideas about infant care (as well as other aspects of life) which we see as "right" or "best." It is very important that we recognize our own cultural "biases."

On the other hand, some of the mothers for whom we care have grown up with cultural beliefs very different from our own. They in turn are likely to feel that their ways are correct and our ways are strange, or that we do not understand their beliefs. The clash of beliefs between nurses and mothers can be a real barrier to health care for infants.

At times the beliefs of other cultural groups, like our own, are helpful; at other times they are detrimental. When we see people practicing beliefs which we feel are detrimental we want to change both belief and action. But ignoring or ridiculing the ideas of other groups is rarely successful in bringing about the changes we desire. Such an approach may very likely break down communication. The mother may simply take her baby home and fail to return. Other barriers between mother and nurse include a lack of knowledge of the ideas of other groups, differences in language, and differences in level of education.

As nurses we can help to lower the barriers to good health for newborn infants in a number of ways.

1. Every mother can be treated with dignity and as a person rather than a case, regardless of how poor she seems to be, how inadequately she speaks English, or any other factor that makes her seem "different."

2. We can talk to each mother so that she can understand. This may mean understanding a different language, such as Spanish, or understanding the idiomatic use of the English language. The latter is equally as important as the former. Conversing with a mother who talks of cooking her "salat" with fat-back and serving it with the "pot-licker" can be as difficult as conversing in a foreign tongue.

3. We can understand the social organization of the families with whom we work, so that we will see why in some families the mother must defer decisions about the baby to the father and in others to the family group.

4. We can recognize the importance of "folk" cultural beliefs in people's lives and realize that ridiculing or ignoring them not only serves no useful purpose but injures the pride of the mother. There are times when these beliefs can be incorporated into the health practices we wish to encourage. For example, suppose we feel that all the water given to a particular baby should be boiled, perhaps because we know that the water supply used by the family comes from a questionable source. But the mother has been lax in boiling the water, and the baby may even have diarrhea. If the mother follows a tradition of giving an herb tea for illness, she can be encouraged to boil the water, to which she can add the tiniest bit of herb, giving the baby only this boiled water. Thus the medical goal has been achieved within the framework of the cultural tradition.

5. By responding to needs felt and expressed first by the mothers, we can begin to bring about practices we feel are important. Both Aichlmayr's work with the reservation Indians and Milio's project in the Detroit ghetto illustrate this well.

6. We can try to understand the role expected of the nurse by mothers of different cultural heritages and work within these expectations in so far as possible. This may mean, for example, that we slow the pace of our activity—admittedly a very difficult thing for

many of us to do — so that we can observe the necessary social amenities essential to rapport. To the mother for whom "el tiempo ando" (time walks), our attitude of "time flies" can seem brusque at the very least. But in the long run, such an approach may prove more economical in terms of time, because if the mother has accepted the health suggestions made and is raising a healthy baby, she will not have to seek our help as frequently.

Working with mothers and babies from a diversity of cultural backgrounds adds richness and depth to our nursing careers. However, if we underestimate the role played by culture in the lives of all people, we will never be able to adequately care for newborn infants and their mothers in the fullest sense. When cultural values differ extensively from our own, we may not even be able to establish basic communication. And if we cannot do this, all of us — mother, baby and nurse — will be losers.

Bibliography

Adair, J., and Deuschle, K. W.: *The People's Health: Medicine and Anthropology in a Navajo Community*. New York, Appleton-Century-Crofts, 1970.

Aichlmayr, R. H.: Cultural Understanding: A Key to Acceptance. *Nursing Outlook*, 17:20, 1969.

Baca, J. E.: Some Health Beliefs of the Spanish Speaking. *American Journal of Nursing*, 69:2172 (October), 1969.

Bartlett, F. H.: *Infants and Children: Their Feeding and Growth*. New York, Farrar and Rinehart, 1932.

Cahill, I. D.: *The Mother From the Slum Neighborhood*. Columbus, Ohio, Ross Laboratories Conference on Maternal and Child Nursing, 1964.

Clark, J.: North Carolina Superstitions. *North Carolina Folklore*, XIV, I:3, 1966.

Clark, M.: *Health in the Mexican-American Culture*. Berkeley, University of California Press, 1959.

Cunningham, M. P., Sanders, H. R., and Weatherly, P.: We Went to Mississippi. *American Journal of Nursing*, 67:801 (April), 1967.

England, N. C., and Daugherty, M. C.: *Prenatal Care In North Florida Negro Dialect*. Unpublished.

Foster, G. M.: *Applied Anthropology*. Boston, Little, Brown and Company, 1969.

Hochstein, G.: Pica: A Study in Medical and Anthropological Explanation. *In* Weaver, T. (ed.): *Essays in Medical Anthropology*. Athens, University of Georgia Press, 1968.

Jacobson, P. M.: The Y Family. *American Journal of Nursing*, 69:1951 (September), 1969.

Kreig, M.: *Green Medicine*. New York, Rand McNally, 1964.

Li, S. and White, R.: The Presence of Geophagy in North Carolina. Unpublished Manuscript.

Marquez, M. N., and Pacheco, C.: Midwifery Lore in New Mexico. *American Journal of Nursing*, 64:81 (September), 1964.

Milio, N.: Project in a Negro Ghetto. *American Journal of Nursing*, 67:1007 (May), 1967.

Obeyesekere, G.: Pregnancy Cravings (Dola-Duka) in Relation to Social Structure in a Sinhalese Village. *American Anthropologist*, 65:323, 1963.

Prugh, P. H.: A Yearning for Clay by Pregnant Women Alarms Some Doctors. *Wall Street Journal*, December 10, 1969.

Ross, C. M., and Van Warmelo, N. J.: Bantu Concepts of Skin Disease: Dermatological Fact and Fiction Amongst the Venda. *Archives of Dermatology, 91*:40, 1965.

Saunders, L., and Hewes, G.: Folk Medicine and Medical Practice. *Journal of Medical Education, 28*:43, 1953.

Seham, M.: Poverty, Illness and the Negro Child. *Pediatrics, 46*:305, 1970.

Starch and Clay as Food. *Science News, 95*:35, 1969.

Watts, W.: Social Class, Ethnic Background and Patient Care. *Nursing Forum, 6*:155, 1967.

White, N. I.: *The Frank C. Brown Collection of North Carolina Folklore.* Volume 6. Durham, Duke University Press, 1961.

Wingert, W. A., Grubbs, J. P., and Friedman, D. B.: Why Johnny's Parents Don't Read. *Clinical Pediatrics, 8*:655, 1969.

Wolfenstein, M.: Trends in Infant Care. *American Journal of Orthopsychiatry, 33*:120, 1953.

Wortis, H., Bardach, J. L., Cutler, R., Rue, R., and Freedman, A.: Child-Rearing Practices in a Low Socioeconomic Group: The Mothers of Premature Infants. *Pediatrics, 32*:298, 1963.

CHAPTER 7

The Care of the Newborn: Where Do We Stand? Where Are We Going?

Infant Mortality

It would be nice to think that an infant born in the United States today had the best of chances for survival and good health. At some times we have believed, or at least hoped, that this was so. Unfortunately, evidence indicates otherwise. Data published by the United Nations Statistical Office indicate that infant mortality rates in the United States in 1968 were higher than in 13 other nations (Fig. 7–4). Only seven of these nations had lower infant mortality in 1955 (Fig. 7–1).

Even more significant is the realization that in recent years many nations have decreased their rates of infant mortality far faster than the United States has (Table 7–1 and Fig. 7–5). Sweden and the Netherlands, where rates were lower in 1955 than those of the United States in 1968, decreased their infant mortality rates by 26 per cent and 32 per cent respectively, while the decrease in the United States during the same period of time was only 18 per cent.

In some areas of the United States infant mortality has been rising rather than falling. Of the ten largest cities, only Houston and Los Angeles had lower infant death rates in 1961 than in 1950. In six of the ten largest cities, infant death rates increased for both whites and

nonwhites. These cities were Chicago, Philadelphia, Detroit, Baltimore, Cleveland, and St. Louis (Donabedia, 1965).

The care of a newborn infant in a hospital nursery can only be one
small part of planning for his well being. It is not too difficult to
realize that good care can apply to a time prior to an infant's conception when nurse or physician offers genetic counseling or family
planning advice. It may be somewhat more difficult to realize that
newborn care is influenced by political and social factors as changes
in systems of delivery of medical care are proposed and evaluated.
Infant mortality rates are sensitive indicators of health and socioeconomic condition in a nation. They may also indicate something
about a nation's values and priorities, at least in a relatively wealthy
nation. For values, to a large extent, determine the amount of money
that is spent for the health and welfare of the people.

Several terms are used in citing mortality rates among infants and
newborns. "Infant mortality rate" refers to the number of infants dying
in the first year of life per 1000 live births. "Neonatal mortality rate"
describes the number of infants dying in the first 28 days of life per
1000 live births. The term "postneonatal mortality" is used to indicate
the number of deaths per 1000 live births for infants between one and
twelve months of age.

A relatively new term, "perinatal mortality," is being used with
increasing frequency to refer to fetal and neonatal deaths influenced
by prenatal conditions or circumstances surrounding delivery. The
period encompassed by perinatal mortality rates is defined in at least
three ways, and any comparison of rates must take these various
definitions into consideration. The period may be defined as covering
the time from the twenty-eighth week of gestational life through the
twenty-eighth day after birth; from the twenty-eighth week of fetal
life through the seventh day after birth, or from the twentieth week of
fetal life to the twenty-eighth day after birth. This last definition is
being used with increasing frequency, but considerable data based
on the first two definitions, exist.

When comparing rates between nations or within a country
during different years we must realize that the various indices of
perinatal, neonatal, and infant mortality do not completely correlate.
Nevertheless the three rates tend to follow similar trends. In the
United States approximately two-thirds of the infant mortality rate is
due to deaths in the first 28 days of life and more than one-third to
deaths in the first day of life.

Infant mortality rates are most easily available for international
comparison. Figures 7–1 to 7–4 summarize the infant mortality rate in
the United States and in those nations with lower rates for the years
1955, 1960, 1965, and 1968. Figure 7–5 and Table 7–1 show the percentage of decrease in several nations during this period.

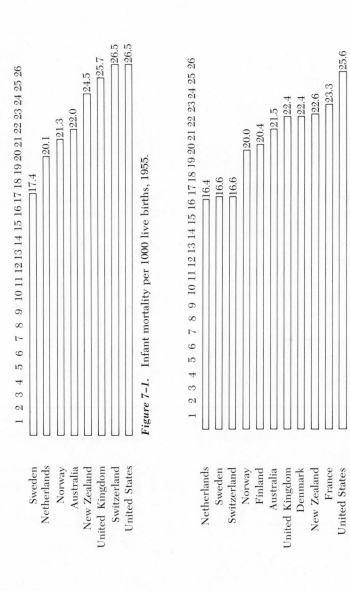

Figure 7-1. Infant mortality per 1000 live births, 1955.

Figure 7-2. Infant mortality per 1000 live births, 1960.

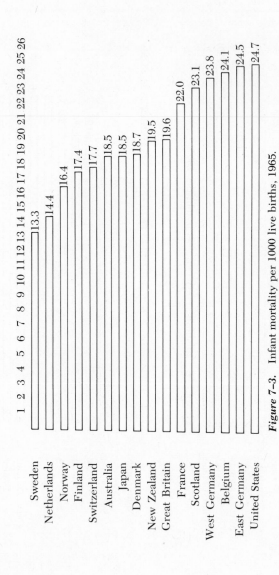

Figure 7–3. Infant mortality per 1000 live births, 1965.

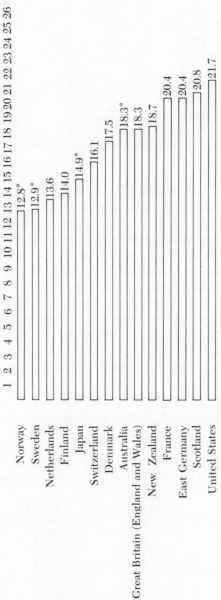

Figure 7–4. Infant mortality per 1000 live births, 1968.

% of Change

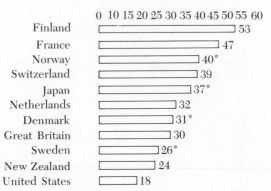

Figure 7–5. Per cent decrease in infant mortality rates, 1955–1968.

Applying the U.S. statistics to the United States as a whole is, of course, somewhat deceptive. On a regional basis, rates in 1967 varied from 19.5 in the Pacific region, which includes Alaska and Hawaii as well as California, Washington, and Oregon, to 27.2 in the central Southeastern region, encompassing Kentucky, Tennessee, Alabama, and Mississippi, the last of which has the dubious distinction of leading the nation with an infant mortality rate of 35.5.

Even greater than regional differences are the differences in white and nonwhite infant mortality. These differences exist in every state and appear regardless of whether the nonwhite population is largely black, as it is in Mississippi where the infant mortality was 47.4 for nonwhites in 1967 compared with a rate of 22.8 for whites,

TABLE 7–1.   *Decrease in Infant Mortality in Selected Nations,*
1955–1968

COUNTRY	1955	1968	PER CENT CHANGE
Finland	29.8	14.0	53
France	38.5	20.4	47
Norway	21.3	12.8°	40
Switzerland	26.5	16.1	39
Japan	39.7	14.9°	37
Netherlands	20.1	13.6	32
Denmark	26.9	17.5°	31
Great Britain	25.7	18.3	30
Sweden	17.4	12.9°	26
New Zealand	24.5	18.7	24
United States	26.5	21.7	18

°1967 data, as noted in Figure 7–5 and Table 7–1.

or largely Indian, as it is in Alaska, where the rate is 51.2 for non-whites and 19.1 for whites.

The very lowest infant mortality in the nation exists in Hawaii, where the 1967 rate was 14.9 for whites and 17.5 for nonwhites. Yet even these rates, considerably lower than any on the mainland, are not as low as those of Sweden, the Netherlands, Finland, and Norway. Whites in Delaware had the lowest rate for any mainland American group (15.9) but were surpassed by Japan and Denmark as well as by the four aforementioned nations. Considering only white infant mortality for the nation as a whole, (19.7) the United States ranked behind ten other nations in 1967.

Nonwhite infant mortality for the nation in 1967 was 35.9 per 1000 live births. This means that nearly 4 per cent of the nonwhite babies born in the United States died before reaching their first birthday. Between 1963 and 1967, nonwhite infant mortality rates increased in Alaska, Massachusetts, Minnesota, Missouri, and Oregon. In Alaska the rate rose from 47.6 in 1963 to a peak of 66.1 in 1965, dropped to 48.8 in 1966, and then rose again to 51.2 in 1967.

CAUSES OF HIGH INFANT MORTALITY

Reasons for high infant mortality in nations with low levels of technological development seem obvious. Some of the factors involved are low levels of nutrition, the continued, though decreasing, prevalence of many infectious diseases, cultural practices such as geophagy (see Chapter 6), and cultural attitudes such as fatalism. It is more difficult, however, to explain the somewhat high rates in nations with advanced technological development, such as the United States, particularly when those rates are both substantial and increasing, in comparison to several other nations.

Prematurity is a major cause of perinatal mortality in developed nations. Approximately 80 per cent of the infants who die within the first 48 hours of life weigh less than 2500 gm., the weight criteria accepted by the World Health Organization in defining prematurity (Stowens, 1966). These premature infants account for 65 per cent of the total perinatal death rate (Brimblecombe, 1968). The percentage of premature infants varies from one population to another. Those nations with a low percentage of premature-by-weight babies have low rates of infant mortality as well.

Reducing perinatal mortality, then, is directly related to reducing prematurity. However, in the United States the percentage of deaths due to prematurity has remained essentially the same for several decades (Hughes, 1967). The fact that rates of prematurity are considerably lower in a number of other nations certainly suggests that prematurity can be reduced. It has been suggested that if all of the existing knowledge of prenatal management were applied to all pregnancies and if all pregnant women cooperated fully, the frequency of low birth weight infants could be reduced by 25 per cent today (Page, 1967).

The suggestion that adequate prenatal care could reduce the incidence of low birth weight babies was strongly supported by a study done in Washington, D.C. which included 30,462 births, nearly 90 per cent of all of the infants born in that city in 1960. Regardless of maternal age, parity, income, or race, there were fewer low birth weight babies born to mothers who had begun prenatal care early in their pregnancies (Schwartz, 1965).

Kohl (1955) also saw inadequate prenatal care as one of several factors responsible for 955 perinatal deaths in New York City. He estimated that 35 per cent of the deaths reviewed were preventable. Factors responsible for deaths in full-term infants were unavoidable disaster, errors in medical judgment, and unsatisfactory pediatric care. The responsible factors in deaths of premature infants were unavoidable disaster, errors in medical judgment, and inadequate prenatal care. Errors in medical technique, unqualified medical attendance, family fault, and intercurrent infection were factors of lesser importance in the deaths of both full-term and premature infants (Kohl, 1955).

If the percentage of low birth weight infants is related to infant mortality, and prenatal care is related to both prematurity and infant mortality, it seems important to examine the way in which prenatal care is delivered in those countries which have been more successful than the United States in reducing low birth weights and prematurity. Actually the delivery of all medical care, not just prenatal care, is important because long-term ill health can present barriers to successful obstetrical performance even when prenatal care is excellent.

SYSTEMS OF HEALTH CARE DELIVERY
IN OTHER COUNTRIES

There are differences between our system of health care and the systems of those nations with consistently low infant mortality. Sweden, long the world leader in low infant mortality, has a highly comprehensive health care program, not only in terms of maternal and child health but also in terms of health care throughout an individual's lifetime. The original impetus for this program was a very low birth rate, which reached the lowest level of any nation in the world in 1934. Since 1938 Sweden has passed legislation which endeavored to give every resident of the country access to maternal and child health care, a goal which became a reality by 1950.

"During a normal pregnancy, these examinations by a physician are considered necessary, one during the early months, one halfway through, and one a month before the anticipated date of confinement. There is one postpartum follow-up visit after six to eight weeks. The mothers are also under supervision of the midwife of the center the entire time. If any complications arise during pregnancy, the nature of these determines the number of required consultations. Women can go to private obstetricians if they prefer, but about 90 per cent go to welfare clinics. Care is free to the patients, and costs the government about \$12 per person per year.

"Hospital delivery is also free and is almost universally used" (Falkner, 1969).

Other maternity benefits include a cash maternity allowance (even if the child is stillborn) an idea hardly applicable to the contemporary U.S. where overpopulation is an increasingly serious problem—three-fourths of the cost of dental care during pregnancy, free prophylactic medicines such as vitamins for expectant and nursing mothers, and three-fourths of travel expenses where they are necessary in order to obtain care.

Norway is another nation with low infant mortality, although rates vary considerably from the large cities, where they are lower, to the rural provinces of the far north. Compulsory national health insurance has been in effect in Norway since 1956. Maternal and child health care, both in clinic and hospital, is free and, as in Sweden, travel costs both to and from the clinic and a cash maternity benefit are available to all mothers, regardless of marital status. The state pays all Norwegian families an annual cash benefit for each child after the first one. This money goes directly to the mother whether or not she is the family breadwinner.

About 85 per cent of the births in Norway take place in hospitals or public maternity clinics. A midwife is in charge of normal deliveries, but a doctor is always on call should complications arise, and the physician bears the ultimate responsibility for mother and baby. The remaining 15 per cent of the deliveries occur in private homes in rural mountainous areas, the babies being delivered by midwives employed by the district.

In addition to the differences in the delivery of health care, between these Scandinavian countries and the United States, there is also some difference in the philosophy concerning labor and delivery. Childbirth is considered a natural event and external interference, such as surgery, forceps, analgesia, and anesthesia are used only when absolutely necessary.

Finland and Denmark, two other nations with low infant mortality rates, also provide for maternity and child care as well as comprehensive health care through state programs. In Finland, care by both physician and midwife at a maternity health center and home visits by the midwife are provided. The use of the services is voluntary and free of charge. Maternity allowances are given to all mothers who ask for them, provided that they follow a maternity care program either through a center or privately. The health insurance system pays daily compensation to expectant mothers after the sixth month. In 1968, 99.2 per cent of the mothers who delivered in Finland were registered at maternity health centers.

In Switzerland, health care has been financed for nearly 50 years through voluntary health associations. In accordance with provisions of the Sickness and Accident Insurance Law of 1911, subsidies are given to recognized voluntary health plans which must meet certain requirements. About 80 to 90 per cent of the population are members of approximately 1110 such associations.

Since 1948 the National Health Service of Britain has made health services available to all of the people without any insurance qualifications. In France, compulsory health care, sponsored by the government and administered locally, finances an average of 80 per cent of the cost of medical care. West Germans may join either an approved voluntary health plan or a government sponsored compulsory health plan.

Of course, the availability of low cost or free care to a majority of the population does not of itself guarantee the quality of such care. But the fact that infant mortality in those countries where such care has been available for a number of years is low and continues to decrease would seem to have some significance.

VARIATIONS IN OBSTETRICAL PRACTICE

Aside from the financing and delivery of health care several of the aforementioned countries follow obstetrical practice which differ from those used in the United States and which may account for lower infant mortality rates. One such difference is a greater involvement of nurses and nurse-midwives in maternity programs. In many countries with low infant mortality, such as Sweden, Norway, England and Wales, nurse-midwives deliver the majority of infants.

Methods of infant delivery also vary. Cesarean section is practiced in 1.25 per cent of all deliveries in the Netherlands and 2.7 per cent of all deliveries in England and Wales. In four studies of obstetrical practice in the United States, cesarean section was found to occur 4.2 to 5.7 per cent of the time (Chase, 1967). In New York City the rate of cesarean section per 1000 live births has risen from 19.9 in 1937 to 50.2 in 1954. This rise is due in part to the fact that in most instances one section leads to another, creating a pyramiding effect. In 1940 only 1 per cent of all sections were due to previous sections; in the New York study 38.7 per cent were due to previous sections. Between 1940 and 1950 the perinatal mortality rate for cesarean section averaged 54.9, a figure 56 per cent above the general rate. A large part, but not all, of this component of mortality was associated with prematurity (Gordon, 1957). About 5 per cent of all infants delivered by cesarean section have some degree of respiratory difficulty for a day or two after birth (McKay, 1969).

Forceps deliveries are reported in only 4.7 per cent of the deliveries in England and Wales and from 20 to 40 per cent of the deliveries in the United States. Episiotomies were reported in 16 per cent of the deliveries in England and Wales and in 65 to 70 per cent of the deliveries in the United States (Chase, 1967). It has already been mentioned that in Norway obstetrical surgery is rare.

There are also apparent differences in the extent to which analgesia or anesthesia is used during labor and delivery, with the United States having a higher incidence of both. In the Netherlands, for example, most mothers prefer not to have analgesia, so that it is rarely used. The same is true in Norway.

The fact that these differences in obstetrical management exist may or may not be significant in terms of infant mortality, but certainly the matter is worth investigating.

Social Factors in Infant Mortality

In addition to those factors just discussed, which might be considered "medical variables," perinatal and infant mortality is also affected by many interrelated "social variables." For example, in one study Kincaid (1965) found that the more siblings a mother had, the more likely she was to experience a stillbirth. Among middle-class women a steep rise in the number of stillbirths occurred when the woman had four or more brothers or sisters. But among women whose fathers were unskilled manual laborers, there was a difference in the rate of stillbirths between women with no siblings and those with one sibling, and also a difference between women with one sibling and women with two or three siblings. Kincaid felt that this difference was probably related to the point at which a scarcity of resources began to have a long-term effect on the growth of the children in matters such as food intake, maternal care, and the like, this in turn would then have the long-term effect of lowering reproductive efficiency.

Vaughan (1968) found that mothers in Lancashire, England, who lost a baby in the perinatal period were more likely to have a poor attitude toward antenatal care, a poor diet, and serious family problems.

Poor attitudes toward antenatal care can encompass a number of additional factors such as transportation problems, child care difficulties, fear of losing time from work, and long waits at the clinic.

Since perinatal mortality is often linked with poverty, the results of a study conducted by Thompson (1968) in Indiana are interesting. When rural-urban residence was controlled, poverty was not the common denominator in reproductive outcome in this study. However, high prematurity and perinatal mortality were associated with urbanization. Whether this is due to the nature of people attracted to large, densely populated, industrialized areas or to the crowded environment itself is a question to be answered by future research.

Race and sex have both been investigated in relation to perinatal mortality. In a California study (Russel, 1967) nonwhite premature infants fared better than whites, with Oriental infants showing the best survival rates. Females of all races had better survival rates than males.

What Are We Doing About Infant Mortality?

An awareness that more newborns can be saved, not only from death but from damaging illness, is the first step toward reducing infant mortality. In recent years several different kinds of programs have been started or accelerated in an attempt to make a concentrated attack on infant mortality in the United States. These include special projects funded by the Children's Bureau, new roles for nurses and paramedical personnel, the increasing use of intensive care nurseries, and the exploration of the relationship of family planning and interconceptual care to infant mortality.

THE CHILDREN'S BUREAU MATERNITY CARE PROJECTS

Within the past several years the Children's Bureau has funded 53 projects aimed at both reducing infant and maternal mortality and cutting the incidence of mental retardation and other handicapping conditions caused by complications associated with childbearing. The projects are located both in large cities and in smaller communities. Ten are in rural areas. In fiscal 1968, 118,000 new maternity patients were included, representing about 3 per cent of the women having babies in the United States during that period. (However, nearly 20 per cent of the babies delivered in this country are born to mothers living in poverty.) One important difference in these projects in comparison to the usual care available to the poor mother is the wider use of allied health personnel, including social workers, nutritionists, and a larger number of aides and assistants of various kinds, in addition to nurses and physicians.

How successful are these projects? In Chicago, in a project involving mothers 15 years of age or younger at the time of conception, neonatal mortality was 19.0 for 2368 project patients and 36.8 for 4400 nonproject patients in the city.

In Dade County, Florida, over a period of three years, the average number of antepartum visits per patient increased from 3.9 to 11.2. The rate of stillbirths per 1000 live births decreased from 27 to 2 and neonatal mortality decreased from 18 to 12 per 1000 live births.

In a Houston project, infant mortality decreased from 27.9 in 1964 to 22.1 in 1967. In New York city, neonatal mortality in 1966 was 13 per cent lower for babies born to mothers under the program than for the city as a whole.

Thirty-six million dollars was appropriated for these maternity care projects by the federal government in 1969. If all of the women in the United States whose incomes are at poverty levels and who need maternity care were included in such projects (approximately 750,000 women per year) it is estimated that an additional 100 million dollars would be needed for the first year, 200 million dollars for the second year, with further increases in the years that follow.

NEW ROLES FOR NURSES AND PARAMEDICAL PERSONNEL

It has become increasingly obvious that nurses and physicians acting only in traditional roles cannot meet the demand for top-rate obstetric and newborn care for our total population. Although birth rates are declining, the number of obstetricians is decreasing at an even faster rate. It has been estimated that by 1980 40 per cent of the babies born in the United States will be delivered of mothers on the wards of municipal and community hospitals in which there are now an insufficient number of physicians; and it is very likely that there will never be an adequate number of doctors to deliver babies in these hospitals or even to properly supervise obstetrical care (Ledney, 1970). Nurses and paramedical personnel will most likely have to assume new roles in filling the gap just to maintain the current level of care.

Consider the following example as one possible new role for nurses in at least some areas of the country. A group of physicians hires a nurse who examines apparently normal newborns in the nursery, visits with mother and baby each day while mother and baby are in hospital, answering the common questions about normal newborn care, and makes at least one home visit to mothers of first babies. The pediatricians who employ her are always available for consultation, but the majority of their time can be devoted to babies with special problems.

At Montefiore Hospital a four-year study explored an expanded role for a public health nurse who worked with a group of obstetricians and pediatricians in the care of their private patients — largely well-educated young women from middle-income families. The role of the nurse included identifying and evaluating both physiological and psychological problems, teaching the mother self care during pregnancy and after delivery and preparing her for hospitalization, providing well-baby care during the first two years of the child's life and care of the sick infant with acute or chronic illness, and counseling parents in relation to family planning and family problems.

Interviews with the mothers who received care from the nurse as well as a physician indicated that 83 per cent of the obstetric patients and 89 per cent of the mothers bringing their children to the pediatricians wanted the services of the nurse again. Perhaps even more important, 71 per cent of the obstetric patients and 81 per cent of the pediatric patients felt that seeing both physician and nurse was preferable to seeing only the physician. Patients said that the doctor–nurse team gave more comprehensive care and showed greater personal interest than did the physician alone.

Attitudes of both physicians and nurses are important in any new role. In the Montefiore study the physician's attitudes changed during the course of the project from "hesitant compliance to confidant cooperation." The nurse's first reaction to the expanded role was anxiety; she was overly cautious, referring problems to the doctor which she could have handled herself. It was not long, however, before she became more secure and was able to manage a variety of problems with confidence (Seacat and Schlachter, 1968).

A nurse might come to this kind of practice by any of several routes. She may be an experienced nurse who has been given supplemental training by the physician or the group for whom she works. She may be a graduate of a pediatric nurse associate program. Although a public health nurse participated in the Montefiore study, it was felt that a professional nurse with additional pediatric and obstetric knowledge could have also fulfilled the role adequately.

In a similar fashion physician's assistants are also supplementing the work of both doctors and nurses. The physician's assistant, working for a doctor in private practice, functions much as the nurse just described. The physician's assistant may also work exclusively within a hospital in the newborn nurseries. What is his role there, and how does this role affect the nurses.

In our hospital the physician's assistant in the nursery is most helpful in performing a number of tasks that might otherwise be delegated to several different people; he collects blood, calibrates and maintains the monitoring equipment and respirators, instructs new personnel in the use of specialized equipment, examines infants, and assists with medical treatment such as umbilical artery catheterization. When newborns are to be transferred from other hospitals within the city to the intensive care nursery, the physician's assistant cares for them enroute, carrying out emergency treatment and making sure that body temperature is maintained. In many ways the physician's assistant, whose sole responsibility is to the newborn nurseries, can give stability and continuity to the medical aspects of newborn care.

Nurse-midwives are hardly new, but an increase in their numbers might make a significant difference in newborn illness and death in the United States. It seems important that in those countries with low infant mortality rates, such as Sweden, nurse-midwives play a far larger role in maternity care than they do in the United States.

In 1970 the American College of Obstetricians and Gynecologists, the Nurses Association of the ACOG, and the American College of Nurse-Midwives formulated a joint statement that said, in part, that in "medically directed teams, qualified nurse-midwives may assume responsibility for the complete care and management of uncomplicated maternity patients."

Like the nurse who assists the physician in caring for the baby after birth, the nurse-midwife may work with an obstetrician or a group in private practice (still a relatively rare situation) or through a clinic. Working with standing orders for normal situations the midwife "manages" the prenatal, labor and delivery, and postnatal aspects of normal pregnancy, thus relieving many hours of obstetrical time for the high risk mother, the mother with complications, and women requiring surgery.

THE INTENSIVE CARE NURSERY

In the mid 1950's, following the realization that the overuse of oxygen had led to retrolental fibroplasia, it became obvious that newborns, and particularly sick or low birth weight babies, needed a special kind of care which they had not been receiving. Concurrently new tools and techniques for evaluating the infant's physiological status, improved ability to control infection, and a change in the "hands off" philosophy of a preceding generation all contributed to the development of neonatal intensive care units (Figs. 7-6 and 7-7).

The number of such units has grown immensely. Swyer (1970) feels that there is now a very real danger that newborn intensive care can become such a status symbol for a hospital that units may be set up in institutions which cannot meet the very stringent requirements of medical, paramedical, and nursing personnel nor provide adequate laboratory facilities, financing, and equipment. An inade-

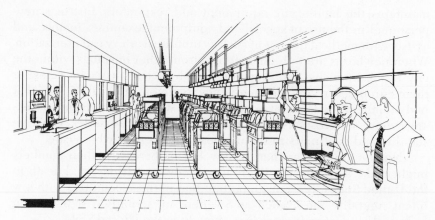

Figure 7–6. The infant care area in the infant intensive care center, University Hospital, San Diego, California, showing overhead service modules and storage wall modules. (From Gluck: *Pediatric Clinics of N. America,* 17:783, 1970.)

quate unit may be worse than no unit at all, in that babies who might have been transferred to a fully qualified unit may be assigned to the care of an inadequately staffed and equipped unit. In relation to the reduction of infant mortality and morbidity "only selective development on regional lines is practical or effective" (Swyer).

Can access to an intensive care truly reduce infant mortality? One set of figures (Table 7–2) indicates that in Quebec it did make a difference.

There are a number of nursing considerations in an intensive care nursery other than the specific care of babies which has been discussed in previous chapters. One is the ratio of nurses to babies. Gluck (1970) suggests one nurse on each shift to care for every three to five babies (or 4.2 nurses for every three to five babies in the nursery, allowing for vacations, days off, and so forth). Staffing has to be flexible enough to adjust the number of nurses to the needs of the babies in the nursery at any given time. Since 40 is considered to be an ideal infant capacity (units with fewer than 20 to 25 infants are felt to be extremely costly in terms of both personnel and money; units with more than 50 babies tend to be unwieldy – Gluck), this means a nursing staff of 42 per 24 hours or ten nurses per shift.

In order to assure that an adequate number of nurses will always be available, nurses from other nurseries or the pediatric units can be rotated through the intensive care nursery. A continuing program of in-service education for intensive care nurses is also essential. In addition, training programs should be available both for other nurses in the hospital where the intensive care nursery is located and for nurses from other area hospitals. Such programs would include formal

Figure 7–7. Overhead service modules such as this one supply oxygen, suction, compressed air, and electricity to the incubator without limiting access, as wall outlets do. (From Gluck: *Pediatric Clinics of N. America, 17:*785, 1970.)

TABLE 7–2. Neonatal Mortality in Hospitals With and Without Access to Neonatal Intensive Care*

	NEONATAL MORTALITY PER 1000 LIVE BIRTHS	
TYPE OF HOSPITAL	1967	1968
Metropolitan hospitals with obstetric/ neonatal intensive care units	6.30	6.42
Metropolitan hospitals referring to external intensive care units	8.48	6.46
Metropolitan hospital with no referral to intensive care unit	10.20	9.64
Nonmetropolitan hospital; no referral	13.69	—

*Adopted from Swyer, P. R.: *Pediatric Clinics of North America, 17:*763, 1970.

classes, attendance at conferences, and guided reading as well as clinical experience.

Since nurses may (and should) have the opportunity to serve on committees planning new neonatal intensive care units, some understanding of space requirements may be in order. From 30 to 50 square feet of space per infant has been suggested in infant care areas, with 20 square feet per infant being an absolute minimum. This area does not include the space needed for the nurses' station, for scrubbing, for storage, and so on. In addition, close to the unit there should be a conference room, rooms for parent teaching and for minor surgery, lounge, utility areas, and office space for the head nurse, resident, and social service personnel. Figure 7–8 illustrates one floor plan which includes many of these ideas. The reader who is interested in specific suggestions concerning the size of these areas is referred to Gluck (1970).

FAMILY PLANNING AND THE REDUCTION OF INFANT MORTALITY

Research into the ways in which an increased understanding of family planning can directly affect infant mortality has been somewhat limited. Yet for two reasons this is an important area of study.

First, there are those who feel that the crisis of overpopulation is such that we cannot afford to reduce death rates until birth rates are

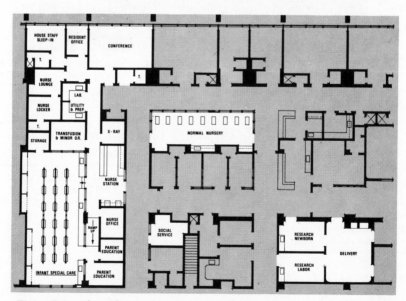

Figure 7–8. Floor plan for the renovation of nursery space at University Hospital, San Diego, California. The shaded area represents the obstetric floor area other than the perinatal center areas. (From Gluck: *Pediatric Clinics of N. America, 17*:783, 1970.)

lowered. Not every demographer (population specialist) agrees with this view, however. Frederiksen (1969) suggests that "a reduction in mortality is a necessary . . . condition for a reduction in fertility." He argues that (1) when mortality is reduced there are compensatory reductions in fertility in order to maintain desired family size and (2) reduction in mortality leads to less uncertainty about survival, and a higher probability of survival leads to reduction in desired family size.

In other words, if a mother expects half of her children to die in infancy or early childhood she will likely want to bear a greater number of children than the mother who feels reasonably certain that each baby will live to grow to adulthood.

Second, there are some rather clear indications that family planning may have a more direct effect on individual instances of perinatal mortality. For example, data from the Maternity and Infant Care project in New York City show that when deliveries occur within a year after the preceding delivery the neonatal death rate is 35 per 1000. If the interval following delivery is one to two years, the neonatal death rate drops to 17 per 1000. With a two- to three-year interval, the rate drops to 7 per 1000. Part of the reason for the high death rate in the first year following delivery is the increased chance of prematurity which exists during that period. In a second study of 16,000 deliveries at the Pennsylvania Hospital, the rate of low birth weight babies when the interval between births was more than 23 months was half the rate which occurred when the interval between births was less than 12 months.

Since 1968 many states have included information about the mother's last previous live birth and last fetal death on birth certificates. The correlation of this information with data about the newborn for whom the certificate is issued could be of value in understanding the relationship between "spacing" and neonatal mortality and damage.

Spacing, however, is not the only way in which family planning may be related to mortality rates. For example, a number of studies indicate that infant mortality is very high among babies born to very young mothers and those born to older mothers. While family planning is not a total answer to this problem, planning can obviously influence the age of the mother at conception.

In addition, planning can help a mother avoid pregnancy at a time when she is physiologically unready. One review of 123 infant deaths and stillbirths in New Orleans in 1964 found that 75 per cent of the deaths could have been prevented by better care. But of the 25 per cent that were judged nonpreventable, the principal reason for the infant's death was a serious medical condition existing in the mother before conception.

It is also known that infant mortality rates increase in children of higher birth order, particularly beyond the level of the fifth child. There are undoubtedly a number of interacting factors affecting this rise, such as the increased age of the mother in later pregnancies and socioeconomic conditions, but family planning should nevertheless be helpful in such situations.

Is the method of family planning a possible factor in pregnancy outcome? Some small studies in relation to birth control pills have been carried out but there is no conclusive evidence as yet. In those countries where legalized abortion is frequent and is often the principal means of family planning, the technique which is used may be a factor in the outcome of subsequent pregnancy. For example, in Yugoslavia where suction is widely used in abortion, there is a high incidence of ectopic pregnancy in the gestations that follow. In Hungary, where the first live birth is often preceded by several abortions, there has been a higher percentage of low birth weight babies and of perinatal mortality. But in Japan, where approximately a million abortions occur each year, but where suction is rarely used, there has been no increase in low birth weight babies (Falkner, 1969).

INTERCONCEPTUAL CARE

More and more we realize that a postpartum check-up for the mother four to six weeks after delivery (if the mother returns at all) is not really adequate if the next pregnancy is to occur when the mother is at optimum health, risk to the newborn is to be decreased. More extensive care between pregnancies, including family planning, counseling, health and nutrition teaching, and supervision to correct existing problems and detect new ones, is important for high risk mothers. Such programs might be in some way combined with the operation of well-baby clinics. How often do we ask a mother at such a session what she is feeding her baby but neglect to inquire about her own nutrition? Yet her own health is tremendously important not only for any future infant but in relation to her ability to care for this present baby. Although this type of care does exist on a very small scale in some parts of the United States; it needs to be expanded to include many more mothers.

Where Are We Going?

The comparison of national mortality rates for newborns and infants does not suggest that we should try to "beat Sweden" or any other nation for the sake of our national prestige. Nor is the method by which another nation delivers health care necessarily the best one for our own country. Rates do indicate, however, that we probably are not utilizing financial and human resources and current available knowledge as well as we could.

It seems likely that if we are really to improve our care of newborns we must not only look at health care alone but also at every aspect of poverty—housing, education, job opportunities and training, and a multitude of other factors. We need to make sure that the care we offer does not mean that the mother must wait for long hours on hard benches in a clinic only to be given a brief, curt, cold examination. We need to consider the environment of all the children growing to adulthood today so that they will be less likely to become the high risk parents of the next generation.

And as we use the information available to us today, all of us — nurses as well as physicians and social scientists—need to be continually testing new ideas and looking for the causes of prematurity and death and injury in the newborn. For only by working together will we achieve our goal of optimum care and opportunity for every newborn infant.

Bibliography

Anderson, E. H., and Lesser, A. J.: Maternity Care in the United States: Gains and Gaps. *American Journal of Nursing, 66*:1539, 1966.

Ashley, D.: Perinatal Mortality in Wales. *British Journal of Preventive and Social Medicine, 22*:132, 1968.

Baumgartner, L., and Pakter, J.: Challenge of Fetal Loss, Prematurity, and Infant Mortality-Assessing the Local Situation. *Journal of the American Medical Association, 167*:936, 1958.

Bean, M. A.: The Nurse-Midwife at Work. *American Journal of Nursing, 71*:949 (May), 1971.

Bébé grandit. Brussels, Belgium; Deuvre Nationale de L'Enfance.

Brimblecombe, F. S., Ashford, J. R., and Fryer, J. C.: Significance of Low Birth Weight in Perinatal Mortality. *British Journal of Preventive and Social Medicine, 22*:27, 1968.

Chase, H. C.: Perinatal and Infant Mortality in the United States and Six Western European Countries. *American Journal of Public Health, 57*:1735, 1967.

Children in Britain. London, Central Office of Information, 1967.

Donabedia, A., Rosenfeld, L., and Southern, E.: Infant Mortality and Socioeconomic Status in a Metropolitan Community. *Public Health Reports, 80*:1083, 1965.

Eliot, M. M.: Deaths Around Birth: The National Score. *Journal of the American Medical Association, 167*:945, 1958.

Evang, K.: *Health Services in Norway.* Oslo; The Norwegian Joint Committee on International Social Policy, 1960.

Evang, K.: Norway. In: *Medical Care and Family Security.* Englewood Cliffs, New Jersey, Prentice Hall, 1963.

Falkner, F.: *Key Issues in Infant Mortality.* Bethesda; National Institute of Child Health and Human Development, 1969.

Frederiksen, H.: Feedbacks in Economic and Demography Transition. *Science, 166*:837, 1969.

Gluck, L.: Design of a Perinatal Center. *Pediatric Clinics of North America, 17*:777, 1970.

Gordon, C. A.: The Maternal and Perinatal Mortality of Cesarian Section. *American Journal of Obstetrics and Gynecology, 73*:65, 1957.

Grossman, M.: Switzerland, Where the Voluntary Insurance Principal Prevails. *In:*

Schoeck, H. (ed.): *Financing Medical Care.* Caldwell, Idaho; The Caxton Printers, 1962.

Heady, J. A., Stevens, C. F., Daly, C., and Morris, J. N.: Social and Biological Factors in Infant Mortality. *Lancet, 1*:499, 1955.

Hughes, E. C.: General Discussion: Perinatal Mortality—Status Quo. *In: Proceedings, AMA National Conference on Infant Mortality.* Chicago; American Medical Association, 1967.

Katz, R. G., White, L. R., Sever, J. L.: Maternal and Congenital Rubella. *Clinical Pediatrics,* 7:323,

Kincaid, J. C.: Social Pathology of Fetal and Infant Loss. *British Medical Journal, 1*: 1057, 1965.

Kohl, S.: *Perinatal Mortality in New York City.* Cambridge, Harvard University Press, 1955.

Langholm, M.: *Family and Child Welfare in Norway.* Oslo, The Norwegian Joint Committee on International Social Policy, 1961.

Ledney, D. M.: Nurse-Midwives: Can They Fill the OB Gap? *RN,* January 30, 1970.

McKay, R. J.: The Fetus and the Newborn Infant. *In* Nelson, W., Vaughan, V., and McKay, R. J. (eds.): *Textbook of Pediatrics.* 9th Edition. Philadelphia, W. B. Saunders, 1969.

Michaelson, M. G.: Medical Students: Healers Become Activists. *Saturday Review,* 16:41, (August) 1969.

Muntendam, P.: *Public Health Care in the Netherlands.* The Hague: Ministry of Social Affairs and Public Health, 1966.

Murray, D. S.: England. In: *Medical Care and Family Security.* Englewood Cliffs, New Jersey, Prentice-Hall, 1963.

Obrig, A.: 1971. A Nurse-Midwife in Practice. *American Journal of Nursing, 71*:953 (May), 1971.

Page, E. W.: Problems of Prematurity: Clues to Prevention. In: *Proceedings, AMA Conference on Infant Mortality.* Chicago, American Medical Association, 1967.

Pearse, W. H.: The Maternity and Infant Care Program. *Obstetrics and Gynecology,* 35:114, 1970.

Russell, K. P.: State Perinatal Study Experience. In: *Proceedings: AMA National Conference on Infant Mortality.* Chicago, American Medical Association, 1967.

Salvesen, K.: *Social Legislation in Norway.* Oslo, Norwegian Joint Committee on International Social Policy, 1967.

Schwartz, S., and Vineyard, J. H.: Prenatal Care and Prematurity. *Public Health Report,* 80:237, 1965.

Seacat, M., and Schlachter, L.: Expanded Nursing Role in Prenatal and Infant Care. *American Journal of Nursing,* 68:822, 1968.

Shapiro, S., and Moriyama, I. M.: International Trends in Infant Mortality and Their Implication for the United States. *American Journal of Public Health,* 53:747, 1963.

Shirer, W. L.: *The Challenge of Scandinavia.* Boston, Little, Brown and Company, 1955.

Social Insurance in Norway. Rikstrygdeverket, The National Insurance Institution, 1970.

Statistical Yearbook. New York, United Nations Publishing Service.

Stowens, D.: *Pediatric Pathology.* Baltimore, Williams and Wilkins, 1966.

Strandberg, O. (ed.): *Social Benefits in Sweden.* Stockholm, The Swedish Institute, 1970.

Swyer, P. R.: The Regional Organization of Special Care for the Neonate. *Pediatric Clinics of North America,* 17:761, 1970.

Thompson, J. F.: Some Observations on the Geographic Distribution of Premature Births and Perinatal Deaths in Indiana. *Obstetrics and Gynecology, 101*:43, 1968.

Vaughan, D. H.: Some Social Factors in Perinatal Mortality. *British Journal of Preventive and Social Medicine,* 22:138, 1968.

Vital Statistics of the United States. U.S. Department of Health, Education and Welfare.

Yleinen terveydenja sairaanhoito Public Health and Medical Care). Helsinki, Finland, National Board of Health, 1970.

Index

Note: Page numbers in *italics* represent illustrations; page numbers followed by t represent tables.

Hypospadias *(Continued)*
surgery for, 121
Hypotension, in newborn, due to anesthesia, 70
Hypoxia, in premature infant, 143

Identification, of infant, checking of, 88
Identification bands, for newborn and mother, 78
Impetigo, 100, *102*
Incubator, cleansing of, 91
transport, 139
Induction, in differentiation, 4
Infant. See also *Newborn.*
bathing, demonstration of, 127
in nursery, 94
change in position of, during birth, *60, 61*
fetal development of, 1–58
gaining weight of, 208
high risk, 131–182. See also *High risk infants* and under names of specific disorders.
identification of, after delivery, 77
checking of, 88
immediate evaluation of, after delivery, 75
influence of culture on, 229–252
mortality, 253–272. See also *Mortality, infant.*
of diabetic mother, 176
characteristics of, 43
premature, characteristics of, 15, 16, 17. See also *Premature infant.*
prophylactic eye drops administered to, 77, 79
with cystic fibrosis, 221
with diaphragmatic hernia, 172. See also *Diaphragmatic hernia.*
with encephalocele, 175
with imperforate anus, 174
care for, 174
with infection, 178
with intestinal obstruction, 173
with meningocele, 175
with meningomyelocele, 175
with omphalocele, 173
with special problems, 131–182. See also *High risk infants* and under names of specific disorders.
with tracheo-esophageal fistula, 169–172, 216. See also *Tracheo-esophageal fistula.*
Infection, convulsions in, 98
in newborn, 178
common, 179t
distention of abdomen as sign of, 119
recognition of, 93

Infection *(Continued)*
in premature infant, prevention of, 133
protection from, 146
maternal, and fetus, 37
Monilia albicans, 114
protection of newborn from, 90–94
resistance to, in premature infant, 143
Infectious agents, as cause of jaundice, 158
Inheritance, dominant, 24
of characteristics, 24–29
recessive, 25
Insulation, in heat retention of newborn, 76
Intensive care nursery, 267, *268*
role in reduction of infant mortality, 268, 269t
Interconceptual care, 272
Intestinal bleeding, in newborn, 123
Intestinal obstruction, infant with, 173
Intestines, herniation of, 9, *10*
Iodine, lack of, cretinism due to, 40
Iron requirements, of newborn, 191
Isochromosomes, 32
Isolette, humidity in, 145
temperature in, 144
Isomil, 198

Jaundice, as sign of infection, 94
causes of, 158
color of, 108
in newborn, 153–156
major causes, 153
influence of breast feeding on, 108
physiologic, causes of, 153
characteristics of, 108
incidence of, 107
treatment for, 109
Jaw, of newborn, abnormality of, *114,* 116

Karyotype, 19, *20*
Kernicterus, 158
cause of, 158
treatment for, 159
Kidneys, development of, in third trimester, 16
function of, in newborn, 184
Klinefelter's syndrome, 34, *34*

Labor, and delivery, hazards of, 68–74
newborn during, 59–86
rapid, delivery following, 74
Lactim, 197
Lambase, 198